Lord Byron
and His Contemporaries

Franz Liszt and His Friends by Joseph Danhauser.
Photo courtesy of The Bettmann Archive, Inc.

Lord Byron
and
His Contemporaries

Essays from
the Sixth International Byron Seminar

Edited by Charles E. Robinson

Newark
University of Delaware Press
London and Toronto: Associated University Presses

Associated University Presses, Inc.
4 Cornwall Drive
East Brunswick, N.J. 08816

Associated University Presses Ltd
69 Fleet Street
London EC4Y 1EU, England

Associated University Presses
Toronto M5E 1A7, Canada

Library of Congress Cataloging in Publication Data

International Byron Seminar (6th : 1979 : University
of Delaware)
Lord Byron and his contemporaries.

Includes bibliographical references and index.
1. Byron, George Gordon Byron, Baron, 1788-1824
—Congresses. 2. Romanticism—Congresses.
3. Poets, English—19th century—Biography—Congresses. I. Robinson, Charles E. II. Title.
PR4381.I5   1979   821'.7 [B]   80-66848
ISBN 0-87413-180-4   AACR2

Printed in the United States of America

To Leslie A. Marchand

Contents

Short Titles and Abbreviations

Unless otherwise noted, quotations from Byron's poetry are taken from the Oxford Standard Authors edition, *Byron: Poetical Works,* ed. Frederick Page, rev. John Jump (London: Oxford University Press, 1970). Other standardized citations in the notes and parenthetically in the text include:

BL&J — *Byron's Letters and Journals,* ed. Leslie A. Marchand, 10 vols. to date (Cambridge, Mass.: The Belknap Press of Harvard University Press, 1973-80).

L&J — *The Works of Lord Byron. Letters and Journals,* ed. Rowland E. Prothero, rev. ed., 6 vols. (London: John Murray, 1898-1901).

Poetry — *The Works of Lord Byron. Poetry*, ed. Ernest Hartley Coleridge, rev. ed., 7 vols. (London: John Murray, 1898-1904).

Preface

In "Lord Byron," his essay in *Fables of Identity: Studies in Poetic Mythology*, Northrop Frye explained the phenomena of Byron and Byronism as a "tremendous cultural force that was life and literature at once": "Byron has probably had more influence outside England than any other English poet except Shakespeare"; moreover, "European nineteenth-century culture is as unthinkable without Byron as its history would be without Napoleon." With such premises explicitly or implicitly in mind, the eleven essayists in this volume explore the extensive literary relations between Byron and his contemporaries. With specific reference to Byron's pivotal role among English writers, Michael G. Cooke contra-distinguishes Byron and Wordsworth by their allegiance to the symbols of the rock and the sea; Andrew Rutherford analyzes Byron's changing responses to Scott and Scotland; James A. Houck employs Hazlitt's aesthetic to question the value and "keeping" of Byron's verse; and Jack C. Wills reminds the reader that Byron's legacy to the nineteenth century had its origins in the spirit and form of such earlier writers as Richard Brinsley Sheridan.

These four essays succeed to four others that demonstrate Byron's presence in continental life and letters: Erwin A. Stürzl details the ignored circumstances of the Austrian Grillparzer's living and writing in the shadow of Byron's reputation; Stefan Treugutt identifies the paradoxical and mythic role that Byron's poetry and politics played in the history of Polish Romantic literature; Nina D'iakonova, with a narrower focus on Lermontov's *A Hero of Our Time,* also testifies to the impact of Byronism on Russian literature; and Ernest Giddey realistically outlines the critical dialogue between Byron and Madame de Staël. Byron and Byronism also affected the sister arts of music and painting: Alice Levine analyzes the elements of Romantic heroism and sensibility in the music inspired by Byron's poetry and the self-conscious Byronism in the life and works of Berlioz and Schumann; and Suzanne Hyman discusses Byron's own contradictory self-consciousness as reflected in contemporary portraits of the poet. Finally, Wilfred S. Dowden, whose complete edition of Thomas Moore's journals will soon be published by the University of Delaware Press, offers manuscript evidence that Byron's letters to Moore (and possibly even a copy of the Memoirs destroyed at John Murray's office) may be extant, yielding additional information on Byron's literary relations with his immediate contemporaries.

Such critical commentaries do validate Frye's judgments about Byron's importance in and for the culture and history of nineteenth-century England and Europe. Interrelating these essays are many more of Byron's contemporaries — e.g., Shelley and Keats, Goethe and Lamartine, Napoleon and Metternich, Beethoven and Liszt, Phillips and Géricault — each defined by and defining the phenomena of Byron and Byronism. Such a biographical and historiographical approach in these essays does not, however, preclude evaluations of Byron's art and artistry. The mental landscape of Byron's "The Dream" is here subjected to vigorous analysis; Byron's satires are illuminated by means of Scottish history, the enlightenment, and contemporary Romantic critical theory; the Byronic hero somehow looms even larger in the shadows of its continental progeny; Byron's letters and journals (as published in 1830) provide a text for analysis of plot and character. In short, these essays confirm Byron's dictum that words are things — to be defined and understood by other things, by contexts that are simultaneously the creators and creations of the art of poetry.

These eleven essays were revised for publication after their refereed selection for and presentation at the Sixth International Byron Seminar held at the University of Delaware, 13-15 July 1979. This seminar on Byron's literary relations with his English and continental contemporaries, like the Missolonghi Seminar in 1976 on the worldwide effects of Byron's death in Greece, addressed an international audience and subject. In Delaware, Byron scholars from Japan, Greece, Poland, Austria, Switzerland, Scotland, Wales, England, and the United States gave evidence of Byron's international reputation and influence. Although Professor D'iakonova could not be present (and her paper, included below, did not arrive in time for the seminar), another paper on Byron and Russia that she had prepared for a different forum was read by Professor Paul G. Trueblood.

This collection of essays cannot pretend to embrace or exhaust all of Byron's literary relations with his contemporaries, but it offers a balanced and representative analysis of such relations, and it may inspire additional scholarship on the cultural and historical significance of Byron's life and letters in the nineteenth century. Thirty professors proposed papers for the seminar and twenty submitted essays, from which these eleven were chosen by a committee of four members from the board of directors of the American Byron Society. In the papers not realized or not selected, Byron was coupled with Keats, Shelley, Erasmus Darwin, the Spanish Romantics, the Venetian satirists, Leopardi, Goethe, the Schlegels, and Liszt. (Ironically and regrettably, the American seminar prompted not a single paper on Byron's literary relations with an American writer.) The variety of such proposals and submissions suggests that Byron's international effects on Western culture still demand critical attention.

In 1976, the Missolonghi Seminar demonstrated the effects of Byron's death in Greece on the consciousness of Byron's contemporaries in Britain, France, Switzerland, Italy, Greece, and the United States (see *The Byron Journal*, 1977, for the details of this seminar). The Delaware Seminar added Poland, Russia, Germany, and Austria to the list of nations that responded to the life and letters of Byron. Collectively, these multiple and varied responses to a single poet draw attention to a frequently overlooked cause of the phenomenon of Byronism: namely, Byron's deliberate seeking of an international audience. Compared with those of the other Romantic poets, Byron's works may not be as syncretic as Blake's, or as unitary as Wordsworth's, or as "ideatic" as Coleridge's, or as philosophically "one-minded" as Shelley's, or as universal as Keats's, but they are more self-consciously international both in letter and spirit. The other Romantics might serve man in general, but Byron chose to serve all or as many men as possible. In this spirit, Byron not only went to Greece and desired to go to America, but he also instructed his contemporaries to leave their private lakes and embark on the ocean of common and therefore international experience. Byron's conjunctions of the Old World with the New, his vistas that sweep from the pre-Adamites to Cain's "son's son's sons, accumulating/In generations like to dust," his rhetorical inclusiveness, his apparently random lists and catalogs of nations and heroes both past and present, Don Juan's trekking through and sailing between the nations of Europe — each and all point to Byron's multeities, his multiplicities, his mobilité that could embrace not only diverse and sometimes contradictory attitudes but also various cultures and different countries.

If not before, certainly after his Grand Tour through Spain, Portugal, Greece, Albania, and Turkey in 1809-11, Byron saw himself as a citizen of the world, and he cultivated that citizenship by his further travels and his writings. Hence, it was not even passing strange when in his "Detached

Thoughts" of May 1822 he wrote: "It is strange — but the Germans say — that I am more popular in Germany by far than in England — and I have heard the Americans say as much of America — the French too have printed a considerable number of translations in prose! with good success" (*BL&J,* 9:52). Byron's frequent adverting to his international fame should make one remember that he merely reaped what he had sown. The essays in this collection may attend more to the bountiful harvest of Byron's works in the nineteenth century, but they also evidence the seeds of Byron's internationalism.

*   *   *   *

More than four hundred individuals were involved in the planning and execution of the Sixth International Byron Seminar, the funding for which was provided by the University of Delaware Library Associates and the University of Delaware, as well as by Ampol and the Hellenic University, both of Wilmington, Delaware. For their generous support, I especially thank Dr. E. Arthur Trabant and Dr. L. Leon Campbell, president and provost of the University of Delaware; Dr. John M. Dawson, director of libraries; Mr. J. Bruce Bredin, Mrs. C. Lalor Burdick, Mr. Edmund N. Carpenter, II, the Choptank Foundation, Mrs. H. B. duPont, Mrs. Ellen Bayard Kennelly, Dr. Samuel Lehner, Mrs. G. Burton Pearson, Jr., Mr. Hugh R. Sharp, Jr., and the other contributors from the University of Delaware Library Associates; Dr. Patricia C. Stetson, Summer/Winter Sessions. I am also grateful for the services provided by Nathaniel H. Puffer, T. Stuart Dick, and Delores Altemus (book exhibit), Mary J. Hempel (publicity), Nancy E. Blake (publications), and David A. Bartley (conferences). Invaluable secretarial and clerical assistance was provided by Nancy E. Diffenderfer, Alison Chandler, Lori Henderson, and Betty McCaughey.

The three-day seminar, for which there were ninety regis-trants, was held in the midst of an international Byron tour of the eastern United States. Byron Society members were received at The Carl H. Pforzheimer Library in New York City; Sleepy Hollow Restorations in Tarrytown; University of Pennsylvania Library, Rosenbach Museum, and Poe House in Philadelphia; Winterthur Museum in Wilmington; Library of Congress, the Capitol, and the Arts Club in Washington, D.C.; and Mount Vernon. I wish to thank the directors and staffs of these institutions for arranging the visits and in most cases preparing exhibits and lectures. Evening receptions were provided by Mr. and Mrs. Jack G. Wasserman and by Mrs. Cherry Cannon in New York City; by Mr. and Mrs. Evan Randolph in Philadelphia; by Dr. Richard H. Howland and by Mr. Michael Pakenham in Washington, D.C. To each of these I express my thanks as well as to Mr. William Smith, Associate Conductor of the Philadelphia Orchestra, who prepared "Contemporary, Romantic, and 20th-Century Settings of Poems by Lord Byron" following a reception and dinner at the University of Delaware on 13 July 1979. Ten of Byron's lyrics were performed by Martha Toney, soprano, Alan Wagner, baritone, and Davyd Booth, pianist. Schoenberg's "Ode to Napoleon Buonaparte" was then performed by the Philarte String Quartet with Davyd Booth, pianist, and William Smith, reciter. Philadelphia provided not only the music but also the memory of Francis Lewis Randolph (1951-74), son of Mr. and Mrs. Evan Randolph and founder of the Byron Society of America. To the Randolphs and other Philadelphians (Mr. Seymour Adelman, Mr. and Mrs. C. Earle Miller, and Professor Stuart Curran), I owe a special debt.

I am also indebted to those who refereed the papers and/or chaired the seminar sessions: Professors John Clubbe (Kentucky), James A. Houck (Youngstown), Jerome J. McGann (Johns Hopkins), Leslie A. Marchand (Emeritus, Rutgers), and Andrew Rutherford (Aberdeen). For her untiring efforts on behalf of the seminar, Marsha M. Manns, honorary secretary of the Byron Society and director of the International Byron Council, deserves special mention. As does my wife, Peggy, without whom the seminar and its related activities would have been impossible.

C.E.R.

Newark, Delaware

Lord Byron and His Contemporaries

Byron and Wordsworth:
The Complementarity of a Rock and the Sea

MICHAEL G. COOKE

In 1807, Wordsworth came before the public for the second time in a poetical way, with his *Poems in Two Volumes,* and Byron for the first time, with his *Hours of Idleness.* Both were in the same situation, on the far outskirts of the temple of fame, and both were accorded the same severe treatment by the temple guardians. But Byron was a stripling of nineteen, still a student at Cambridge, offering work ostensibly tossed off as occasion served, whereas Wordsworth, whose *Lyrical Ballads* had already gone gingerly into a fourth edition and who was harboring at home a full book of *The Recluse* and a full-scale version of *The Prelude,* was at thirty-seven nearly twice as old, a patently and, to some, offensively dedicated poet.[1]

Wordsworth was aware of Byron's work, or at least of its reception; he expressed "disgust at the unhandsome treatment of the *minor* Lord by the *Edinburgh Review.*"[2] This reaction is worthy of scrutiny. For Wordsworth is coming out on behalf of the man — or really the youth — who had, in a review in the *Monthly Literary Recreations,* joined the chorus of dispraise against his own *Poems in Two Volumes.* Was his

19

thoughtfulness toward Byron, then, insincere? A maneuver for getting at the *Edinburgh Review,* where Wordsworth himself had been all but keelhauled by Jeffrey? Is the reported stress on the word "minor" a mark of mischief? Or a kind of understated, underplayed magnanimity and guarded fellow-felling?

Something like magnanimity — qualified, paradoxical — manifests itself again when Byron captivates literary London and, indeed, all London in 1812, with *Childe Harold's Pilgrimage,* Cantos I and II. At twenty-four, Byron, according to his own immortal phrase, "awoke to find [himself] famous." Wordsworth, then forty-two, was "almost lionized by the literary households" of London.[3] This on the public front. In a personal, introspective moment, just a year earlier, he had sounded not like a "lion," but like an aspirant struggling with diffidence and disenchantment:

> I seem to have lost all personal interest in everything which I have composed. When I read my poems, I often think that they are such as I should have admired and been delighted with if they had been produced by another, yet, as I cannot ascertain how much of this approbation is owing to self-love, and how much to what my own powers and knowledge supply to complete what is imperfect in the poems themselves, upon the whole my own works at present interest me little, far too little.[4]

One readily recognizes a fault line between the public condition of being lionized and the inner conviction of being ineffectual, undistinguished. It is not within such a fault line that one would look for a flowering of magnanimity, but Wordsworth immediately grants the "power" of the young man who seemed to come forward suddenly and outstrip him.

Wordsworth sounds another note on occasion, expressing a fear that Byron might be "somewhat cracked," and in a harsher vein calling for him to be (a) denounced for the temper of the 1816 valedictory poems on his domestic embranglements,[5] and (b) "branded" for *Don Juan* (which, as Wordsworth saw it, would "do more harm to the English character than anything of our time").[6] But what I have called magnanimity and, even at points of friction or distaste, a measured and judicious quality must be taken as the hallmark of Wordsworth's treatment of Byron.

Byron does not reciprocate. The nineteen-year-old tyro dismissed his elder's *Poems in Two Volumes* as "namby-pamby,"[7] and the creator of *Childe Harold* and the Turkish Tales designates the author of *The Excursion* as "this Arch-Apostle of mystery & mysticism," and further charges him with "a peevish affectation ... of despising a popularity which he will never obtain."[8] This last remark serves as an accidental, uncanny gloss on Wordsworth's declaration of poetical indifference, cited above; but the main interest must fall on the prevailing tone of exasperation and derogation in Byron's remarks. For one brief period, with Shelley's help, he appears to have attuned his spirit to Wordsworth's; but even this Byron made light of, recalling that "Shelley, when I was in Switzerland, used to dose me with Wordsworth physic even to nausea."[9] It is typical for him to refer to Wordsworth with asperity, going from pitch to pitch of virtuosity and vehemence.

In 1819 and 1820, Byron seems to make a veritable campaign of flying in Wordsworth's face. He terms Wordsworth an "imposter" and "renegado rascal" (*BL&J,* 7:82, 253), a "poetical charlatan and political parasite,"[10] and repeatedly, dinning in his own clever transmogrification of the other's name, "Turdsworth" (*BL&J,* 7:158, 167, 168, 253). He hales Wordsworth into his odd and — on both sides — somewhat foolish quarrel with Southey, excoriating him in the Dedication to *Don Juan,* in a Preface to that Dedication, and in his Reply to the *Blackwood's* review of that poem.[11]

All of Byron's vociferation betrays nothing so much as a preoccupation with Wordsworth, and proves ironic when, on the occasion of his one and only meeting with Wordsworth, in 1815, he remained virtually dumbstruck with feelings of *"reverence!"*[12] This response may be forecast in Byron's statement, a year earlier, that "there can be no doubt of his [Wordsworth's] powers to do about any thing" (*BL&J,* 4:167). In a complementary irony, Wordsworth, the laconic one, "tried to talk his best" before Byron, "and talked too much."[13]

Byron and Wordsworth clearly harbored for each other a certain measure of respect and admiration, but the opposition between them is more salient. When this opposition intensifies in 1819 and 1820, the reason comes readily to hand. With *Don Juan,* Byron is bidding for a new independence and authority as a poet, challenging alike poetic tradition and English social custom, and Wordsworth is the one he sees as the figure to reckon with, the authority figure. Byron seems to say that Wordsworth is influencing English poetry for the bad (*L&J,* 6:381), but the issue goes beyond critical analysis and perhaps beyond poetry. Byron had been writing with fluency and variety and power for years, had established a place of his own. He can hardly have felt himself forbidden his ground. But he appears to have been affected by Wordsworth's proprietary manner, and he evinces a primary, irrational need to break Wordsworth's authority. Only such a profound and intense association seems capable of explaining his equation of Wordsworth with Castlereagh as a repressive power. And Wordsworth, in turn, dreads Byron's departure from the bounds of propriety,[14] his power to captivate and to lead (or, as Wordsworth might think, lead astray).

Clearly, there is a question of authority both ways, and an unspoken vying for power. Having regard not just to their personal deportment, but at a deeper level to the favorite figures and key images of their poetry, one is tempted to summarize their relationship as a conflict between a person endowed with years and with an austere stability, and a person bursting with gifts and with an aggressive mobility —

in short, a relationship between a rock and the sea.

One's first impulse may be to ask how two such antithetical characters can belong to one period and movement. But in spite of their opposition in poetic and personal style, Byron and Wordsworth share an underlying intimacy whereby each, in testing, complements and orients the other. When they are considered together, the rock and the moving waters will be seen to inter-respond as part of a single seascape. Something in the essence of Romanticism seemed to call for the confrontation, if not reconciliation, of opposite and discordant personalities, as well as qualities. Thus, and thus only, could the world of Romanticism be complete, as in the scientific world of the time it was felt, and proved, that ultraviolet rays had to exist if infrared rays were known.

The peculiar complementary opposition between Wordsworth and Byron comes out best perhaps in terms of the neo-Freudian treatment of the theory of primary and secondary processes in mental-imaginative functioning. Freud postulates "two fundamentally different kinds of psychical processes" in dreams: the primary one is self-absorbed and concerned with direct wish fulfillment by way of hallucinated satisfactions, whereas the secondary one entails "voluntary movement" to "alter the external world" and "arrive at a real perception of the object of satisfaction."[15] The primary process might be summarized as relentless fixation, the secondary process as mature compromise and adaptation. Commentators such as Kris and Rycroft tend to give an aesthetic turn to primary and secondary processes, and they are wary of trying to keep strict separation between them.[16] Wordsworth's concern with and for the old, his predisposition toward the mountain, and his adoption of a duteous sternness may be taken as putting an emphasis on secondary process, whereas Byron's preoccupation with the young, his identification with the ocean, and his experimental habits show a leaning toward the primary process.

Many other features of their work seem consonant with these dispositions: a fondness for gender ambiguity and disguise and role confusion in Byron, as against formalization and stabilization and an attendant dread for the indifferentiated openness and vulnerability of childhood in Wordsworth.[17] The latter is frank about his dread of the "abyss of idealism" and absorption, and manifests it passionately in the *Memorials of a Tour on the Continent, 1820,* especially in "Processions." If he seems more at ease about dissolving into the all in "Tintern Abbey" (ll. 37 ff.), it may be stressed that at the height of communion he insists on his separateness: his ideal comes with the act of *seeing* "into the life of things," where to see is to be separate from. Even the use of the plural "we" gives a stronger sense of all-embracing unity than in fact applies (l. 49). Wordsworth is, somewhat tendentiously, attributing *his* convictions to us, and acknowledges as much with his concern that his may be "a vain belief" (l. 50).[18]

Granting a difference in emphasis rather than absolute station between Byron and Wordsworth, one readily sees how crucial a presence, as a sort of measure and check, the favored figure of each enjoys in the work of the other. Mazeppa is Byronic as an impetuous, irreverent youth, Wordsworthian as a chastened and devoted warrior in old age. What makes him Byron's is not the absence of restraint, discipline, resignation, but the ceaseless undercurrent of treacherous passion — he still hates and loves with the force of youth, still is associated with the horse that, for all the trappings of domesticity, conveys what Calvin Hall calls "a pristine symbol of wild, lawless, licentious animal passion."[19]

The young boy in "Nutting" or the young poet in "Resolution and Independence" is in turn Wordsworthian in ability and willingness to take tempering and the scabbard of reflection, but Byronic in every primary impulse of self-seeking, self-pity, and cruelty at frustration. Each of these protagonists is Wordsworth's by virtue of raising his personal setbacks into generic laws, embracing not the heady figments of passion but the austere forms of justice and compassion. It is striking that in both instances Wordsworth pits against the youth's self-absorbed impetuosity a still and passive figure (the old man as stone or sea-beast, the hazel-grove as young woman) who yet prevails in the contest; the rock withstands the sea. And just as Byron draws the grizzled old warrior, Mazeppa, back into the throes of passion and "alarming impulsiveness,"[20] so Wordsworth may be said to cut down the range of water as amorphous force in the shrinking of the leech pond, and to draw the water's creature, the sea beast, up on the rigorous land as something more than stranded, as something ascended and by implication evolved.

Wordsworth's sense of the sea as unpredictable and thus inimical occurs again and again, as in "Elegiac Stanzas" ("Peele Castle"), the Arab dream in Book V of *The Prelude,* "Fish-Women" in *Memorials of a Tour on the Continent, 1820.* This unpredictable sea is only slightly counteracted by the pristine sea of the "Ode: Intimations of Immortality," while it is amply reinforced elsewhere. Even his devotion to "These waters, rolling from their mountain-springs/With a soft inland murmur" ("Tintern Abbey," ll. 3-4), provides reinforcement, since nothing but the water's origin in the mountain and its continent passage will account for Wordsworth's favor. Blunt reinforcement comes from *Evening Voluntaries* X, "Composed by the Sea-Shore"; Wordsworth cites various forms of frustration, confusion, despair, and contends that "The Sailor knows" them, qua sailor:

> he best, whose lot is cast
> On the relentless sea that holds him fast
> On chance dependent, and the fickle star
> Of power, through long and melancholy war.
> O sad it is, in sight of foreign shores,
> Daily to think on old familiar doors,
> ... tossed about along a waste of foam.
> [Ll. 5-12]

At times, the two writers' personal differences and bents all but reverse themselves, as though their belonging to the same time frame bound them to the same mind set. This is an idea proposed as a general principle by John Keats: "a mighty providence subdues the mightiest Minds to the service of the time being."[21] Occasionally, Wordsworth treats the water and Byron the mountain as the field of opportunity. In the rowboat episode (*The Prelude,* Book I), the mountain ostensibly gives Wordsworth his comeuppance. And does Byron not gravitate toward the mountain, rather than the sea, in *Manfred* and in *Childe Harold,* especially in the passage on the tannen growing in adversity (IV. xx)?

On close inspection, for all the intricacy of the relationship between lake and mountain peak, the rowboat episode evinces a typical Wordsworthian predisposition toward the mountain. The water entices the boy into license and confusion, and the peak, seeming to domineer over him, reorients and leads him back to firm ground and wholesome ways. The peak itself serves as an illustrative anticipation of his knowledge of "huge and mighty forms." It affords a beginning of understanding and rectified relationship to the essence and substance ("forms") of things. Throughout *The Prelude* the mountains will check presumption in Wordsworth, as repeatedly in Book VI, at the peak of the Alps or in the Simplon Pass. But this check is part of a process of education, indeed of revelation, the mountain serving as an agent for stripping away false hope and pride (the rowboat episode) or error (the Simplon Pass); and, on the other hand, most especially in the ascent of Mount Snowdon, for placing Wordsworth lucidly and commandingly in relation to the sea and all its analogues of aimlessness, despair, animality (the dog and hedgehog), and local will.

When Byron seems to adopt the Wordsworthian citadel of the mountain, the gesture proves topical rather than radical. For Byron, "he who ascends to mountain-tops, shall find/The loftiest peaks most wrapt in clouds and snow"

(*Childe Harold* III.xlv). Manfred goes to the mountain for such starkness, even barrenness, to reflect his inner state, just as the passage on the tannen flourishing in rock finds the mountain appealing for its reflection of severity, not for its fostering, enlightening possibilities. Byron hardly finds what Wordsworth celebrates in "A Narrow Girdle of Rough Stones," namely, the "crags" that form "a rude and natural causeway" and interpose "between the water" and Grasmere, leaving the latter "safe in its own privacy." As soon as his moods of hostile severity pass, Byron, as it were, reverts to his more answerable habitat, the sea. He looks, at the end of *Childe Harold,* "from the Alban Mount," which is but a convenient locus, out on "Our friend of youth, [the] ocean" (IV.clxxv). The phrase, "friend of youth,"[22] proves nicely ambiguous, including Byron himself as a youth and likewise all who share in or espouse the condition of youth.

The ocean proves more than Byron's friend. It is the force that might "roll" him the one dearest to his heart and also the immediate and focused member of the "elements! in whose ennobling stir/I feel myself exalted" (IV.clxxvii). It is Byron's "image of Eternity," where for his part Wordsworth finds in the Snowdon scene his "emblem of a mind/That feeds upon infinity" and his "type/Of a majestic intellect" (*The Prelude,* XIV.66-71). Alike in what they seek, Byron and Wordsworth differ in where and how they seek it.

What, then, are the implications of their particular choices? Is there something salient in the work of either arising from Byron's approach as frank champion of the "friend of youth" and Wordsworth's as tacit champion of age, Byron's identification with the sea and Wordsworth's with the rock or mountain? Obviously, one may cite Wordsworth's incessant pressing of the young toward sobriety and age, in poems as varied as "The Westmoreland Girl" and "Tintern Abbey," and on the other hand Byron's defiant or romantic favoring of youth in the Tales or *The Island.* Subtler effects may also be involved. Wordsworth takes his stand on traditional, conservative blank verse and regular quatrain patterns, with the thoroughly domesticated sonnet for variety, while Byron early breaks free of the orthodox couplet, using it significantly again for the unusual purpose of romance in *The Island,* and embarks on the foreign *ottava rima* and on the nine-line stanza that remains so far from naturalization that it is more properly identified with Spenser than with the English tradition. The difference, present also in their very methods of composition, with Byron so spontaneous and uproarious and Wordsworth so measured and deliberate,[23] is reminiscent of that between the sea and the rock. Yet blank verse allows Wordsworth a variegation of style and multiplication of voices in *The Prelude,* and *ottava rima,* with all its surface strictness, furnishes Byron with ironic rhyme-play and in general a subtle means of investigating the demise *and* the necessity of traditional heroism: "I want a hero." Apparent strictness, in Wordsworth, gives room for invention and variety; apparent license, in Byron, bases itself on strictness.

That sensitive difference is further enunciated in Byron's fate as the poet in exile, the man who loved the water and, calling it the image of eternity, proved himself the pilgrim of eternity; and in Wordsworth's repudiation not of travel — he continued all his life to write memorials of tours hither and yon — but of the implications of travel. His very use of the word *memorials* suggests a monumental fixity and refusal of animation and change. Certainly he repudiated the exotic adventure of the French Revolution and its domestic analogue in the liaison with Annette Vallon. And he seems to repudiate the implications of travel, namely exposure and propensity to the new, in the Lucy series:

> I travelled among unknown men,
> In lands beyond the sea;
> Nor, England! did I know till then
> What love I bore to thee.

'Tis past, that melancholy dream!
Nor will I quit thy shore
A second time; for still I seem
To love thee more and more.

Onorato acutely observes that "most of Wordsworth's significant realizations ... take place while he is actually or figuratively a traveller,"[24] but the discoveries do not seem to come in or from traveling. On the whole, Wordsworth does not take travel as a matter of opportunity and revelation, though it proves, even in the grimly undertaken ascent of Mount Snowdon, such a thing for him.

Byron, however, eagerly undertakes travel, even in the grim circumstances of *Childe Harold* III. For him, travel produces a critique of England[25] rather than a capitulation to it. Don Juan's circumstances, especially in the shipwreck episode, might seem to augur an aversion to travel and the ocean. But the ocean brings out the best in Juan, and brings him whole to Haidée. Its capacity for destruction is never denied by Byron, but it seems more ruthless to those who hold to false or presumptuous or domineering principles than to one who trusts to its billows. Byron's ultimate equanimity in the flow of time significantly qualifies his perpetual attachment to things of his youth. His relative equanimity at removal from England is part of what makes him cosmopolitan, and a bit mysterious. Wordsworth's response seems more familiar to the modern American, who discovers his nationalism by going abroad. Even so, he remains vulnerable to the dual construction of the qualifier "still" in the phrase, "still I seem." One must only remember, matching his "stillness" and austere stability with Byron's notorious "mobility," that each had its price as well as its virtues.

Byron may have recognized his own bent toward the sea of youth and Wordsworth's toward the rock of age. During the critical year of 1820 he writes: "I am still the youngest of the fifteen hundred first of living poets — as Wm Turdsworth is the oldest'' (*BL&J*, 7:168). Ultimately, their distinct bents affect the very substance or subject matter of their work. Although each was instantly recognized as an egotistical or, perhaps better, self-originating poet, one may do better to consider where they are tending, rather than where they start from. It seems to me that Wordsworth tends toward an intensity of principle and commitment that approaches sublimity, and that Byron tends toward an intensity of experimentation and reflection that fosters nothing so much as irony. In general, Wordsworth bases his commitment on home ground, on biography or an individual life-pattern, as distinct from Byron's basing his investigation on outside and even on remote ground, on history. Peter Manning has observed that "for Byron inquiry into the self and inquiry into history are parallel."[26] Perhaps we may see them as reciprocal and interchangeable. Byron, as befits one who emphasizes primary-process reactions, wants continually to merge and fuse with people, with nature, and even with time; his exploration of his failure to do so, of the reason and meaning of that failure, and of its place in the human historical scheme gives a singular depth and resonance to his work.[27]

Wordsworth, more in the spirit of secondary-process reaction, seeks to define relationship with people, with nature, and with life (rather than time), and that relationship is based on separation into identity within common principles and commitments (Wordsworth is the poet who finds, in maturity, "abundant recompense" for the "loss" of fusion with nature). Byronic fusion occurs in the Lucy poems, but in a dreadful form:

> No motion has she now, no force;
> She neither hears nor sees,
> Rolled round in earth's diurnal course
> With rocks, and stones, and trees.
>   ["A slumber did my spirit seal"]

And recognition of radical Wordsworthian separation is

manifest at the end of *Childe Harold* IV, but in an almost pathological form ("Oh! that the Desert were my dwelling-place"), and with a stubborn wish to be accorded "one fair Spirit for my minister," a soul-mate in effect and partner in fusion (clxxvii).

It might almost seem that Byron is able to deal explicitly and directly with war and time as subjects because of his reverent familiarity with the ocean ("For I was as it were a child of thee,/And trusted to thy billows far and near,/And laid my hand upon thy mane — as I do here" [*Childe Harold* IV.clxxxiv]). What monuments are to Wordsworth, with his radiant local habitation, empires are to Byron. The difference is one of scale, not value, but it deserves to be acknowledged. Coleridge wished Wordsworth to deal with man in history, but instead he makes the past personal memory,[28] in *Tintern Abbey* and *The Prelude* alike, and balks at being taken up in and by the surge and sweep of the departicularizing revolution.

Wordsworth is disturbed to find his own place in the Revolution unclear, and then by the shifting form and goal of the action in France. He is as skeptical of formal, cultural authority as Byron is. He finds authority, by a spontaneous biographical process, in his own experience and in its canonical connection and communication with the individual human pattern. Byron makes the past a subject of contemplation, probing its claims to authority, and finds consolation and strength in a growing sense of lucid participation and independence. Seeking to sort himself from what is other, before relating himself to it, Wordsworth treats synthesis as chaos, analysis as a source of identity. Seeking to merge with what is other while preserving himself in it, Byron treats synthesis as cohesion, analysis as a form of fragmentation.

Byron's oceanic propensities and their apparent corollary, his historical perspective, meet in a formal consideration of man and time in *Don Juan,* Canto XV. The culminating passage is familiar, but rich enough to bear fresh quotation:

> Between two worlds life hovers like a star,
> 'Twixt night and morn, upon the horizon's verge.
> How little do we know that which we are!
> How less what we may be! The eternal surge
> Of time and tide rolls on, and bears afar
> Our bubbles; as the old burst, new emerge,
> Lash'd from the foam of ages; while the graves
> Of empires heave but like some passing waves.
>
> [xcix]

His forthright concern with time as a concept, as a problematical field for the application of the self, appears as early as *Childe Harold* I (xxii) and leads to the confrontation of time as beautifier, corrector, and avenger in Canto IV (cxxx) as well as to a tour de force of mordant pathos in the great *ubi sunt* and *carpe diem* passage that begins with the unprecedented cry: " 'Where is the world . . .?' " (*Don Juan* XI.lxxvi-lxxxvi). Neither Shelley on Ozymandias and Rousseau and Prometheus, nor Keats on Hyperion surpasses Byron in contemplation of the issue of time. Wordsworth, however, does not attempt it. In compensation, with his biographical focus, he is able to give a stability[29] to the experience of a lifetime that Byron, for all his ironic insouciance, would dearly love to achieve. Byron does not subscribe to Vico's theory of the life-pattern of nations and civilization, and he does not arrive at Wordsworth's independent position on the life-pattern of individuals.

And yet, Byron once clearly met Wordsworth on his own ground, writing a poem in blank verse and embodying a normative sense if not a theory of individual life, on a principle of reflective mysticism. "The Dream," produced under the agonizing stress of his marital breakdown and unofficial exile from England, is Byron's counterpart to "Tintern Abbey," as the poem "To Edward Noel Long, Esq." is his tribute to that poem.[30] The importance of "The Dream" in Byron's oeuvre has not been overlooked. Critics have turned to it again and again to explain Byron's mood or mentality in 1816.[31] The biographical approach is best summarized in McGann's comment that Byron's "own history and psychology determine nearly the entire meaning and form of an apparently objective narrative."[32] The basic thrust and novel character of Byron's use of autobiographical material in this poem has been noted chiefly by Robert F. Gleckner, who points to its element of "myth" and "not mere self-revelation or the display of a bleeding heart."[33]

The myth or norm of biography in "The Dream," like that in "Tintern Abbey," takes personal experience as its ground, not its goal. Wordsworth's is a norm of restoration, and unfolds in a dynamic process before his eyes. He has experienced personal and public discomfiture, even failure, and begins by doubting the evidences of a consolation and grace that he desperately needs. Doubt leads to reaffirmation (his is not a "vain belief," and he will not suffer his "genial spirits to decay"); and affirmation leads to clarified and broadened vision of his own life-pattern, and of the legitimacy and necessity of that pattern in human life. He prophesies it for Dorothy, and summons her to embrace it, indicating that will, as much as nature, underlies it. "Tintern Abbey" maintains a nice continuum between concrete observation and the contemplative, even imaginary, cave; between hard experience and enduring principles and values.

"The Dream" seems at first devoid of "reality" and of any principles and values save desolate denial and confusion. Beside the fact that "dream" may be, after "imagination," the most complex term in the English Romantic lexicon, there is a direct caution in the poem against relegating its content to the world of sleep-imagery. The poem is neither a Chaucerian dream-vision nor yet a modern dream. Byron's "The Dream," however, is associated with "vision" — an insight into reality beyond the scope of what in convention passes for reality; it may or may not have occurred in sleep; and if it had, it would still have the value of "slumbering thought," that is, of thought intrinsically and of slumber only conditionally, with the ability to hold years together and concentrate (Byron says "curdle") a long life into one hour. In sum, the idea of "the dream" seems to apply not so much to the quality of concrete events, as to the sudden, preternatural grasp of the generic pattern and meaning of those events.[34] This singular grasp accounts for the philosophical authority and, as Ridenour observes ("Byron in 1816," pp. 459-60), the *originality* of the opening section: "Our life is twofold: Sleep hath its own world,/A boundary between the things misnamed/Death and existence" (ll. 1-3). Wordsworth attains a comparable authority only at the end of "Tintern Abbey," but Byron does not put his early assurances to any great advantage. He knows much about time ("heralds of eternity," "spirits of the past," "Sibyls of the future"), and he knows about the mind (which "can make/Substance, and people planets of its own/With beings brighter than have been"); but his knowledge is impotent, barren, and in that sense also like a dream, leaving "a weight" like an incubus (ll.7-21).

The dream itself is divided into seven stages, which could be seen as an antithesis for the days of creation or the optimism of the seven-pointed star. But only the first phase (ii) offers a bright spot, and it is specious. The boy and the maiden only seem to share a favorable setting and relationship. His soul is hers, her heart belongs to another, and this division intensifies through the poem. The overall movement is as negative or privative as the action of "Tintern Abbey" is positive and restorative. To say that Byron is confronting and defying Wordsworth, writing at the same age, twenty-eight, at which Wordsworth composed "Tintern Abbey," would require a certain critical license. But he is distinctly going across his ground, dealing with

a most living landscape, and the wave
Of woods and corn-fields, and the abodes of men

Scatter'd at intervals, and wreathing smoke
Arising from such rustic roofs.

[Ll. 32-35]

Furthermore, in his adherence to this landscape, Byron partially suppresses his own "oceanic" impulses. He takes pains to assure his reader that "there was no sea to lave" the base of his "gentle hill," although the original young woman in "The Dream" is the "ocean to the river" of the young boy's "thoughts," who causes his "blood [to] ebb and flow"[35] with a touch (ll. 28-31, 57-59). A Byronic desire for mystical-physical unity is felt by the young man, but in a Wordsworthian setting where Byron's most intimate icon, the sea, is displaced by "the wave/Of woods and corn-fields" or reduced to a mere metaphor of adolescent sexuality.

But the natural setting is not all Wordsworth. The association of the young woman with Diana, the "moon" governing the movement of the young boy's "blood," confirms a pagan-classical feature of the landscape: "a peculiar diadem/Of trees, in circular array" (ll. 36-37). Moreover, where Wordsworth in "Tintern Abbey" makes the natural setting control and redeem its ostensible rival, "the city," Byron has two other settings that oppose and in effect undo the first pristine scene. The first scene, of hill and woods and cornfields, is strongly identified with youth, not only because of the age of the original pair, but subtly also because the hill is "green," and "the last," implying youngest, and because the moon is "sweet." The counter-settings are heavily identified with age: "an ancient mansion" (l. 76); and "fiery climes" in a period after "noontide" and marked by "fallen columns" and "ruin'd walls" (ll. 107-17).

Byron's dread of age as a symbol (he was fond of autumnal beauty in women) comes forth sharply here. Not only the place but the state of youth is lost, with a distinctly un-Wordsworthian finality. Still Byron continues to levy on

Wordsworth. The figure the young boy grows into becomes "The Wanderer," in a blatant borrowing from *The Excursion*. Considering that Byron would in another few years call *The Excursion* a "drowsy frowzy poem" (*Don Juan* III.xciv), the appropriation of one of its major characters here seems either a high-handed stroke, or a low blow. It is striking that where Wordsworth's Wanderer is a "Man of reverend age," with his "face/Turned toward the sun ... setting" (*Excursion* I, 33, 40), Byron instinctively makes his a young man in fiery climes, implying rampant, even irreverent energy.

There is a fourth setting in "The Dream," one that is neither all-but-pristine nature (woods and cornfields), nor immemorial architecture (the ancient mansion), nor yet the decay and perversion of these ("fiery climes" with "fallen columns" and "ruin'd walls"). This setting occurs in the mind and takes on a character both deeper and truer than the others. With its philosophical declarations, the poem has begun in the mind; with its pretensions to the value of a myth or norm it may have been necessary to end there. This mind at the end — for there is one mind, bifurcated into two people — is the mind that, as Satan says, constitutes its own place. And, as Satan finds, for such a mind that place is hell. For the aged maiden only "a fantastic realm" remains, a state of "frenzy" (ll. 173, 177), and for the aging youth only "blight and desolation," "Hatred and Contention" (ll. 188-89). In these terms of starkness one readily recognizes the conditions under which Byron gravitates towards the mountains, not as a Wordsworthian healing ground but as a mirror of isolation and independence. And thus it proves. The poem says the aging man "made ... friends of mountains" (l. 195). Only Wallace Stevens, in works like "The Rock," captures a similarly alluring bleakness in the mountain.

"The Dream" ends on a Faustian note:

            with the stars
    And the quick Spirit of the Universe
    He held his dialogues; and they did teach
    To him the magic of their mysteries;
    To him the book of Night was open'd wide,
    And voices from the deep abyss reveal'd
    A marvel and a secret.

                                              [Ll. 195-201]

One may be tempted to associate this passage with
Wordsworth's great profession of abstraction from
pedestrian phenomena, "laid asleep/In body," with "the
burthen of the mystery . . . lightened" ("Tintern Abbey," ll.
38-49). But Byron's line, having more of a ring of bravado,
might as again in *Manfred* seem a bit gratuitous.

    Whether he legitimizes the second myth or not, Byron gives
away the fact that he has myth on his mind. "The Dream"
generates a private myth of personality, which it allusively
connects with an external cultural myth of personality. Its
own myth involves a relentless decline from innocent
aspiration to insupportable loss, a depiction of fulfillment
(the maiden's marriage) as but an alternative and specious
curve from a given position in a circle of doom. This myth
unfolds within a frame of nature insidiously affected by the
"sport . . . of man" (l. 38), and otherwise vicious (as the
indifferent moon sways the captivated blood of the youth) or
ruinous (in fiery climes). The relation of the indigenous myth
to the imported one affords a final gloss on the meaning of
"dream," as on the ultimate mood of the poem. For the
Faustian note suggests access to, confrontation of dark and
strenuous knowledge.

    The woman in her "fantastic realm" has had a similar
experience:

    What is [melancholy] but the telescope of truth?
    Which strips the distance of its fantasies,
    And brings life near in utter nakedness,
    Making the cold reality too real!

                                              [Ll. 180-83]

Here fantasy defeats, rather than intensifies, fantasy;[36] the woman cannot cope with it, perhaps, but she is closer to truth than when she tantalized the mooning boy and "loved another" who proved not to love her enough (ll. 71, 127-28). Her peculiar fantasy overrides reality in a sense; it also surpasses it and this occasions her frenzy. In a line that vividly anticipates Eliot's contention that "Mankind cannot bear too much reality," Byron treats mad melancholy as the result of the telescope's "Making the cold reality too real" (l. 183).

The form of the dream, by analogy, proffers a knowledge not perhaps within the bounds of reality, conventionally taken, but within "a wide realm of wild reality" (l. 4). This is the speaker's knowledge, which also becomes that of the original pair inside the poem's action, as it is by allusion part of Faustian knowledge. The sum of that knowledge proves negative, its effect disconsolate. But the poem also manifests an attitude toward knowledge, apart from its disconsolate tenor, and that attitude is at worst resigned, as indicated in the last line of the dream proper: "Be it so." The poem's speaker could seem proud, in an austere way: he knows "a marvel and a secret," albeit a grim one. "The Dream" might in this light not be interpreted as a poem of despair and cynicism, but as a poem of undefeated desolation, reflecting the quality of one who "made ... friends of mountains." If this is not a Wordsworthian mountain, it is because Byron seems not to have detected the subtle versatility of the mountainous state, harboring flowers and birds and gracious private valleys, that Wordsworth records in poems like "Joanna's Rock" and *The Prelude* (1805: XIII.233) and "Michael." Then again one may observe that the sea in "The Fish-Women" (*Memorials of a Tour on the Continent, 1820*) falls short of a Byronic one.

How far investigation of the peculiar and, for Romanticism, crucial relation between Wordsworth and Byron can go it would not be proper here to try to say. But one may observe in passing that *Don Juan,* without adopting the same eventualist teleology, evinces the same formal mobility and surprise as *The Prelude,* though Byron cannot have known Wordsworth's work, and in turn Wordsworth cannot have made use of Byron's.[37] Further interest would attach to unfolding the intricacies of their politics, with the lord a liberal and losing his life around a revolutionary struggle, while the commoner proves an arch-conservative; or of their divergent critical views; or of their treatment of religion; or of their sexual lives, one charged with and the other surreptitiously suspected of incest, each engendering an illegitimate daughter, and one ending up disapproving of any sexual irregularity while the other seemed unable to put an end to his liaisons; or of their use, and critique, of the figure of the guide.

Even in extending such an investigation, one might not soon come to the question of mathematics. And yet it would seem grievous to omit Wordsworth's fondness for mathematics, and Byron's antipathy to it, at least as an instrument of the bluestockings and, in particular, of his "Princess of Parallelograms." Wordsworth took to mathematics where Byron took to mountains, in times of tumult and stress, at once quieting and tempering his mind with its purity of form and absolute self-containment. It is striking that Byron also had need for a comparable nostrum in social terms, and, typically at once sharing and differing with Wordsworth, he turned for the purpose to the Armenian language. The more they are the same, the more they differ, giving rise to a complementary opposition that holds out one of the quandaries and one of the clues in the intricate framework of Romanticism.

NOTES

1. See Mary Moorman, *William Wordsworth, A Biography: The Later Years, 1803-1850* (Oxford: Clarendon Press, 1965), p. 269.

2. Henry Crabb Robinson, *On Books and Their Writers,* ed. Edith J. Morley (London: J. M. Dent and Sons, 1938), 2:736.

3. Moorman, *William Wordsworth,* p. 209.

4. Quoted in ibid., pp. 268-69.

5. *The Letters of William and Dorothy Wordsworth: The Middle Years,* ed. Ernest de Selincourt (Oxford: Clarendon Press, 1937), 2:734.

6. See Moorman, *William Wordsworth,* p. 211.

7. The review (*L&J,* 1:341-43) is full of gracious condescension and exhortations tinged with reproof.

8. *BL&J,* 4:324, 325. It is only fair to remark that Byron was for most of his life reluctant to take "poesy" for his "passion predominant" (p. 115) and affected greater indifference than he felt when his popularity waned and adverse criticism mined his path.

9. *Medwin's Conversations of Lord Byron,* ed. Ernest J. Lovell, Jr. (Princeton, N.J.: Princeton University Press, 1966), p. 194.

10. See *Poetry,* 6:5n.

11. For the Preface, see *L&J,* 6:381-83; for the Reply, see *L&J,* 4: appendix 9, esp. pp. 486ff. In 1847 Wordsworth especially remembered and resented the "public poetical attacks" in *Don Juan* because he thought they would prove "most enduring" (*The Letters of William and Dorothy Wordsworth: The Later Years, 1821-1850,* ed. Ernest de Selincourt [Oxford: Clarendon Press, 1939], 3:1306).

12. See *His Very Self and Voice: Collected Conversations of Lord Byron,* ed. Ernest J. Lovell, Jr. (New York: MacMillan Co., 1954), p. 129. Note also Leigh Hunt's remark that Byron "pretended to think worse of" Wordsworth than in fact "he did" (p. 333).

13. Robinson, *On Books and Their Writers,* 1:436.

14. It is striking that the Wordsworthian revolt against the canons of eighteenth-century poetry emerges as a *conservative* one. In his "Preface" to *Lyrical Ballads,* espousing "a selection of language really used by men, and ... [withal] a colouring of imagination ... in a state of excitement," Wordsworth opts for what is perennial and universal in interest, rather than what is confined to a particular time or class. His principle, which may resemble neo-naturalism in relation to Pope, encases restoration in revolution.

15. Freud's original views are set forth in *The Interpretation of Dreams,* ch. 6, sec. E.

16. See Ernst Kris, *Selected Papers* (New Haven, Conn.: Yale University Press, 1975), pp. 153, 159, 308, 363; and Charles Rycroft, *The Innocence of Dreams* (New York: Pantheon Books, 1979), pp. 153ff.

17. The immediacy and depth of this state give power to Wordsworth's poems about people who do not grow up: the boy of Winander, Lucy, H. C. (in poems referring to the period of childhood), Ellen ("The Childless Father"), the "departed child" (in "Maternal Grief"); and to cognate poems like "Alice Fell," "The Idiot Boy," "The Danish Boy," "Her Eyes Are Wild," "The Reverie of Poor Susan,"

"Ruth," "Surprised by Joy." Wallace W. Douglas generally favors the idea that Wordsworth gives himself to primary-process incorporation (*Wordsworth: The Construction of a Personality* [Kent, Ohio: Kent State University Press, 1968], pp. 133-36). He deals with it, certainly, but less as an ideal or good than as a siren attraction or loss.

18. Quotations from Wordsworth are from *The Poetical Works of Wordsworth,* ed. Thomas Hutchinson, rev. Ernest de Selincourt (London: Oxford University Press, 1966).

19. Calvin Hall, *The Meaning of Dreams* (New York: McGraw-Hill, 1966), p. 56.

20. Ibid.

21. *The Letters of John Keats,* ed. Hyder Edward Rollins (Cambridge, Mass.: Harvard University Press, 1958), 1:282.

22. This phrase may embody a particular autobiographical reference to the Scottish highlands, where the boy Byron was sent from Aberdeen to speed his recovery from scarlet fever. He remembered the mountains with gratitude and may have reverted to them in spiritual crises because of their service in physical disease. The spirit may be soothed from without; it is cured from within. The adult Byron, however, may have affected the mountain with his distress more than it touched him with healing. Concerning the Highland holiday, Leslie A. Marchand stresses Byron's sporting in the estuaries of the Dee and the Don, rather than any contact with "Loch-na-garr and Morven . . . visible in the distance" (*Byron: A Portrait* [New York: Alfred A. Knopf, 1970], p. 15).

23. This may have been a learned response for Wordsworth. "Resolution and Independence" certainly presents him as a conspicuously poeticizing character, and in "Summer Vacation," Book IV of *The Prelude,* his terrier has to give him a signal when people are approaching so that he can quit spouting off and not be "suspected" of being "crazed in brain." But this "craziness" is elsewhere identified with "the boyish spirit," the giving over (or going under) of which is at issue. Byron remains headstrong, but Wordsworth takes up the position of one "willing, nay — nay, wishing to be led" (*The Prelude,* IV. 66, 93-130).

24. Richard J. Onorato, *The Character of the Poet: Wordsworth in The Prelude* (Princeton, N.J.: Princeton University Press, 1971), pp. 17-18.

25. G. Wilson Knight remarks that "Byron is cosmopolitan and international; he is not, in any usual sense, English" (*Byron and Shakespeare* [New York: Barnes & Noble, 1966], p. 338).

26. Peter J. Manning, *Byron and His Fictions* (Detroit, Mich.: Wayne State University Press, 1978), p. 65.

27. Knight, in two of the chapters of *Byron and Shakespeare,* suggests various ways in which Byron evinced interest in "seraphic" unity and in all-inclusive "plastic form" (see "Sonnets and Seraphs," and "Tempests, Lear, Prospero"). Robert F. Gleckner also comments tellingly on Byron's persistent and ungratified desire for "unity transcending time, space, and all separability" (*Byron and the Ruins of Paradise* [Baltimore, Md.: Johns Hopkins Press, 1967], p. 201).

28. According to Lady Blessington, in a discussion of Rogers's *The Pleasures of Memory,* Byron declared that "memory . . . never offered any pleasures to me" (*Lady Blessington's Conversations of Lord Byron,* ed. Ernest J. Lovell, Jr. [Princeton, N.J.: Princeton University Press, 1969], p. 201).

29. By using Emily as a biographical center, Wordsworth is able to impose a sense

of stability on history in *The White Doe of Rylstone.*

30. For discussion of this connection, see Michael G. Cooke, *The Blind Man Traces the Circle: On the Patterns and Philosophy of Byron's Poetry* (Princeton, N.J.: Princeton University Press, 1969), pp. 17-20.

31. See Charles du Bos, *Byron and the Need of Fatality,* trans. Ethel Coburn Mayne (New York: Putnam, 1932), pp. 50-51, 83; George M. Ridenour, "Byron in 1816: Four Poems from Diodati," in Frederick W. Hilles and Harold Bloom, eds., *From Sensibility to Romanticism* (New York: Oxford University Press, 1965), pp. 459ff. In "Byron and the Mind of Man: *Childe Harold* III-IV and *Manfred,*" Ward Pafford treats the poem in terms of radical conflict between reason and imagination in Byron (*Studies in Romanticism* 1 [1962]: 115ff., 124).

32. Jerome J. McGann, *Fiery Dust: Byron's Poetic Development* (Chicago: University of Chicago Press, 1968), p. 280.

33. Gleckner, *Byron and the Ruins of Paradise,* p. 251.

34. Perhaps this same value inheres in Wordsworth's calling his experience in "I Travelled among Unknown Men" a "melancholy dream."

35. Actually, Byron has suggested that the young woman is Diana ("As the sweet moon ... shining on" the young man, ll. 44-49). The image of "ebb and flow" chimes with *that* reference.

36. The overall poetic "dream" or "fantasy" seems a classic representation of Freud's definition of the phenomenon of fantasy:

The relation of phantasies to time is altogether of great importance. One may say that a phantasy at one and the same moment hovers between three periods of time — the three periods of our ideation. The activity of phantasy in the mind is linked up with some current impression, occasioned by some event in the present, which had the power to rouse an intense desire. From there it wanders back to the memory of an early experience, generally belonging to infancy, in which this wish was fulfilled. Then it creates for itself a situation which is to emerge in the future, representing the fulfillment of the wish — this is the day-dream of phantasy, which now carries in it traces both of the occasion which engendered it and of some past memory. So past, present and future are threaded, as it were, on the string of the wish that runs through them all. [See *On Creativity and the Unconscious: Papers on the Psychology of Art, Literature, Love, Religion,* ed. Benjamin Nelson (New York: Harper Torchbook, 1958), pp. 48-49.]

37. Fuller discussion of the relation between these two great epics of English Romanticism is available in Michael G. Cooke, *Acts of Inclusion: Studies Bearing on an Elementary Theory of Romanticism* (New Haven, Conn.: Yale University Press, 1979), pp. 223ff., 227, 235.

Byron, Scott, and Scotland

ANDREW RUTHERFORD

One of the reddest or most tartan herrings ever dragged across the trail of Byron criticism is T. S. Eliot's suggestion that Byron should be considered "as a Scottish poet," on the basis of a strained comparison between his satiric invective against Southey and the "flytings" of late medieval Scots verse. More convincingly, however, Eliot suggests the case for a comparison between Byron and Scott — "the one poet of his time with whom he could be considered to be in competition, a poet of whom he spoke invariably with the highest respect." Yet the comparison that he himself proceeds to offer is of a trivializing kind:

> I have always seen, or imagined that I saw, in busts of the two poets, a certain resemblance in the shape of the head. The comparison does honour to Byron, and when you examine the two faces, there is no further resemblance. Were one a person who liked to have busts about, a bust of Scott would be something one could live with. There is an air of nobility about that head, an air of magnanimity, and of that inner and perhaps unconscious serenity that belongs to great writers who are also great men. But Byron — that pudgy face suggesting a tendency to corpulence, that weakly sensual mouth, that restless triviality of expression, and worst of all that blind look of the self-conscious beauty; the bust of Byron is that of a man who was every inch the touring tragedian.

I do not think it is just changes in critical fashion that make this seem an unprofitable line of approach. Yet Eliot goes on to make the very valid point that Byron's Scottish antecedents are important for "his peculiar diabolism, his delight in posing as a damned creature," his Satanism, all of which derive "from the religious background of a people steeped in Calvinist theology."[1] What we are left with, I think, is a sense that the cluster of topics Eliot proposes — Byron, Scott and Scotland — is potentially interesting, even if the interest is not fully established by that essay.

The same comment may, of course, seem applicable to this essay. All I can offer in defense is a disclaimer and a statement of intention. I do not propose to offer an exhaustive treatment of the subject, but instead wish to argue a specific case: that Byron's changing attitudes to Scotland and the Scots provide a kind of index to his own growth to maturity as a man and as a poet, and that Scott's writings, especially his novels, played a significant part in that progression.

Most people know that Byron spent the first ten years of his life in North-East Scotland. What use does he make of these early experiences in his poetry? In his first volume Byron presents himself to the public as a young nobleman, with heavy emphasis on both his youth and his nobility — an emphasis for which the *Edinburgh Review* was soon to take him ruthlessly to task. His descent from the Byrons of Newstead is proudly asserted: the first poem in all four versions of this publication is "On Leaving Newstead Abbey," and his pride in his specifically English ancestry is reasserted elsewhere in the volume. Yet he also proudly acknowledges a Scottish dimension in his experience and ancestry: a subordinate but important aspect of his poetic self is, he suggests in *Hours of Idleness,* his growing up in the Highlands. "Though accustomed, in my younger days," he writes in the Preface, "to rove a careless mountaineer on the Highlands of Scotland, I have not, of late years, had the benefit of such pure air, or so elevated a residence.'' This theme is taken up in his fine lyric on Loch na Garr — "certainly," he remarks in a note to the poem, "one of the most sublime and picturesque amongst our 'Caledonian Alps'. . . . Near Lachin y Gair I spent some of the early part of my life." That part of his life, and the sensibility it nurtured, are commemorated by the poem itself:

> Ah! there my young footsteps in infancy wander'd:
> > My cap was the bonnet, my cloak was the plaid;
> On chieftains long perish'd my memory ponder'd,
> > As daily I strode through the pine-cover'd glade;
> . . . .
> England! thy beauties are tame and domestic
> > To one who has roved o'er the mountains afar:
> Oh for the crags that are wild and majestic!
> > The steep frowning glories of dark Loch na Garr.
> > > > > [Ll. 9-12, 37-40]

He takes the opportunity of stressing in a note the royal connections of his "maternal ancestors, 'the *Gordons*'" and in the next edition (*Poems Original and Translated*) he returns to the image of his youthful self as a Highland figure in a Highland landscape:

> When I roved a young Highlander o'er the dark heath,
> > And climb'd thy steep summit, oh Morven of snow!
> To gaze on the torrent that thunder'd beneath,
> > Or the mist of the tempest that gather'd below.
> > > > > [Ll. 1-4]

In another poem in the same collection he elaborates the contrast drawn in "Lachin y Gair" between Scottish bleakness and freedom on the one hand, English riches and servility on the other:

> > I would I were a careless child,
> > > Still dwelling in my Highland cave,
> > Or roaming through the dusky wild,
> > > Or bounding o'er the dark blue wave;

The cumbrous pomp of Saxon pride
    Accords not with the freeborn soul,
Which loves the mountain's craggy side,
    And seeks the rocks where billows roll.
                                            [Ll. 1-8]

In such poems Byron articulates, with varying success, emotions that he genuinely felt — his sense of isolation, his delight in solitude, his imaginative response to the bleak grandeur of mountain scenery, and his conviction that such an environment fosters freedom and integrity in contrast to the corruption and servility of civilized society. These are themes to which he was to return, and which he was to orchestrate much more impressively in later works. Yet as they are reiterated here, we become aware of an anomaly. "I would I were a careless child,/Still dwelling in my Highland cave," exclaims the poet; and the same phraseology was to appear in "The Adieu" — "Why did I quit my Highland cave, /.../ To seek a Sotheron home!" (ll. 28-30). We know, however, though we make appropriate allowances for poetic license, that he dwelt not in a Highland cave but in a modest dwelling-house in Broad Street, in the center of Aberdeen. He did indeed rove "o'er the dark heath" and may well have climbed the steep summit of Morven, but this was in the course of occasional summer holidays on Deeside, while he lived for most of his boyhood in Aberdeen itself and its environs — an area that was not then, and had not been for centuries, Highland in language, culture, costume, or social organization. Hence, these early poems of Byron's involve an element of *suggestio falsi*, since he claims to have been a member of or inward with a Celtic culture of which in fact he knew extremely little. The superficiality of his knowledge shows in his repeated misuse of the term *pibroch,* which he obviously thought meant "bagpipes," whereas any Highlander would have known that it refers to the greatest form of music composed for that instrument. As the *Edinburgh Review* unkindly commented on his having spent part of his youth at Loch na Garr, "he . . . might have learnt [there] that *pibroch* is not a bagpipe, any more than duet means a fiddle."[2]

This *suggestio falsi* is accompanied by a significant, indeed a revelatory *suppressio veri.* If we juxtapose these early lyrics with Byron's 1821 account of his schooldays in Aberdeen, we see at once that in the former he is suppressing, editing out, much of the social-psychological reality of his boyhood experience. He writes freely if polemically about Cambridge, fully and nostalgically about Harrow, sentimentally or angrily about Southwell affairs; but his childish recollections do not seem to go back further than his years in England, while his Scottish boyhood is presented in this very selective, glamorized, romantic way. This suggests first a youthful and quite understandable snobbery: Newstead Abbey and Harrow were backgrounds easy to acknowledge publicly, Broad Street and the Grammar School much less so — not to mention Bodsy Bowers, who did not teach him to read; Mr. Ross, who did; or Paterson the shoemaker's son, who gave him the rudiments of Latin grammar. Second, the suppression of his Aberdonian experience suggests that life really began for him, in many ways, with his accession to the title. One would not wish to exaggerate the hardships of his early life, but he and his mother did live in comparatively humble circumstances, in a rather constricting, provincial environment, and his removal to the south was a kind of liberation — even a rebirth to a completely new life — while the old one is to a significant extent obliterated from the record. And third, it tells something, I suspect, about his emotional life. He had always a great capacity for friendship; his poems about Harrow often celebrate his boyhood affections; and the absence of any such poems relating to his young companions in Aberdeen suggests to me that he was rather a lonely, isolated little boy. (It is for the psychiatrists to say whether or not this may have influenced his personality in later life.)

Byron's portrayal of himself as a Highlander is of historical as well as biographical interest: already, by 1806-7, the Highlander had come to seem a romantic figure instead of what he had been for centuries in Lowland Scotland as well as in England — an object of hatred, fear, ridicule, and contempt. This traditional attitude of derisive loathing was current in England well into the second half of the eighteenth century, sharpened of course by the memory of successive Jacobite rebellions; but it tended to merge with a detestation of Scots in general — because they were on the make, because they were commercially sharp, because at times they seemed to have an undue share of political power and patronage. Boswell in his *London Journal* tells with indignation how he in 1762 saw two Highland officers, just back from active service in the Havanas, hissed by an anti-Scottish mob at Covent Garden. On a different cultural level the satirist Charles Churchill, whom Byron was later to admire, and whose grave he visited when leaving England in 1816, published a poem in 1763 called *The Prophecy of Famine: A Scots Pastoral*. It is virulently anti-Scottish: in a mock-pastoral dialogue between two Highland shepherds he reiterates the old charges of poverty, savagery, uncouthness, indecency, and disloyalty. Then the goddess of Famine, appropriate to such a foul, beggarly country, appears to them, linking their Jacobite lament to the theme of revenge, with Scots and Famine taking over England like a kind of tartan mafia. And here it is Scots in general, not only Highlanders, who are his target, though the Highlanders epitomize the faults of the Scots in general. The poem was enormously popular; and it was presumably the prevalence of this kind of feeling in London that led John Macmurray, in 1768, to drop the Mac from his name when he set up as a publisher and founded the House of Murray. His friend General Sir Robert Gordon wrote to him from India as follows: "My best compliments to Mrs. Murray, who I suppose will not be sorry for your laying aside the wild Highland 'Mac' as unfashionable and even dangerous in the circuit of Wilkes's mob."[3] Half a century later, however, this had changed completely, and no one man did so much to change it as Scott himself. His presentation of Highlanders and clan life in *The Lady of the Lake,* and still more in novels like *Waverley* and *Rob Roy,* did much to establish the nineteenth-century cult of the Highlands — to give High-landers themselves a romantic, heroic reputation, and to make them appear representative, in many ways, of Scottish-ness itself. The extent of the change can be seen from the fact that when George IV visited Scotland in 1822 (the first reigning monarch to do so since 1651), taking part in ceremonies stage-managed by Scott himself, he wore Highland dress — a thing quite inconceivable in any former period.

Although this event provided rich material for satirists (like Byron himself in the conclusion to *The Age of Bronze*), it marks a complete revolution in ways of regarding Scotland and the Scots; and the cultural-historical interest of Byron's early "Highland" lyrics is that they document one stage in this long process — they show how far it had proceeded before Scott had even begun to publish on Highland themes. (*The Lady of the Lake* was not to appear until 1810, or *Waverley* until 1814.) Earlier influences, not explored here, would include, first, the glory won on battlefields throughout the world by Highland regiments who, as the elder Pitt said, "served with fidelity as they fought with valour";[4] and it is noteworthy that the noblemen who raised or officered such regiments in the later eighteenth century often had themselves painted in the full panoply of Highland dress, as if reasserting their traditional role of clan chiefs. Second, there was the popularity of James Macpherson's supposed translations of Ossian, with their blend of the epic and elegiac in their portrayal of the Celtic past — their vision of courage, nobility, conflict, doom, sorrow, and regret, which colored the Highlands in the imagination of Britain and Europe for two generations. These works were certainly one of Byron's early enthusiasms (although Scott had no time for them), and the cult is associated with that strain of eighteenth-century thought that connected the primitive not with the savage and uncouth, but with the noble, the unspoiled — and also with the greatest capacity for poetry. "For many circumstances," wrote Hugh Blair, "of those times which we call barbarous, are favourable to the poetical spirit. That state, in which human nature shoots wild and free, though unfit for other improvements, certainly encourages the high exertions of fancy and passion."[5] This is why Byron saw a specifically Highland childhood as so thoroughly appropriate for a poet, just as Scott, in *The Lay of the Last Minstrel,* hailed "Caledonia! stern and wild" as "Meet nurse for a poetic child!"[6] But this is to digress.

Having left Aberdeen in 1798, Byron never showed any disposition to return, nor for many years even to refer to his life there. If he alludes in early letters to his Scottish experience, it is as a picturesque tourist, a connoisseur of Highland scenery, as in his letter of August 1805 to Charles David Gordon: "I suppose you will soon have a view of the eternal Snows that surround the top of Lachin y gair, which towers so majestically above the rest of our *Northern Alps.* I still remember with pleasure the admiration which filled my mind, when I first beheld it, and further on the dark frowning mountains which rise near Invercauld, together with the romantic rocks that overshadow Mar Lodge a seat of Lord Fifes, and the cataract of the Dee, which dashes down the declivity with impetuous violence, in the Grounds adjoining to the house" (*BL&J,* 1:75). He never returned to Scotland, though he did in 1807 have a project, which came to nothing, of visiting Edinburgh, the Western Highlands and the Hebrides — like Johnson and Boswell. And he also told Elizabeth Pigot that he meant "to collect all the Erse traditions, poems, &. &c. & translate, or expand the subjects, to fill a volume, which may appear next Spring, under the denomination of '*the Highland*

Harp' or some title equally *picturesque''* (*BL&J,* 1:132). This has the air of an attempt to follow in Macpherson's Ossianic footsteps: he too had made a tour of the Highlands to collect the materials (supposedly) for his translations; but it was a task for which Byron was quite unfitted, linguistically and in other ways. The project was, however, only one of many that he entertained in the euphoria induced by the favorable reception of *Hours of Idleness,* and that he abandoned after the shock of the *Edinburgh*'s review.

That review, as is well known, was a shattering blow to his self-esteem and to his aspirations in both politics and poetry. It is also a landmark in the charting of his attitudes to Scotland. The *Edinburgh* was the supreme arbiter of taste; it was also a main organ of the Whigs, with whom he proposed to align himself in Parliament. "As an author," he told Hobhouse, "I am cut to atoms by the E Review, it is just out, and has completely demolished my little fabric of fame, this is rather scurvy treatment from a Whig Review, but politics and poetry are different things, & I am no adept in either" (*BL&J,* 1:158-59). It is ironic that his professed views on poetry as well as on politics were so close to the *Edinburgh*'s own. He had already drafted a satire on contemporary poetry (*British Bards*) and though the text of this original version is not extant — E. H. Coleridge's bibliographical note is quite mistaken on this point — even the published text of *English Bards and Scotch Reviewers* shows the affinity between his judgments and those of the Scotch Reviewers. For evidence, I note the *Edinburgh*'s articles on Southey's *Thalaba* and *Madoc,* Scott's *Lay of the Last Minstrel* and *Marmion,* Moore's *Anacreon* and *Epistles, Odes and Other Poems,* Strangford's *Camoëns,* Bowles's *Spirit of Discovery,* and Wordsworth's *Poems, In Two Volumes.* I am not suggesting that the *Edinburgh* was Byron's only source for these opinions: he was drawing on commonplaces of conservative literary taste that were available in contemporary parodies and satires (like Richard Mant's *Simpliciad* and Lady Anne

Hamilton's *Epics of the Ton*), as well as in other journals; but he certainly read and used the *Edinburgh*'s articles. In a footnote to line 297 of *English Bards,* he even explains a joke about Strangford by giving a page reference to the *Edinburgh*. His main criticisms of Scott (except for the charge of venality, which Jeffrey was too gentlemanly to make) are those of the *Edinburgh* itself, which was severely critical of the goblin page (derived from Gilpin Horner), the spirits of river and mountain, the limited interest of "the feuds of Border chieftains," and the incongruity of the character of Marmion as villain-hero. At some points one seems to identify a verbal echo: Byron's "mountain spirits *prate* to river sprites" (l. 155) is very close indeed to the *Edinburgh*'s reference to "the *prattlement* of the river and mountain spirits."[7] We all accept, I suppose, the satirist's right to adopt a persona distinct from his own personality in actual life; and we should therefore simply note in passing that the conservative stance Byron adopts in this poem involves some distortion of his own response to poetry — Moore's in particular — though we may also feel that it constrains his characteristic liveliness. It could, however, well be argued that there is an *internal* inconsistency in his attacking Scotch Reviewers with such fierceness when their views on English Bards (himself excepted) are so like his own. Originating in different impulses, these elements of the poem are not fused to satiric unity, but we hardly notice this as we are carried along by the vigor of his attack.

Byron denounces "the oat-fed phalanx" of Reviewers with a rhetoric that seems at times to embrace the whole Scottish nation, and that certainly draws on a tradition of anti-Scottish as well as Dunciadic polemic. A Caledonian goddess of dullness is introduced to save and exhort Jeffrey, after which "the kilted goddess kiss'd/Her son and vanish'd in a Scottish mist" (ll. 508, 526-27). "I ought to apologise to the worthy deities," runs Byron's note to these lines, "for introducing a new goddess with short petticoats to their

notice: but, alas! what was to be done? I could not say
Caledonia's genius, it being well known there is no such
genius to be found from Clackmannan to Caithness." There
is a tribute to Burns in spite of this, and qualified praise of
Scott, who is seen as capable of better things; but his anti-
Scottish bias is intensified in *The Curse of Minerva,* written
in Athens in March 1811. To his continuing resentment at the
Scotch Reviewers is now added his new sense of outrage at
the depredations of Lords Aberdeen and Elgin in their
removal of Greek antiquities. In *English Bards and Scotch
Reviewers* he had jeered at their wasting "useless thousands
on their Phidian freaks,/Misshapen monuments and maim'd
antiques" (ll. 1029-30); but now, having observed their
activities for himself, he saw them as acts of international
brigandage. He had denounced them in *Childe Harold,*
Canto II, in terms that made clear the peculiarly Scottish
dimension of the crime: "The last, the worst, dull spoiler,
who was he?/Blush, Caledonia! such thy son could
be!/England! I joy no child he was of thine" (xi). In *The
Curse of Minerva* he elaborates the charge, in an exuberant
denunciation of both Scotland and the Scots:

> "Daughter of Jove! in Britain's injured name,
> A true-born Briton may the deed disclaim.
> Frown not on England; England owns him not:
> Athena, no! thy plunderer was a Scot.
> Ask'st thou the difference? From fair Phyle's towers
> Survey Bœotia; — Caledonia's ours.
> And well I know within that bastard land
> Hath Wisdom's goddess never held command;
> A barren soil, where Nature's germs, confined
> To stern sterility, can stint the mind;
> Whose thistle well betrays the niggard earth,
> Emblem of all to whom the land gives birth;
> Each genial influence nurtured to resist;
> A land of meanness, sophistry, and mist.
> Each breeze from foggy mount and marshy plain
> Dilutes with drivel every drizzly brain,
> Till, burst at length, each wat'ry head o'erflows,

Foul as their soil, and frigid as their snows.
Then thousand schemes of petulance and pride
Despatch her scheming children far and wide:
Some east, some west, some everywhere but north,
In quest of lawless gain, they issue forth.
And thus — accursed be the day and year!
She sent a Pict to play the felon here."

[Ll. 125-48]

This is as virulent as anything Charles Churchill ever wrote, and I like to quote it to cultural nationalists who try to persuade me (sometimes citing Eliot as their authority) that Byron is "really" a Scottish poet; but he does go on to concede reluctantly that

... "Caledonia claims some native worth,
As dull Bœotia gave a Pindar birth;
So may her few, the letter'd and the brave,
Bound to no clime, and victors of the grave,
Shake off the sordid dust of such a land,
And shine like children of a happier strand;
As once, of yore, in some obnoxious place,
Ten names (if found) had saved a wretched race."

[Ll. 149-56]

At any rate, in the years that followed, Byron found two such names — those of Jeffrey and Scott, both of whom he had treated so offensively. He returned to England willing and eager to resume the fray; but he was mellowed by the success of *Childe Harold,* Cantos I and II, and disarmed by Jeffrey's generous review of the poem, coupled with his refusal to prolong the unnecessary quarrel. "Jeffrey has behaved most handsomely," Byron acknowledged in May 1812, and he was deeply gratified by the other's subsequent reviews of the verse-tales. "Many a man will retract praise," he noted in March 1814; "none but a high-spirited mind will revoke its censure, or *can* praise the man it has once attacked. ... I admire him for *this* — not because he has *praised me* ... but because he is, perhaps, the *only man* who, under the relations in which he and I stand, or stood, with regard to each other, would have had the liberality to act thus; none but a great soul dared hazard it" (*BL&J*, 2:178, 3:252-53). With the occasion of offense removed, Byron abandoned forever his attack on all things Scottish. His "Address Intended to be Recited at the Caledonian Meeting" in London in 1814 was written in support of a fund for educating and supporting orphans of Scottish soldiers and sailors who had died in action. It foreshadows the tribute to the gallantry of Highland regiments in the Waterloo stanzas of *Childe Harold,* Canto III. And indeed, far from damning the whole nation on account of the Scotch Reviewers, he now thought of coming north to meet their editor-in-chief. "Perhaps you and Mrs. Moore will pay us a visit at Seaham in the course of the autumn," he suggested to Thomas Moore in July 1815. "If so, you and I (*without* our *wives*) will take a *lark* to Edinburgh and embrace Jeffrey" (*BL&J*, 4:303).

Byron's rapprochement with Scott in 1812 was even more important; and their unflawed friendship — in spite of political, religious, and temperamental differences — is one that does both men the greatest credit. Highpoints in their relationship were Scott's sympathetic review in the *Quarterly* of *Childe Harold,* Canto III, and his acceptance of the dedication of the controversial *Cain* — both gestures of support to Byron at times when he was the subject of widespread and intemperate attacks. Their mutual respect was literary as well as personal in nature. Byron had, even in *English Bards,* seen Scott as capable of poetic greatness:

> Thy country's voice, the voice of all the nine,
> Demand a hallow'd harp — that harp is thine.
> [Ll. 933-34]

He knew Scott's poetry well: Ali Pasha's court at Tepaleen had immediately reminded him of Branksome Castle in *The Lay of the Last Minstrel*; and Childe Harold's "Goodnight" in Canto I was suggested by a ballad in the *Minstrelsy of the*

Scottish Border.[8] "I see the 'Lady of the Lake' advertised,"
he had written to Hodgson in October 1810: "of course it is
in his old ballad style, and pretty, after all Scott is the best of
them. — The end of all scribblement is to amuse, and he
certainly succeeds there, I long to read his new Romance"
(*BL&J,* 2:20). *Hints from Horace* had a few unsympathetic
comments in the notes, but in the text Byron praises Scott for
his mastery of the octosyllabic couplet in his verse tales:

> Though at first view eight feet may seem in vain
> Form'd, save in ode, to bear a serious strain,
> Yet Scott has shown our wondering isle of late
> This measure shrinks not from a theme of weight,
> And, varied skilfully, surpasses far
> Heroic rhyme, but most in love and war,
> Whose fluctuations, tender or sublime,
> Are curb'd too much by long-recurring rhyme.
>
> [Ll. 405-12]

This praise has obvious implications for Byron's own choice
of meter for many of his own verse-tales, just as Marmion,
"Not quite a Felon, yet but half a Knight," with his "acts of
darkness" and his mistress disguised as a page, is an obvious
prototype for Lara. Byron had, in fact, long enjoyed Scott's
poetry in spite of the criticisms he had made of it in *English
Bards*: now, after the rapprochement of 1812, he acknowledges that enjoyment freely. "I like the man — and
admire his works to what Mr Braham calls *Entusymusy,"* he
writes in November 1813. "He is undoubtedly the Monarch
of Parnassus, and the most *English* of bards" (*BL&J,* 3:209,
219-20).

Much more important for my present theme, however, is
Byron's unstinted admiration for Scott's novels, which
involved delighted recognition of their authentic rendering of
the Scottish social scene — the Scottish world that he himself
had known in boyhood. This is explicit from the very outset:
"Waverley," Byron wrote to Murray in July 1814, "is the
best & most interesting novel I have redde since — I don't

know when ... besides — it is all easy to me — because I have been in Scotland so much — (though then young enough too) and feel at home with the people lowland and Gael'' (*BL&J*, 4:146). His admiration for Scott's poetry was never to be repudiated, but it was qualified by his later conviction that the Romantic innovators were all on the wrong lines (himself included), whereas his enthusiasm for the novels flourished and increased. He reads them and re-reads them constantly; he quotes from them repeatedly in his letters; and his praise of them is unequivocal. ''I have more of Scott's novels (for surely they are Scott's),'' he writes to William Bankes in February 1820, ''and am more and more delighted. I think that I even prefer them to his poetry.'' ''Pray send me W. Scott's new novels,'' he tells Murray soon afterwards: ''what are their names and characters? I read some of his former ones at least once a day for an hour or so. ... Pray make him write at least two a year. — I like no reading so well'' (*BL&J,* 7:45, 48). In his journal for January 1821 he notes: ''Read the conclusion, for the fiftieth time (I have read all W. Scott's novels at least fifty times) of the third series of 'Tales of my Landlord', — grand work — Scotch Fielding, as well as great English poet — wonderful man! I long to get drunk with him.'' And again: ''Scott is certainly the most wonderful writer of the day. His novels are a new literature in themselves, and his poetry as good as any — if not better (only on an erroneous system). ... I like him, too, for his manliness of character, for the extreme pleasantness of his conversation, and his good-nature towards myself, personally. May he prosper! — for he deserves it. I know no reading to which I fall with such alacrity as a work of W. Scott's.'' ''Give my love to Sir W. Scott,'' he writes to Murray in March of that same year, ''& tell him to write more novels; — pray send out Waverley and the Guy M [annering] — and the Antiquary — It's five years since I have had a copy —— I have read all the others forty times'' (*BL&J*, 8:13, 23, 88).

If we ask why Byron found these novels so congenial, our answers must to some extent be speculative; but two features seem immediately relevant. In the first place, almost every novelist of the eighteenth and nineteenth centuries had to decide, consciously or unconsciously, on the emphasis to be given in his work to the claims of what we should see as realism and romance; and one can easily see why Scott's particular blend of the two in *his* novels would appeal to Byron. Scott deals very often with romance themes and romantic situations, but he treats them realistically. If he presents Highland clansmen in *Waverley,* for example, or Highland outlaws in *Rob Roy,* he does so with considerable knowledge of history and social circumstance: he establishes the prosaic detail of their lives and does not shrink from showing the cruel, the dishonest, the ignoble aspects of their lives and characters, as well as the attractive or the noble. He shares with Byron what one Scott critic has described as "a shrewd, even tough realism."[9] Secondly, modern critics have explored the dialectic in Scott's novels between the values of the Scottish present and Scottish past — the profit and loss account, imaginative, emotional, and moral, which he offers in portraying the savage, heroic world of conflict and the civilized, profitable one of progress. Yet Scott is in the last analysis concerned with synthesis as much as with antithesis: living as he did in the era of the French Revolution, the Napoleonic Wars, and subsequent unrest, he could see that many values of the past — courage, for example, and the spirit of the loyalty that he found in Fergus's clansmen — were very relevant to the present, if its civilization and prosperity were to be preserved. And furthermore, he was drawn, for his fiction, to periods or situations when the worlds of present and past, or, more fundamentally, peace and conflict, order and violence, civilization and savagery, were juxtaposed, so that a young man like Edward Waverley, Henry Morton, or Francis Osbaldistone could pass from one to another. Which is just what Byron sought to do throughout his life, in his early travels, in his involvement with the Carbonari in Italy, and in his commitment to the insurrectionists in the Greek War of Independence.

These seem to be important factors in his admiration for Scott's novels, but there is a third, relating quite specifically to the portrayal of Scottish life and character. The Union of the Crowns in 1603 had removed the Scottish Court from Edinburgh to London, with far-reaching effects on Scottish culture. The Union of the Parliaments in 1707 had removed the Scottish parliament as well, and the effects of this, it has often been suggested, went even further. Already mentioned were the anti-Scottish as well as anti-Highland feelings prevalent in England for much of the eighteenth century. There was also a loss of national confidence among Scots. In the century that followed the Union, they were in many ways being assimilated to England: many, for example, took pains to purge their speech of Scotticisms; and although national sentiment was still strong, a sense of inferiority coexisted with their pride. This was a further reason for Byron's playing down his Aberdeen background in his early poetry. Scott, however, set out quite deliberately in his novels to rectify this situation. He was struck, he writes, by

> the extended and well-merited fame of Miss Edgeworth, whose Irish characters have gone so far to make the English familiar with the character of their gay and kind-hearted neighbours of Ireland, that she may be truly said to have done more towards completing the Union than perhaps all the legislative enactments by which it has been followed up. . . . I felt that something might be attempted for my own country of the same kind with that which Miss Edgeworth so fortunately achieved for Ireland — something which might introduce her natives to those of the sister kingdom in a more favourable light than they had been placed hitherto, and tend to procure sympathy for their virtues and indulgence for their foibles. I thought also that much of what I wanted in talent might be made up by the intimate acquaintance with the subject which I could lay claim to possess, as having travelled through most parts of Scotland, both Highland and Lowland; having been familiar with the elder as

well as the modern race; and having had from my infancy free
and unrestrained communication with my countrymen, from the
Scottish peer to the Scottish ploughman.[10]

It was an endeavor that met with quite remarkable success.
He did a superb public relations job for Scotland and the
Scots, imprinting a more favorable image of them on the
English, the American, the European, and, indeed, the world
imagination. He also helped to articulate for Scots themselves
their national consciousness — a sense of Scottishness to be
asserted proudly, not at all apologetically. And this was an
aspect of his work that had a deep appeal for Byron. In a
letter to Scott in January 1822 he wrote:

> I don't like to bore you about the Scotch novels ... but nothing
> can or could ever persuade me since I was the first ten minutes in
> your company that you are *not* the Man.——To me those novels
> have so much of "Auld lang syne" (I was bred a canny Scot till
> ten years old) that I never move without them — and when I
> removed from Ravenna to Pisa the other day — and sent on my
> library before — they were the only books that I kept by me —
> although I already knew them by heart.

He goes on, after speaking of the bitterness he feels towards
England and the English,

> But my "heart warms to the Tartan" or to any thing of Scotland
> which reminds me of Aberdeen and other parts not so far from
> the Highlands as that town — (about Invercauld & Braemar
> where I was sent to drink Goat's *Fey* in 1795-6 [following a?]
> threatened decline after the scarlet fever).   [*BL&J,* 9:86-87]

Notice here not just the nostalgia, frankly acknowledged, but
the accuracy, the authenticity, the truthfulness of his
recollections, which guard the nostalgia against any danger of
lapsing into sentimentality. There is no pretense here of his
having been a picturesque young Highland chieftain: instead
he describes himself as "bred a canny Scot" and records the
simple memory of spending a summer's convalescence in the
Highlands, with his emotion all the more effective for its not

being orchestrated in a more pretentious way. Notice too his use of the North-East dialect form *fey* for *whey,* in contrast to an earlier unease about Scotticisms, glimpsed in *Hours of Idleness* in his self-conscious gloss on *gloaming* as "the Scottish word for twilight ... recommended by many eminent literary men, particularly by Dr Moore in his Letters to Burns."[11] This letter can be linked to his long note of 1821 on "Aberdeen — Old and New or the Auldtoun & Newtoun":

For several years of my earliest childhood I was in that City — but have never revisited it since I was ten years old. — I was sent at five years old or earlier to a School kept by a Mr. *Bowers* — who was called "*Bodsy* Bowers" by reason of his dapperness. — It was a School for both sexes — I learned little there — except to repeat by rote the first lesson of Monosyllables — "God made man — let us love him" by hearing it often repeated — without acquiring a letter. — Whenever proof was made of my progress at home — I repeated these words with the most rapid fluency, but on turning over a new leaf — I continued to repeat them — so that the narrow boundaries of my first year's accomplishments were detected — my ears boxed — (which they did not deserve — seeing that it was by *ear* only that I had acquired my letters) — and my intellects consigned to a new preceptor. — He was a very decent — clever — little Clergyman — named Ross — afterwards Minister of one of the kirks (*East* I think) [;] under *him* — I made an astonishing progress — and I recollect to this day his mild manners & good-natured painstaking. — The moment I could read — my grand passion was *history* — and why I know not — but I was particularly taken with the battle near the Lake Regillus in the Roman History — put into my hands the first. —— Four years ago when standing on the heights of Tusculum — & looking down upon the little round Lake that was once Regillus & which dots the immense expanse below — I remembered my young enthusiasm & my old instructor. —— Afterwards I had a very serious — saturnine — but kind young man named Paterson for a Tutor — he was the son of my Shoemaker — but a good Scholar as is common with the Scotch. — He was a rigid Presbyterian also. — With him I began Latin in Ruddiman's Grammar — & continued till I went to the "Grammar School" (*Scotice* "*Schule*" — *Aberdonice* "*Squeel*") where I threaded all the classes to the *fourth* — when I was re-called to England (where I had been hatched) by the demise of my Uncle. — I had acquired this hand writing which I can hardly read myself under the fair copies of Mr. Duncan of the same city. — I don't think that he would plume himself upon my progress. — However I wrote much better then than I have ever done since; — haste and agitation of one kind or another have quite spoilt as pretty a scrawl as ever scratched over a frank.   [*BL&J,* 8:107-8]

Here is a vivid, uncensored, lively recollection of his childhood — socially authentic and unpretentious, and linguistically accurate, as in his rendering of the Aberdonian pronunciation "squeel" for "school" — undistorted by literary stereotypes or literary conventions. Indeed, one might claim that it has been liberated from stereotypes and conventions partly at least by Scott's example. In his novels he showed Byron how to come to terms with his Scottish background and experience, how to acknowledge them without embarrassment or inhibition, and how to appreciate them without romantic distortion.

It is rather disappointing that this new affectionate awareness of Scotland as she really is finds little expression in his poetry: perhaps it was an awareness better suited to the more sensitive medium of his prose. He can revert to the satiric mode, when faced with the sycophancy and absurdity of George IV's visit to Edinburgh:

> where is "Fum" the Fourth, our "royal bird"?
> Gone down, it seems, to Scotland, to be fiddled
>   Unto by Sawney's violin, we have heard:
> "Caw me, caw thee" — for six months has been hatching
> This scene of royal itch and loyal scratching.[12]
>
> [*Don Juan* XI.lxxviii]

Byron can also revert to the histrionic, as when he touches in *The Island* on the effect of childhood memories in later life:

> He who first met the Highlands' swelling blue
> Will love each peak that shows a kindred hue,
> Hail in each crag a friend's familiar face,

And clasp the mountain in his mind's embrace.
Long have I roamed through lands which are not mine,
Adored the Alp, and loved the Apennine,
Revered Parnassus, and beheld the steep
Jove's Ida and Olympus crown the deep:
But 'twas not all long ages' lore, nor all
Their nature held me in their thrilling thrall;
The infant rapture still survived the boy,
And Loch-na-gar with Ida look'd o'er Troy,
Mix'd Celtic memories with the Phrygian mount,
And Highland linns with Castalie's clear fount.
Forgive me, Homer's universal shade!
Forgive me, Phoebus! that my fancy stray'd;
The north and nature taught me to adore
Your scenes sublime, from those beloved before.

[II. 280-97]

Here the stilted versification and clumsy, inept phraseology obscure the sentiments, instead of giving them full, adequate expression; and one turns with pleasure to the unaffected lucidity of Byron's footnote: "When very young, about eight years of age, after an attack of the scarlet fever at Aberdeen, I was removed by medical advice into the Highlands. Here I passed occasionally some summers, and from this period I date my love of mountainous countries."

When all is said and done, it is only in his *ottava rima* poetry that Byron finds a medium to do justice to the flexibility of tone, the modulations of feeling, the combination of witty common sense and deep emotion, the vitality of linguistic usage, that characterized his conversation, letters, and informal prose. It is not surprising, therefore, that it is to *Don Juan* we must turn for the one adequate summation of his feelings about Scotland. The passage is familiar, but I shall not apologize for quoting it, with all its nostalgia, its inclusiveness, its honesty, its self-criticism, its emotional integrity:

And all our little feuds, at least all *mine,*
Dear Jeffrey, once my most redoubted foe

(As far as rhyme and criticism combine
        To make such puppets of us things below),
Are over: Here's a health to "Auld Lang Syne!"
        I do not know you, and may never know
Your face — but you have acted on the whole
Most nobly, and I own it from my soul.

And when I use the phrase of "Auld Lang Syne!"
        'Tis not addressed to you — the more's the pity
For me, for I would rather take my wine
        With you, than aught (save Scott) in your proud city.
But somehow — it may seem a schoolboy's whine,
        And yet I seek not to be grand nor witty,
But I am half a Scot by birth, and bred
A whole one, and my heart flies to my head, —

As "Auld Lang Syne" brings Scotland, one and all,
        Scotch plaids, Scotch snoods, the blue hills, and
            clear streams,
The Dee, the Don, Balgounie's brig's *black wall,*
        All my boy feelings, all my gentler dreams
Of what I *then dreamt,* clothed in their own pall,
        Like Banquo's offspring: — floating past me seems
My childhood, in this childishness of mine:
I care not — 'tis a glimpse of *"Auld Lang Syne."*

And though, as you remember, in a fit
        Of wrath and rhyme, when juvenile and curly,
I rail'd at Scots to show my wrath and wit,
        Which must be own'd was sensitive and surly,
Yet 'tis in vain such sallies to permit,
        They cannot quench young feelings fresh and early:
I *"scotch'd* not killed" the Scotchman in my blood,
And love the land of "mountain and of flood."

[X.xvi-xix]

The last phrase, incidentally, is a quotation from *The Lay of the Last Minstrel.*

To sum up, it is my contention that the attitudes to Scotland in Byron's early lyrics are those of an adolescent who is rebelling against the true facts of his childhood; that the attitudes to Scotland in his early satires are those of an angry young man, launching indiscriminate attacks on a world that had failed to appreciate his genius; but that the attitudes in the passage above from *Don Juan* are those of an adult who has come to terms with his own past, and that Scott has helped him to attain to this maturity.

NOTES

1. T. S. Eliot, *On Poetry and Poets* (London: Faber and Faber, 1957), pp. 194-95.

2. *The Edinburgh Review* 11 (1807-8): 288.

3. Samuel Smiles, *A Publisher and His Friends* (London: John Murray, 1891), 1:7.

4. Quoted by John Prebble, *Mutiny: Highland Regiments in Revolt, 1743-1804* (London: Secker & Warburg, 1975), p. 93.

5. Hugh Blair, *A Critical Dissertation on the Poems of Ossian, the Son of Fingal* (London: T. Becket and P. A. De Hondt, 1763), p. 2.

6. Sir Walter Scott, *Selected Poems,* ed. Thomas Crawford (Oxford: Clarendon Press, 1972), p. 123.

7. *The Edinburgh Review* 6 (1805): 6 (my italics).

8. See *BL&J,* 1:227; and "Preface" to *Childe Harold* I and II.

9. A. O. J. Cockshut, *The Achievement of Walter Scott* (London: Collins, 1969), p. 122.

10. Sir Walter Scott, *Waverley,* Centenary Edition (Edinburgh: Adam and Charles Black, 1889), pp. 9-10.

11. Byron's note to l. 34 of "Elegy on Newstead Abbey."

12. Many of Byron's Scots words and phrases in his letters derive from the Waverley Novels, and although "Caw me, caw thee" could be a childish recollection of Scots usage, it probably stems from a footnote in *A Legend of Montrose*: "In Old English, *ka me ka thee, i.e.* mutually serving each other" (Centenary Edition, 6 [1890], 130n).

Byron and William Hazlitt

JAMES A. HOUCK

The literary relations between Lord Byron and William Hazlitt have never received detailed examination. Hazlitt's relations, literary and personal, with most of his famous contemporaries have been well explored: his profound influence upon Keats, his tangled relations with Wordsworth and Coleridge, his copious writings on Scott, his connections with Lamb — all have inspired detailed and frequent investigation. Few are the books dealing with any of his other major contemporaries that do not contain references to Hazlitt (albeit often unflattering ones). Yet even a passing allusion to Hazlitt in the work of Byron scholars is more the exception than the rule, and Hazlittians have been equally chary in regard to their subject's writings on the noble poet. The fact is a curious one. Hazlitt is with increasing frequency being accorded again today the recognition that many of his contemporaries gave him, however grudgingly in some cases, as the finest practicing critic of his day, and some see him as rivaling Coleridge as a critical theorist. Walter Jackson Bate has recently declared Hazlitt "easily the most representative of the major British critics writing during the period of 'High Romanticism' (1790-1830)."[1] One should be interested in what the period's "most representative" critic has to say about its most popular poet.

That such an examination has apparently been deemed unprofitable may be traced to three causes. First, with Byron — alone among his most famous literary contemporaries — Hazlitt had no personal relations. While yet a young man he had met and been powerfully affected by Coleridge, who in turn introduced him to Wordsworth, though as with many of Hazlitt's friendships, those with the two poets were subsequently to sour. His avuncular interest in Keats was one of the most important events in the young poet's brief life, and his long friendship with Lamb has often been celebrated. Hazlitt was at least tenuously connected with Shelley through their mutual friend Leigh Hunt in a way that was never true of Byron, even during their mutual "association" in *The Liberal*. Indeed, Hazlitt offended Byron in his first extended criticism of him. In "On the Living Poets," the last of the *Lectures on the English Poets* (1818), Hazlitt — in a memorably amusing manner — accuses Byron of vacillating on Napoleon: "There is one subject on which Lord Byron is fond of writing, on which I wish he would not write — Buonaparte. Not that I quarrel with his writing for him, or against him, but with his writing both for him and against him." Worse, he accuses the poet of praising Napoleon when he was successful and attacking him when he was defeated.[2] The accusation probably called forth Byron's famous observation that Hazlitt "*talks pimples*" (*BL&J,* 8:38), a reference to the long and cruel *Blackwood's* campaign against "pimpled Hazlitt," and it occasions a lengthy defense by Byron in a note appended to the first canto of *Don Juan* (see *BL&J,* 6:100 and n). Though Leigh Hunt, in a letter to his brother John in the fall of 1822, contends that "Lord B. admires Hazlitt's writings," a year later Henry Muir records that Byron "expressed himself in the most bitter terms" in regard to Hazlitt, "and would not allow that he could write good English."[3] It has been suggested that Scamp the Lecturer in *The Blues,* written at about this time, is Hazlitt.[4] And in 1828 in *Lord Byron and Some of His Contem-*

poraries, Hunt charges that though Hazlitt thought Byron liked him, in fact the poet merely feared him.[5]

A second reason for the lack of attention to Hazlitt's discussions of Byron is that Hazlitt reviewed few of Byron's works. Indeed, only six places in Hazlitt's writings contain extended discussion of Byron. However, Hazlitt frequently remarks on Byron throughout his writings, and these briefer observations, if only made *en passant,* often merit consideration. Byron appears in Hazlitt's pages notably more frequently, for example, than either Shelley or Keats, though more has been written about his views of these two contemporaries.

But a third consideration most tellingly explains the paucity of comment on the Byron-Hazlitt relations. It seems generally accepted by students of both the poet and the critic that Hazlitt did not really like or understand Byron's work and that his discussions of it are of only passing interest as reflecting commonplace prejudices of the time or one or another of Hazlitt's own well-known "prejudices." Samuel Chew, for example, devotes a scant three pages in his *Byron in England* to a summary of Hazlitt's discussions of the poet, noting that the critic was "curiously unaware of the real Byron."[6] Perhaps Robert Gleckner best sums it up when he asserts "Hazlitt's general lack of sympathy with Byron's verse."[7] But I wonder — or at least I would certainly hesitate before agreeing to attribute to Hazlitt a lack of sympathy for anything. The catholicity of his taste is astounding, and he could separate the wheat from the chaff — especially in regard to his contemporaries, a notoriously difficult task. His perceptive criticism makes him at the least a man whose ideas should be listened to, and his remarks on Byron can illuminate certain important theoretical positions of Hazlitt and pinpoint what may in fact be deficient in some of Byron's work. These remarks will also show Hazlitt rounding back on himself and coming to admire a major work — and a major poet — he had before thought significantly flawed.

The references to Byron in Hazlitt's writings appear over a period of almost seventeen years, from a passing comment on the "softness and the wildness of character of the popular poet of the East" in an art review for the *Morning Chronicle* in the spring of 1814 (18:19) to an allusion to the poet's lack of sympathy for Cowper in "The Letter-Bell," posthumously published in March 1831 in the *Monthly Magazine* (17:382).[8] In 1815 Hazlitt ventures a passing jest about the poet, who then disappears from Hazlitt's published writings until 1818; but from this year onward only one year passes without some observations on Byron. In 1818 comes "On the Living Poets," and in the spring of the same year Hazlitt reviews the fourth canto of *Childe Harold* for the *Yellow Dwarf* and goes out of his way to praise the "mighty poet" in an *Edinburgh Review* piece on Walpole's correspondence. There is silence in 1819, but the essays of 1820, especially those in the *Table Talk* series, are peppered with references to Byron. In the *London Magazine* for May 1821, Hazlitt reviews, unfavorably, *Marino Faliero,* and in the issue for the next month he discusses at length the Pope-Byron-Bowles controversy. Only a few scattered references appear in the writings of 1822; 1823 brings a review of *Heaven and Earth,* though it was heavily edited and revised by Jeffrey before its appearance in the February *Edinburgh.* Hazlitt's anthology *Select British Poets,* with its generous Byron selections, appears in 1824; 1825 dates the appearance of Hazlitt's most famous discussion of Byron in *The Spirit of the Age,* which also contains numerous comments on the poet outside the essay devoted to him. The travel essays appearing through 1824-25 and later gathered as *Notes of a Journey* often mention Byron, and some of the essays in the *New Monthly Magazine* for 1825, later to appear in *The Plain Speaker,* also refer to him. From 1826 to 1829 Byron will occasionally — and, I think, significantly — appear in the papers later gathered as *Conversations of James Northcote,* as well as in other miscellaneous essays for a variety of publications from this time until Hazlitt's death in 1830. The last extended discussion is an essay entitled "Byron and Wordsworth" for the *London Weekly Review* in April 1828. And this survey omits occasions when Byron is merely quoted or appears simply as a name in a list.

Certainly Hazlitt's opinions of Byron are occasionally tinted by extra-literary influences and associations, as is the case with any critic. Long noted by students of Hazlitt is his period of withdrawal, melancholy, and pessimism (cynicism, some would insist) between 1819 and 1823, brought on by the increasingly vicious attacks on him in the Tory journals, the seeming desertion of his friends, the deaths of his father and his idol Napoleon, and the *"Liber Amoris* affair," his infatuation with the young daughter of his landlord that subsequently led to his divorce from his first wife and, upon learning the girl was a mere flirt and jilt, a period of what he himself subsequently saw as a kind of insanity that he "wrote out" in his still moving — and still sadly underrated — *Liber Amoris.* During this time, he has little patience with what he once irritably perceives as Byron's *"got-up* ill-humour" (19:64). Also coloring his criticism is his background as the son of a dissenting minister: one may anticipate from a dissenter little sympathy for the whims of an aristocrat. And certainly influencing some of his querulous later remarks are what Hazlitt saw as Byron's capitulation to the urgings of his friends that he dissociate himself from the "Cockneys" Hazlitt and Hunt, who labored with him on *The Liberal.*

But the most important elements of Hazlitt's view of Byron and his writings, especially the oriental tales with their "Byronic" heroes, are derived from deeply held and perceptive beliefs about the nature and function of literature and about the nature and functioning of those who create it. Most central in Hazlitt's assessments of Byron and his work is the critic's continuing emphasis upon the difficulties and the temptations posed when one is a Noble Poet. Over and over through the years Hazlitt returns to the fact that Byron is doubly an aristocrat, both by birth and by virtue of his genius. He is "a spoiled child of nature and fortune" (19:62; see also 19:35; 11:75, 94). He is both Poet and Peer (8:210; see also 11:70; 17:159, 194n). That he is a great poet, "one of the proudest pages of our annals" (16:149), Hazlitt frequently asserts.[9] But he equally insists — at least until his final years when, I shall later suggest, he changes his mind about *Don Juan* — that Byron has not fulfilled his promise, that he has misused his gifts. Byron is not, though he could and should have been, the greatest poet of his age. Hazlitt seems to locate the cause of the poet's (relative) failure in his double nature as lord and poetic genius, the weaknesses of each re-enforcing those of the other.

At times Hazlitt's use of the point seems unfair and testy, as in a *Table Talk* essay of 1820, "On the Aristocracy of Letters":

> What a fine addition is ten thousand a year and a title to the flaunting pretensions of a modern rhapsodist! His name so accompanied becomes the mouth well: it is repeated thousands of times, instead of hundreds, because the reader in being familiar with the Poet's works seems to claim acquaintance with the Lord. [8:209]

The observation embodies a keen psychological insight, though it is ill-natured. But Hazlitt continues, unfairly, to suggest that Byron's popular reputation is due solely to his noble rank. "He sustains two lofty and imposing characters; and in order to simplify the process of our admiration," Hazlitt asserts, "we equalise his pretensions, and take it for granted that he must be as superior to other men in genius as he is in birth" (8:210). But Hazlitt's spleen has been aroused by the noble poet's seeming invulnerability to criticism because of his title: "the poet Keats had not this sort of protection for his person" (8:211; see also 20:159). And of course this was written at a time when Hazlitt was being savaged monthly by the Tory press and thus made to pay dearly for his liberal opinions while Byron was hit only obliquely and reluctantly in the *Quarterly* and was awarded compensating praise in *Blackwood's*. Hazlitt occasionally voices frustrated resentment at Byron's privileged position, at which times the dissenter comes most clearly to the fore.

But most frequently when Byron's dual aristocracy is adduced, the motive is neither frustrated envy nor a doctrinaire dissenting posture. Rather, Hazlitt is calling attention — Byron's attention as well as his readers', at least until the poet's death — to the double danger thus imposed upon the Noble Bard. As I have elsewhere suggested,[10] Hazlitt's criticism is informed by a psychology of literary genius. Hazlitt is aware of genius's weaknesses, its craving for praise, its fear of attack and censure, its love of power, its egotism, its tendency to go to extremes. He insists that a critic must by sympathetically aware of this psychological profile and adapt his criticism accordingly, meting out praise when it is due — and when it is needed — defending genius against unfair and partisan attack, chastising it when it weakens or wanders from its true bent or is carried to unwarrantable extremes. A genius is always in a dangerous and vulnerable position. But an aristocratic genius faces even greater difficulties and temptations. Hazlitt is equally shrewd in his analysis of the aristocratic character and temperament. Desires are fulfilled with too little personal effort to make their gratification seem worthwhile; honors are paid without the exacting of merit or accomplishment; necessities are supplied without work, resulting in ennui and "the want of something to do"; and an exaggerated sense of self-importance and self-worth accompanies a noble title, joined with disdain for the untitled.[11] Hence, the many contradictions in Byron. The liberal poet defends freedom for all and courts revolution, while the aristocrat shelters behind his title and fears the rabble.[12] The poetic genius desires praise and approbation, but the noble lord disdains to subject himself to the opinions of those beneath him: "when we come to offer him our demonstrations of good will,"

Hazlitt complains, "he should not kick us down stairs" (19:65). And elsewhere: "His Lordship is hard to please: he is equally averse to notice or neglect, enraged at censure and scorning praise. He tries the patience of the town to the very utmost, and when they show signs of weariness or disgust, threatens to *discard* them" (11:76). Byron's genius will, unless subject to a sense of propriety enforced by sympathetic criticism, naturally run into extremes, yet he is a lord and impervious to criticism and common opinion and thus to the healthy check that could temper his more wayward impulses.

According to Hazlitt, Byron's genius and privileged status occasion his egotism, his gloomy and ungovernable passions, his "undramatic" character — all of which mar many of his works. Byron cannot be a poet of the very highest order because his dual nature causes him habitually to interrupt what Hazlitt seems to perceive as a four-stage process of poetic creativity. It may be sketched only briefly here: a particular aspect of nature matches the conformation of the poet's mind, his natural bias, and its impressions on his mind are thus especially vivid and hence arouse an interest, which leads to feeling or passion being connected with the perception. The imagination is thus engaged and, through a passionate involvement, a *grappling* with the object or experience, the imagination perceives its essence and heightens it by associating with it other ideas or images that, while related to it by similarity of feeling or passion, have the effect of intensifying or elevating it. Words then arise and must be selected and arranged. There are thus four stages to the process that the greatest poets at least have followed: the initial perception and choice of object;[13] the arising of natural interest, feeling, and passion and the engaging of the imagination; the imaginative grappling with the object; and the arising of words. But, Hazlitt suggests, Byron curtails the natural development of a poem at the second stage; he does not move on to the passionate grappling with the object until the impression is objectified and unified. The real force of

Hazlitt's critique of Byron is lost, unless one sees it in terms of this process.

The intimacy and intensity of the greatest poets' imaginative involvement with nature Hazlitt describes in highly physical terms. A few examples must suffice. All great art, he remarks as early as 1814, is "the result of that strength which had grappled with nature" (18:42). Shakespeare's plays are superior to his poems, Hazlitt suggests, because only in the former has he grappled with nature (4:14, 228, 358). Homer grappled with his subject (5:15), and Moore is superficial because he is unable to grapple with his (5:151). During this "grappling," objects must take "hold of the mind" (5:12; 16:136) or of the imagination (12:259). Or else they must "stagger" and "strike" them.[14] But Byron does not enter into this process, Hazlitt asserts. Byron does not allow the object to twine round his mind but rather "flings his own views or feelings upon outward objects" (16:412). In the "Byronic" poems, there is no "twining of the heart round any object"; all is the result of first impressions. The procedure is the reverse of Wordsworth's, for whom "recurrence" is all, which ultimately defines the superiority of Wordsworth to his aristocratic contemporary. Byron's birth and high station make him "impatient of any but the most inordinate and immediate stimulus," and his noble background causes him to disdain common objects (20:155-56, 252).

Byron thus molds objects and experiences according to subjective responses, rather than allowing his associations to be guided by the object (for example, 11:71). Hence the charge, as in *The Spirit of the Age,* that the noble poet disdains nature: "He raises his subject to himself, or tramples on it; he neither stoops to, nor loses himself in it" (11:69; see also 19:72). Byron thus falsifies nature, Hazlitt continues: "he hangs the cloud, the film of his existence over all outward things" (11:71). Insofar as he ever grapples with his subject, it is merely to charge it with "the electric force of his own feelings" (11:72). It thus follows as a necessary corollary that all of Byron's characters are a reflection of himself: "Lord Byron makes man after his own image, woman after his own heart . . . he makes out everlasting centos of himself" (11:71; 5:153).

Hazlitt designates Byron a "poet of passion," one sometimes at the mercy of his passions. An object, usually not a common one, arouses an interest, passion ensues, and Byron immediately allows it free rein. The imagination's associative process is not governed by the result of a grappling with the initial object but rather by the passions of the poet. From this follow the extravagances and exaggerations, albeit sometimes "splendid" ones (20:211), which Hazlitt so often decries in Byron's work (for example, 11:159, 170, 188; 16:445), for no natural limits or strictures are imposed upon the imagination when governed by passion. From this circumstance too comes the monotony with which Hazlitt charges Byron; the passions, at least in the "Byronic" earlier poems, Hazlitt insists, are always the same: violent, fierce, sullen, gloomy. "Whatever he does, he must do in a more decided and daring manner than any one else," writes Hazlitt, continuing with amusing exaggeration: "he lounges with extravagance, and yawns so as to alarm the reader" (11:70). These are not the passions of a mind in conflict, or even in communication, with the world, but rather of "a mind preying upon itself, and disgusted with, or indifferent to all other things." Hazlitt objects to Byron's egotism, the absorption of all the universe in "the ruling passion and moody abstraction of a single mind" (5:153). Byron, he asserts, "obstinately and invariably shuts himself up in the Bastile of his own ruling passions" (11:71); this "restlessness" in his poetry fails to "satisfy" and give the mind "repose"; such must be the result if the imagination is subservient to passion. Byron's poems lack *keeping,* or possess it within only a narrow range, and thus cannot finally leave either the poet or his readers satisfied and at rest.

Hazlitt elsewhere suggests that an organic image, the growth of a flower, best represents "the slow and perfect growth of works of imagination" (16:209-10). But this cannot be the case when first impressions and immediate passions rule all; then there can be no keeping and momentum. *Keeping* is a favorite term with Hazlitt. It is most frequently used within the context of the drama but is applicable to poetry as well. *Keeping* is Hazlitt's word for harmony, consistency, proportion (and, in drama, truth of character). It is, as he applies it, equivalent to the neoclassical concept of decorum, save that while decorum was to be guaranteed by the judgment, the comparing faculty, keeping is to be achieved only through unity of emotion. Only a directed imagination resulting from a grappling with the object will ensure keeping, and with keeping comes momentum. *Momentum* is "massing," "accumulation," "impulse," a slow accretion of detail that results in a consistent and unifying thread of feeling and effect, such as Hazlitt finds in Wordsworth's poetry, for example.[15]

The perfection of art is for Hazlitt the creation of the ideal, "that which we wish any thing to be" (8:321), the point at which the audience's expectations and desires have been fulfilled. Hazlitt repeatedly in his criticism uses images of plenitude and "filling." He insists that a work must "fill the moulds of the imagination" (see 8:41; 9:134) or "fill up" an idea in the mind (10:44; 20:211, 302). The necessity of "filling" the mind and thus satisfying the cravings of the reader's will and imagination requires the poet to have sympathy, to avoid egotism. If, as with Byron in Hazlitt's view, the associations of the poet with an object are merely personal or if he has chosen an object unfamiliar to most, his productions will fail to satisfy the expectations of most readers, will fail to "fill up" an idea in their minds. Hazlitt insists that, despite the immediate contemporary popularity of many "Byronic" poems because of their color and flash and the notoriety of their creator, they are not destined to live, to appeal to an audience removed from the influences of the times and the fascinating spectacle of the adventures of the poet himself. He has proved correct.

Hazlitt's expressions of Byron's shortcomings in the oriental tales and the dramas, then, are more than mere impressionistic dicta or the common cant of his day. Because Byron yields to his passions and allows them to govern his imaginative associations, his poetry must often lack keeping, or, where the initial passion is sufficiently powerful to unify the associations, it will be keeping of a narrow range (for example, 5:153). But even then there can be no ultimate satisfaction, for Byron has imposed his own passions upon the object and thus no "natural" heightening can take place — hence the complaints of exaggerations and distortions. Hence too Hazlitt's charges of falsified descriptions, as with the treatment in canto four of *Childe Harold* of the Falls of Terni: "The poetry is fine," Hazlitt notes, "but not like" (10:258). If the description is not true to nature, it cannot be carried to the stage of the ideal and thus satisfy the mind. And as Byron's passions are always the same, he can ultimately satisfy only those who share his own moods, especially the unhappy and the cynical (16:412). Though Hazlitt refers here to the oriental tales, the point applies equally to Byron's dramas. It comes once again to the poet's egotism, his "unaccommodating selfishness" (5:153), his unsympathetic refusal to go outside himself. Thus Byron is undramatic, even in his dramas. "They want the essence of the drama," Hazlitt charges. "They abound in speeches and descriptions, such as he himself might make either to himself or others, lolling on his couch of a morning, but do not carry the reader out of the poet's mind to the scenes and events recorded" (11:74). Hazlitt is not here merely parroting the conventional ideas of the age, as is sometimes charged,[16] but his objections are derived from and based upon his own detailed theory of literature, which should be better served by a poet who "has a seat in the House of Lords, a niche in the

Temple of Fame'' (11:77).

But to say that Byron is primarily a poet of passion rather than of imagination — or, like Wordsworth, of sensibility — is not for Hazlitt to say that he is no poet at all, or that he is an insignificant one. Hazlitt's writings on the poet are filled throughout with perceptive appreciation, indeed often a relish, of this passion. The distinctive quality of Byron's work upon which the critic focuses in the brief critical notice devoted to the poet in *Select British Poets* is its "intensity" (9:244; see also 20:128), and Hazlitt is always an admirer of this quality, whether in a poet, a juggler, or a fives-player. He notes appreciatively that Byron is "an *out-and-outer*" (17:169), that he is not "effeminate" (8:254) nor *mimminee-pimminee* (19:72), perhaps the most opprobrious term in Hazlitt's critical lexicon. Byron is, in many ways, as Ralph Wardle has observed, "Hazlitt's kind of man."[17] But Byron's despair and cynicism are to Hazlitt a morbid mental disease, one exacerbated by his aristocratic status; and the disease is all the more dangerous because of the appealing energy with which it is expressed. He condemns Byron's "cynical truisms" (17:233) and harbors no sympathy for a Childe Harold — or a Lord Byron — who, seemingly having everything, begins to crave impossibilities (19:36) like Camus's Caligula; "we are tired of the monotony of his Lordship's griefs, of which we can perceive neither beginning nor end," Hazlitt writes in 1818 in his review of *Childe Harold,* and he continues, with exasperated amusement:

> He volunteers his own Pilgrimage, — appoints his own penance, — makes his own confession, — and all, — for nothing. He is in despair, because he has nothing to complain of — miserable, because he is in want of nothing. 'He has tasted of all earth's bliss, both living and loving,' and therefore he describes himself as suffering the tortures of the damned. He is in love with misery, because he has possessed every enjoyment; and because he has had his will in every thing, is inconsolable because he cannot have impossibilities. His Lordship, in fact, makes out his own hard case to be, that he has attained all those objects that

the rest of the world admire; that he has met with none of those disasters which embitter their lives; and he calls upon us to sympathise with his griefs and his despair. [19:35-36]

The complaint may be read as a jejune and superficial assertion that the rich should all be happy and that anguish of soul and mind are of little account. But Hazlitt was neither jejune nor superficial, and even in 1818 he is sufficiently familiar with the legitimacy of the pains of a wounded spirit. Hazlitt is also pointedly aware, in this year before Peterloo, of the physical and social needs of the great mass of the English people and is surely indignant at the concern and pity lavished by the reading public upon the aristocratic sufferer rather than upon those who could more readily benefit from it. In any case Hazlitt distrusts Byron's sincerity; and even if he is sincere, Hazlitt is too shrewd a psychologist not to realize that Byron's mental torments are too often of his own creation. He would doubtless have seconded Carlyle's suggestion that happiness may as well be increased by decreasing one's denominator as by increasing one's numerator. The point is after all a very commonsensical one. And Hazlitt is concerned with the moral effects of the Byronic stance.

Literature is for Hazlitt preeminently a teacher of morality. "Who is there that has not been the better, the wiser, and happier man for these fine and inexhaustible productions of genius?" he exclaims of the novels of Scott (19:85), and he makes the same point about Shakespeare's tragedies (12:245). Hazlitt has no use for strictly didactic literature, and he attacks Byron for defending it and does so at length (19:65-69). Literature teaches morality by presenting a selective but accurate picture of nature, an imaginative but true depiction of the way things are. Sympathetic identification with others provides the chief means by which literature inculcates morality. This makes Scott "one of the greatest teachers of morality that ever lived" because he takes us out of ourselves, enlarges and deepens our sympathies. Byron, even in his dramas, never does so. Shakespeare is not only the greatest dramatist but the greatest moralist as well. He "did not intend to be moral," Hazlitt explains, "yet he could not be otherwise as long as he adhered to the path of nature. Morality only teaches us our duty by showing us the natural consequences of our actions" (11:267; see also 4:346-47). A part of Hazlitt's objections to Byron's works in this regard, especially to *Don Juan,* is clarified by an observation he makes comparing Shakespeare with Beaumont and Fletcher. Shakespeare, he asserts is "manly and bracing"; he "never disturbs the ground of moral principles; but leaves his characters . . . to be judged by our common sense and natural feeling." But Beaumont and Fletcher, "in the hey-day of their youthful ardour," use their characters to conduct moral experiments. They construct ambivalent characters and place them into difficult moral situations in order to see what will happen. "They are not safe teachers of morality: they tamper with it, like an experiment tried *in corpore vili*; and seem, to regard the decomposition of the common affections, and the dissolution of the strict bonds of society, as an agreeable study and a careless pastime." They present equivocal characters and set them into equivocal situations — their morality or immorality is thus unclear (6:248-50). Though never spelled out quite so specifically, this is also Hazlitt's objection to Byron's works, most notably *Don Juan,* but others as well (see, for example, 11:71). Of the author of *Don Juan* Hazlitt writes in *The Spirit of the Age*:

> He hallows in order to desecrate; takes a pleasure in defacing the images of beauty his hands have wrought; and raises our hopes and our belief in goodness to Heaven only to dash them to the earth again, and break them in pieces the more effectually from the very height they have fallen. Our enthusiasm for genius or virtue is thus turned into a jest by the very person who has kindled it. . . . It is not that Lord Byron is sometimes serious and sometimes trifling, sometimes profligate and sometimes moral — but when he is most serious and most moral, he is only preparing to mortify the unsuspecting reader by putting a pitiful *hoax* upon him. [11:75]

If this were Hazlitt's final word on Byron's greatest achievement, Hazlitt might be admired today for having firmer philosophical underpinnings for his moral objections than most others who decried the "immorality" of *Don Juan,* but one would surely feel that for all his sensitivity and perception in regard to the earlier "Byronic" poems, Hazlitt had rather missed the point here. But this is not the last word. At about the time of Byron's death or shortly afterward, Hazlitt's attitude is changing. The travel essays appearing in 1824-25 contain many good-natured and complimentary allusions to Byron; Thomas Medwin recounts that when he visited Hazlitt in Switzerland in 1827 the critic spoke at length of Byron and his works. While he had not altered his view of the earlier works, according to Medwin, Hazlitt singled out *Don Juan* as his favorite of all Byron's poems.[18] And an essay appearing in *The Atlas* in 1829, "Trifles Light as Air," while still berating Byron for his egotism and "presumption," also notes that the continued popularity of *Don Juan* indicates that the "senseless fastidiousness" growing within the reading public has not yet driven out such attacks upon vice as Byron's poem and *Tom Jones* (20:280-81). And also in 1829, in one of the "Conversations of James Northcote," there is something close to a repudiation of the earlier criticism. The discussion, put into the mouth of Northcote but surely revealing Hazlitt's own views, merits full quotation:

> no one can deny the force, the spirit of it [*Don Juan*]; and there is such a fund of drollery mixed up with the serious part. Nobody understood the tragi-comedy of poetry so well. ... in Lord Byron [the comic story and the tragic story] are brought together, just as they are in nature. In like manner, if you go to an execution at the very moment when the criminal is going to be turned off, and all eyes are fixed upon him, an old apple-woman and her stall are overturned, and all the spectators fall a-laughing. In real life the most ludicrous incidents border on the most affecting and shocking. How fine that is of the cask of butter in the storm! Some critics have objected to it as turning the whole into burlesque; on the contrary, it is that which stamps

the character of the scene more than any thing else. What did the people in the boat care about the rainbow, which he has described in such vivid colours; or even about their fellow-passengers who were thrown overboard, when they only wanted to eat them? No, it was the loss of the firkin of butter that affected them more than all the rest; and it is the mention of this circumstance that adds a hardened levity and a sort of ghastly horror to the scene. It shows the master-hand — there is such a boldness and sagacity and superiority to ordinary rules in it! [11:279-80]

In this passage, which Byron scholars generally have overlooked, Hazlitt presents Northcote as still asserting the "immorality or misanthropy" of the poem, but Hazlitt has clearly moved to a mature and perceptive understanding of Byron's finest achievement, which tacitly recants his earlier cavils.

Why the change? There are several possible reasons. Most commonsensically, it may well be that at the time of his writing the attack upon the poem in *Spirit of the Age,* Hazlitt had not actually read more than the opening cantos. A footnote, presumably added after the essay had been completed, notes that the censure applies "to the first Cantos of Don Juan much more than to the last" (11:75n), and one wonders if perhaps the later cantos have but recently received their first reading by the critic. If so, Hazlitt is among the first to comment on Byron's change of purpose and focus as the poem progressed. In addition, this perception may well have been eased by a change in the critic's own outlook. John Kinnaird, in his new book on Hazlitt, contends persuasively that Hazlitt during the 1820s is losing his earlier faith in the powers of the imagination and genius and democracy, that he is approaching a type of modern realism in his outlook, that his later essays reveal an attempt to penetrate imagination's illusions and the subtle deceptions of the self. Significantly, he parenthetically notes a parallel with what Byron is attempting in *Don Juan.*[19]

What one may find in Hazlitt's writings on Byron, then, is

a perceptive analysis of the shortcomings of the "Byronic" poems and dramas, found wanting according to Hazlitt's psychological theory of literature and poetic creativity. And at the same time his writings give a glimpse at least of a major critic changing his mind and moving toward an appreciation for and a recognition of what is now seen as one of the major literary productions of his time. Hazlitt has important things to tell about Byron; in turn, these reactions and insights reveal important things about Hazlitt himself.

NOTES

1. W. Jackson Bate, review of John L. Mahoney, *The Logic of Passion: The Literary Criticism of William Hazlitt,* in *Keats-Shelley Journal* 28 (1979): 156.

2. 5:153-54. All Hazlitt citations refer to *The Complete Works of William Hazlitt,* ed. P. P. Howe, 21 vols. (New York: J. M. Dent and Sons, 1930-34). Subsequent references will be parenthetical in my text.

3. *His Very Self and Voice: Collected Conversations of Lord Byron,* ed. Ernest J. Lovell, Jr. (New York: Macmillan Co., 1954), pp. 327, 451.

4. *Poetry,* 4:570.

5. Leigh Hunt, *Lord Byron and Some of His Contemporaries; with Recollections of the Author's Life, and of His Visit to Italy* (London: Henry Colburn, 1828), p. 63.

6. Samuel C. Chew, *Byron in England: His Fame and After-Fame* (London: John Murray, 1924), p. 138.

7. Robert F. Gleckner, *Byron and the Ruins of Paradise* (Baltimore, Md.: Johns Hopkins Press, 1967), p. 285.

8. Curiously, Hazlitt seems afflicted with a sort of tic in regard to the matter, bringing it up with indignation on three separate occasions. I suspect that this, coupled with his frequently expressed fondness for the poet, might reflect both a nostalgic remembrance of an early favorite and a personal identification with many aspects of the character and life of Cowper.

9. Hazlitt observes in his *English Poets* that Byron has perhaps "suffered too much" to be a great poet, but the suggestion is advanced for rhetorical force within the context of the discussion and is never repeated.

10. James A. Houck, "Hazlitt on the Obligations of the Critic," *The Wordsworth Circle* 4 (1973): 250-58.

11. The point is made frequently in Hazlitt's writings, but see especially "On the Aristocracy of Letters" (8:205-14) and "On the Conversation of Lords" (17:162-74).

12. See especially 11:70-71 and 12:378-80.

13. Much of the point of Hazlitt's review of Byron's *Letter on Bowles* (19:62-84) is that Byron is wrong in his defense of artificial over natural objects as the best subject matter for poetry and that in any case his own practice is in conflict with his theory, Byron's subjects being taken from nature.

14. For example, 6:129; 16:76; 17:150, 196; 18:310; 19:325.

15. For example, 2:270; 5:14, 17, 151; 11:173; 16:321; 19:41. Hazlitt extends the concept to analyses of individual mental characters. See, for example, his observations on Coleridge (16:102), Brougham (17:8-9), and the French (17:240; 10:162n; 12:327-28).

16. For example, Anne Barton, "'A Light to Lesson Ages': Byron's Political Plays," in *Byron: A Symposium,* ed. John D. Jump (New York: Macmillan, 1975), pp. 142-43.

17. Ralph M. Wardle, *Hazlitt* (Lincoln, Neb.: University of Nebraska Press, 1971), p. 223.

18. Thomas Medwin, "Hazlitt in Switzerland: A Conversation," *Fraser's Magazine* 19 (1839):281.

19. John Kinnaird, *William Hazlitt: Critic of Power* (New York: Columbia University Press, 1978), p. 270. Kinnaird also suggests *passim* some interesting parallels in character and thought between the two men. He suggests as well that Hazlitt may be correct in locating some of Byron's shortcomings in his aristocratic "affectation of 'superiority,'" but hints that Hazlitt may have failed to see that this "affectation" gives freedom and force to the satire of *Don Juan* (p. 318). Although Hazlitt never specifically sets forth the idea, I suspect that he is in his final years moving toward the understanding that Byron's strength lies in his weakness and that his aristocratic position in fact helps to make possible *Don Juan*.

Lord Byron and "Poor Dear Sherry," Richard Brinsley Sheridan

JACK C. WILLS

When he dined at Samuel Rogers's home one evening in the spring of 1813, Lord Byron began a relatively short but significant association. Among the company was the aging and dissipated, but still alert and witty, Richard Brinsley Sheridan, whom the young poet had admired for years as a man of letters and a statesman. Despite Lady Byron's complaint that Sheridan was a bad influence on her husband, for the next three years the friendship would be the source of considerable satisfaction to both men.[1]

Students of Byron are generally familiar with his "Monody on the Death of the Right Hon. R. B. Sheridan," the drinking bouts of the two at the home of Rogers and at other places, and Byron's extravagant praise of the older author, which brought tears to Sheridan's eyes when he was told of it:

> "Whatever Sheridan has done or chosen to do has been, *par excellence,* always the *best* of its kind. He has written the *best* comedy (School for Scandal), the *best* drama [*The Duenna*] (in my mind, far before that St. Giles's lampoon, the Beggar's Opera), the best farce (the *Critic* — it is only too good for a farce), and the best Address (Monologue on Garrick), and, to crown all, delivered the very best Oration (the famous Begum Speech) ever conceived or heard in this country." [*BL&J,* 3:239]

But few, I suspect, realize to what extent Byron's thought and works were affected by this voice from a bygone era. Sheridan, in turn, must have perceived in Byron a sympathetic understanding of his nature, since he once expressed a desire that the poet become his biographer.[2]

The appreciation of Byron and Sheridan for each other began long before the dinner at Rogers's, however. Byron records that at Harrow he and his classmates "used to show his name — R. B. Sheridan, 1765 — as an honour to the walls" (*BL&J,* 6:68). Later at Cambridge in 1807, he lists Lyttelton, Glover, Young, Sheridan, and Fox among those orators he "may imitate ... [but] never equal" (*BL&J,* 1:113). Over the years Byron's continuing interest in Sheridan is reflected in frequent quotations from the plays in his letters and journals, as well as specific allusions to the author and his works in the poems. Among the better known of the latter are the lines from *English Bards and Scotch Reviewers,* where the author of the tragedy *Pizarro* is exhorted to "Let Comedy assume her throne again" and to "Give, as thy last memorial to the age,/One classic drama, and reform the stage" (ll. 581, 584-85). Sheridan is also mentioned in "The Irish Avatar" (l. 114), "The Waltz" (l. 217), *Don Juan* (XI.lxxvii), and, of course, the "Monody on the Death of the Hon. R. B. Sheridan." Sheridan's liking of him, according to Byron, "was founded upon 'English Bards & S[cotch] Reviewers.'"[3]

A curious coincidence preceded the actual meeting of Byron and Sheridan in 1812. After Drury Lane was destroyed by fire in 1809, the chief financial backer of the new theater, the brewer Samuel Whitbread, was determined to exclude Sheridan from the management. Accordingly, a new governing body, called the Sub-committee of Management, was created, and among its members was the rising young poet Lord Byron.[4] With different people this circumstance might have been a source of resentment, but the two men apparently liked each other almost immediately. Byron's view of Sheridan as a kindred spirit, inspired by his reading of the plays, was confirmed by his acquaintance with the man. As for Sheridan's reaction, there is Thomas Moore's testimony that "the presence of the young poet . . . seemed to bring back his own youth and wit."[5]

Several of the evenings the two men spent together are chronicled in Byron's letters and journals. Of these accounts Leslie A. Marchand remarks that while Byron recorded "much amusing gossip about Sheridan" and other personalities of this period, "it is more than gossip; it is a fresh and generally sympathetic examination of the inner springs of other personalities as they impinged on his own" (*BL&J*, 1:19). Some of the more delightful and revealing of these incidents, as one might suspect, involve drinking sprees. On one such occasion, Byron reported to Moore on October 31, 1815, that he and Douglas Kinnaird "had to conduct Sheridan down a d——d corkscrew staircase, which had certainly been constructed before the discovery of fermented liquors." In this same letter Byron recounts one of his favorite Sheridan stories, one which typifies the wry sense of humor of both men:

> Perhaps you heard of a late answer of Sheridan to the watchman who found him bereft of that "divine particle of air," called reason, ********** He, the watchman, found Sherry in the street, fuddled and bewildered, and almost insensible. "Who are you, sir?" — no answer. "What's your name?" — a hiccup. "What's your name?" — Answer, in a slow, deliberate, and impassive tone — "Wilberforce!!!" [noted for being a strict Evangelical and teetotaller] Is not that Sherry all over? — and, to my mind, excellent. Poor fellow, *his* very dregs are better than the "first sprightly runnings" of others. [*BL&J*, 4:327]

A characteristic portrait of the two during these years, as painted by Byron, comically depicts the rapport between them and helps explain why Lady Byron was so angered by the relationship: "Poor fellow! he got drunk very thoroughly and very soon. — It occasionally fell to my lot to convey him home — no sinecure — for he was so tipsy that I was obliged to put on his cock'd hat for him — to be sure it tumbled off again and I was not myself so sober as to be able to pick it up again" (*BL&J,* 9:15).

Probably more than any other person of his time Byron perceived and understood the paradox that was Richard Brinsley Sheridan. "What a wreck is that man!" Byron noted in his journal on November 16, 1813, "and all from bad pilotage; for no one had ever better gales, though now and then a little too squally. Poor dear Sherry!" (*BL&J,* 3:207). Almost a decade later, speaking with Medwin in Italy, Byron more dramatically imaged the contrast between Sheridan's genius and his shortcomings as a man: "Sheridan was an extraordinary compound of contradictions. ... The upper part of Sheridan's face was that of a god — a forehead most expansive, an eye of peculiar brilliancy and fire; but below he shewed the satyr."[6]

The friendship of Byron and Sheridan was cemented by their philosophical and aesthetic kinship, a kinship revealed in their liberal political sentiments, dislike of cant and hypocrisy, incisive satire, and vitality and wit. Both men, as Sheridan's biographer Walter Sichel has pointed out, "scathed hypocrisy." Both "loved to contrast profession with motive, and practice with pretext, to unravel the skeins of personal pique, to knock down the screens of political cant and to expose the frail realities behind them."[7] They shared likewise an intense hatred of tyranny and injustice. And — for sometimes different reasons — both fought these evils not only in the writer's study but also in the political arena or, in the case of Byron, on the battlefield. This activist set of mind, which contributed to Sheridan's decision to seek a seat in Parliament at the height of his fame as a dramatist, is most clearly articulated in Byron's declaring, "I do think the preference of *writers* to *agents* ... a sign of effeminacy, degeneracy, and weakness. Who would write, who had any thing better to do?" (*BL&J,* 3:220).

Liberal convictions and family connections resulted in both

men's allying themselves with the Whig opposition, the party embraced by such reformers as Fox, Horne Tooke, and Burdett; more explicitly, they led Sheridan to speak out for the Begums of Oude, Byron to defend the Nottingham frame breakers, and both to support the French Revolution and Catholic emancipation. Both, too, were adversely criticized for their unwavering political stands, as they were for their conduct in general. It is understandable, therefore, that one detects a personal note in Byron's defense of Sheridan against his detractors. "The Whigs abuse him," he complained to Moore in 1818; "however, he never left them." Contrasting Sheridan with "the pensioner Burke" and "the coalitioner Fox," Byron insisted that "he beat them all, in all he ever attempted. But alas," he concluded ruefully, "poor human nature!" (*BL&J,* 6:47-48).

One specific facet of politics shared by Byron and Sheridan was, of course, their fascination with oratory. Sheridan, one of the greatest in an age of good orators, had come by his interest quite naturally through his father's teaching of elocution and his own association with the theater. As was to be the case with Byron, however, his maiden speech, answering a charge against his own election, was not universally acclaimed.[8] Nevertheless, Sheridan believed in his oratorical abilities, and the Parliamentary speech became "the main expression of his conviction."[9] In his most famous speech against Warren Hastings on February 7, 1787, the "astonishing oration," so powerful that "at its conclusion, the whole of the assembly joined in a loud and continued tumult of applause," elicited praise from supporters and opponents alike. The most satisfying acclaim must have been from his constant critic, Pitt, who said that the speech "surpassed all the eloquence of ancient and modern times."[10] And, although Sheridan never reached such heights again, as late as 1802 Lady Melbourne could write to Lord Cowper, "Sheridan made a most brilliant speech . . . it is impossible to say too much of the Wit and ability display'd."[11] Byron, who insisted that he had never heard anyone who fulfilled his ideal of an orator, added that Sheridan was the only one he ever "wished to hear at greater length" (*BL&J,* 9:14). A more elaborate tribute is the "Monody," where Sheridan's "words were sparks of Immortality," the "delegated voice of God!/Which shook the nations" (ll. 44-45, 104).

From his Harrow years until the publication of *Childe Harold's Pilgrimage,* Byron's determination to become just such an orator was as strong as his desire to be known as a great poet. "My qualities," he once wrote, "were much more oratorical and martial — than poetical; and Dr. D[rury] my grand patron — (our head-master) had a great notion that I should turn out an Orator — from my fluency — my turbulence — my voice — my copiousness of declamation — and my action." His interest was whetted by a holiday trip to London in 1805 where he heard with equal pleasure the declamations of the leading actors and the orations in the House of Commons. Inspired by his experience to compose a declamation for Speech Day at Harrow, he "astonished [Dr. Drury] into some unwonted ... and sudden compliments" in the presence of the declaimers at rehearsal (*BL&J,* 9:42-43).

Byron's maiden — and best-known — speech was delivered within a few weeks of the appearance of *Childe Harold's Pilgrimage,* the poem that was to make him famous. The Nottingham Frame-breaking Bill had been introduced in the House of Commons on February 14, 1812, and shortly thereafter in the House of Lords. Byron spoke against the bill on its second reading before the Lords on February 27. According to R. C. Dallas, to whom he gave the original manuscript, the speech "produced a considerable effect ..., and he received many compliments from the Opposition Peers."[12] The speech reinforced Sheridan's belief, held from the time he had read *English Bards* in 1809, that Byron "should make an Orator if [he] would but take to speaking and grow a parliament man" (*BL&J,* 9:16). The opinion was not unanimous, however. Lord Holland found the speech not "at all suited to our common notions of Parliamentary eloquence," and Dallas thought that he so altered his natural tone of voice and contorted his features that he became "a youth declaiming a task."[13] Byron himself, while boasting that Sir Francis Burdett had called it "the best speech by a *Lord* since the 'Lord knows when,' " admitted that his presentation had been "perhaps a little theatrical" (*BL&J,* 2:167).

An exhaustive analysis of the speeches of Byron and Sheridan would be impractical because (if for no other reason) of the huge volume of Sheridan's orations as against Byron's three. Even a comparison of the best known oration of each is hampered by the differences in length, topics, and ends; nonetheless, a few parallels are worth noting. Marchand, for instance, citing Sheridan along with Pitt and Burke as Byron's models, specifically mentions his "rhetorical questions and balanced sentences, with rolling periods and reasoned arguments as well as ironic contrasts."[14] And both Byron and Sheridan, as one might expect, have a penchant for dramatic and comic strategies.[15] The ultimate kinship of these two speeches, however, is their "imaginative rendering of the abstract issue, the conflict between charity and deliberate tyranny."[16] With the same "dislike of high-handed authority"[17] engendered in them by an overbearing parent and the British public school (Byron had defended smaller schoolboys at Harrow and Sheridan had championed Elizabeth Linley), both men sympathized with the underdog. Byron, however, losing interest in his career as an orator and enjoying the acclaim he received from *Childe Harold,* soon left off speaking entirely, telling Augusta Leigh, "I hate the thing altogether — & have no intention to 'strut another hour' on that stage" (*BL&J,* 3:32).

Despite Byron's statement that his abilities were more oratorical and martial than poetical, he remarked that poetry and oratory were "so nearly similar, as to require in a great measure the same Talents, & he who excels in the one, would on application succeed in the other."[18] However true in general, this proposition is put to the test in the monodies, or addresses, written by Byron and Sheridan and spoken at Drury Lane. Mary Ann Yates gave the first public reading of Sheridan's "Verses to the Memory of Garrick" on the evening of March 11, 1779. The leading periodicals of the day described it as an "elegant and affecting tribute" and reported that it "was received with uncommon applause."[19] Byron, whose "Address" celebrating the re-opening of Drury Lane in 1812 was spoken from the same stage, wrote his "Monody on the Death of the Right Hon. R. B. Sheridan" ten days after Sheridan's death at the request of Douglas Kinnaird. It was read — over his objections — on September 7, 1816, by Maria Rebecca Davison, who, fittingly, played the part of Lady Teazle in the evening's production, *The School for Scandal* (*BL&J,* 5:82n).

Under the circumstances, it is not surprising that the two addresses are alike in several respects, most noticeably in their heroic couplets and the characteristic modes of wit that inevitably accompany balanced sentences and antitheses. Such an eighteenth-century form might be expected from Sheridan, but he was actually breaking precedent (see Garrick's English cantata, "Ode Upon Dedicating a Building and Erecting a Statue to Shakespeare at Stratford-Upon-Avon," the most recent antecedent to Sheridan's address).[20] Whether Byron accepted the tradition that Sheridan had begun or simply believed the couplets appropriate to his subject, he chose a form that had fallen rather out of fashion. Jack D. Durant's thorough treatment of the metrical and persuasive elements of Sheridan's poem makes any further comment on this matter superfluous, especially since he concludes that Byron's "close metrical imitation of Sheridan's poem clearly attested to [his] view that the monody on Garrick was the best 'address' in the language."[21]

Several other parallels exist, although many of them result from the similarity of the subject matter and from clichés of the time.[22] But certain of these features, while arguably commonplaces, suggest the influence of Sheridan's address on Byron's. One is a catalog of the powers of the deceased, wherein Byron's lines on Sheridan (27-30) echo Sheridan's on Garrick (63-74) in structure as well as content. Another parallel involves the two poets' conviction that the place of the departed can not be filled: Garrick's art "no model leaves behind" (1. 62); to Sheridan's hour of light "no likeness is bequeath'd" (1. 25). Most telling are the two poets' similar uses of the imagery of fire and lightning. Sheridan, having earlier in his poem spoken of "the Poet's bosom fire" (1. 41), likens the evanescence of the actor's art to lightning: "like th' electric fire,/But strike the frame, and, as they strike, expire;/Incense too pure a bodied flame to bear,/Its fragrance charms the sense, and blends the air" (ll. 75-78). The same image in Byron's "Monody" dominates the description of Sheridan as orator, playwright, and earthly sufferer. In his defense of the people of India, Sheridan was "the thunder . . . The wrath . . . Which shook the nations . . . and blazed/Till vanquish'd senates trembled as they praised" (ll. 43-46); as the writer of sparkling comedies he was "Bright with the hues of his Promethean heat;/A halo of the light of other days" (ll. 56-57). Unlike Sheridan's Garrick, however, Byron's Sheridan suffered a sky-change reminiscent of the Byronic hero:

> Breasts to whom all the strength of feeling given
> Bear hearts electric — charged with fire from Heaven,
> Black with the rude collision, inly torn,
> By clouds surrounded, and on whirlwinds borne,
> Driven o'er the lowering atmosphere that nurst
> Thoughts which have turn'd to thunder — scorch, and burst.
>
> [Ll. 89-94]

Sheridan had died on July 7, 1816, just two-and-one-half months after Byron left England for good. For the older man, Byron's attention had been as fitting a tribute to the end of a successful career as Dr. Johnson's had been to the beginning. Byron, in turn, had received the genuine approval of an established author whose opinions he respected. He came to appreciate Sheridan as a person, in spite of his weaknesses; and he would continue to write under the influence of Sheridan's works.

In general, Byron saw Sheridan as the living repository of the eighteenth-century manners and ethos he so revered. Bored by the inanities of Regency society, Byron "preferred the wit and intellect he encountered at the home of Rogers, where Sheridan, Mackintosh, and 'Conversation' Sharp turned to anecdotes of a former time."[23] Byron's letters and journals support this conclusion: for example, "On Tuesday [March 10, 1814] dined with Rogers, — Mackintosh, Sheridan, Sharpe, — much talk, and good, — all, except my own little prattlement. Much of old times — Horne Tooke — the Trials — evidence of Sheridan, and anecdotes of those times when *I*, alas! was an infant." He adds, of a production he had just seen of *A Trip to Scarborough*, Sheridan's adaptation of *The Relapse*, "*What plays*! what wit! — helas! Congreve and Vanbrugh are your only comedy. Our society is too insipid now for the like copy" (*BL&J*, 3:248-49). More revealing is Byron's lament to Lady Melbourne on October 1, 1813: "I would give the world to pass a month with Sheridan or any lady or gentleman of the old school — & hear them talk every day & all day of themselves & acquaintance — & all they have heard & seen in their lives" (*BL&J*, 3:129). Byron's view of his relationship to this tradition is described by John Clubbe in his study of Byron's letters:

> The literary tradition which emerges most vividly from a reading of the letters — at least those in the first volumes — is a Restoration, neoclassical, and late Augustan one. Byron saw himself continuing the tradition he inherited, not as a participant in another.

With the many allusions to Restoration and eighteenth-century comedies in his letters to Lady Melbourne, Byron transforms his pursuit of Lady Frances Wedderburn Webster into "a comedy worthy to stand beside the writers he so greatly admired."[24]

Sharing with Sheridan many ideas on the form and function of drama,[25] Byron was delighted by the elder writer's comedies. Each man possessed a lively wit that could, while unmasking hypocrisy and deflating pomposity, maintain a spirit of perfect good humor: their satire was above all humane. Moreover, as Marchand has observed, it was "more as a wit" that Byron admired Sheridan than anything else.[26] And their ultimate motive for writing comic satires was probably the same. Sichel, noting of Sheridan that "a constitutional melancholy neighboured his mirth," states that the dramatist would have agreed with Byron's lines from *Don Juan,* "And if I laugh at any mortal thing,/'Tis that I may not weep" (IV.iv).[27] Humor is always a good defense against pain and disillusionment, of which these men had more than their share.

The key to the spirit, at least, of the comic theory shared by Byron and Sheridan is suggested by John Loftis's contention that *The School for Scandal* "is an embodiment of the neoclassical reinterpretation of Aristotle's theory of comedy, just as it is an embodiment of neoclassical wit, as defined by Pope in *An Essay on Criticism.*"[28] An important Aristotelian concept evident in this play as in other comic writings of Byron and Sheridan is the value of laughter for its own sake. Comedy, Sheridan tells his audience in the tenth-night prologue to *The Rivals,* was not intended to preach, but "To charm the fancy and yet reach the heart" (l. 20). Byron is even less equivocal. "Do you suppose," he asked Murray in August 1819, "I could have any intention [in writing *Don Juan*] but to giggle and make giggle?" (*BL&J,* 6:208). Similarly, while damning most popular stage entertainments in *Hints from Horace,* Byron excepted farce because of its power to evoke laughter: "Whoever loves a laugh must sigh for Foote'' (l. 336). In his study of Aristotle's theory of comedy, Lane Cooper explains that ''there is a comic, as well as a tragic, catharsis.''[29] Byron and Sheridan seem to agree.

In both authors this attitude toward laughing comedy contributed to an appreciation and utilization of burlesque. A. B. England's recent study has demonstrated that this is a major thread in *Don Juan*, and Loftis has argued that ''many of the difficulties spectators or readers of the comedies experience in evaluating them would disappear if they recognized that Sheridan was above all a master of burlesque.''[30] But aside from providing amusement, as England has noted, burlesque also ''enforces a special kind of world view.''[31] Because both Byron and Sheridan were intensely aware of the gulf between the ideal and the actual, satire became their mode of expression. ''But now I'm going to be immoral,'' the narrator of *Don Juan* announces in a reversal of the dictum of Sophocles; ''I mean to show things really as they are,/Not as they ought to be'' (XII.xl). This determination to show things as they really are helps to explain Byron's and Sheridan's satire on pretension and hypocrisy: compare, for example, the scene in which Juan, the product of Donna Inez's narrow program of education, is discovered in Donna Julia's bedroom and sent running naked into the night, with the famous screen scene in *The School for Scandal,* where Charles Surface drags the Teazles from their hiding-places and exposes Joseph's villainy.

Insisting on full and unadorned truth, Byron and Sheridan in their works adopt the role of improviser: they perform in full view of the audience.[32] For instance, having used the Latin phrase *inter nos,* the narrator of *Don Juan* admits, ''(This should be *entre nous,* for Julia thought/In French, but then the rhyme would go for naught)'' (I. lxxxiv). Whatever other reasons Byron has for employing this casual technique, one is to imply that there is nothing mysterious about his craft, that he has nothing to hide. Sheridan's giving the audience a look backstage in *The Critic* makes essentially the same point: like Charles Surface, he is throwing aside the screen, unmasking the pompousness and incompetence of dramatists like Cumberland and Kelly.[33] Conversely, Byron and Sheridan delight in such characters as "Fighting Bob" Acres and Sir Fretful Plagiary (Byron quotes these characters frequently in his letters and journals, especially Acres's boast that in his country they "kill a man a week" and Sir Fretful's complaint that if there is any abuse of a person, he "is always sure to hear of it from one damned good-natured friend or another"), because, in addition to their sheer preposterousness, they illustrate in such a refreshingly humorous way the deceits we all practice on ourselves and others.

The other major strain in Byron's and Sheridan's comic satires — the Popean wit alluded to by Loftis — involves the matter of voice. Ronald Bottrall's 1939 study connects the two authors in this tradition by arguing that the voice in Byron's satires is less that of Frere, Casti, and Pulci, whose *ottava rima* form he borrowed, than "that aristocratic colloquial speech which had been the heritage of the English nobility from the Restoration down to Chesterfield and Sheridan." Byron, he adds, "is the last great writer to make use of it greatly."[34] A. B. England has taken Bottrall's thesis a step further, demonstrating *Don Juan*'s affinity with Augustan literature by a precise rhetorical analysis of it.[35] Byron's comments on Sheridan's verbal deftness indicate that the man he met at Rogers's was the living embodiment of a tradition of wit that he admired in life and letters.

But more specific evidence of Sheridan's influence can also be found in Byron's comic poems. Among the more amusing examples in the lesser-known works is "The Waltz," reminiscent of Sheridan's shorter poem "The Walse." Ironically, both womanizers thought the dance, introduced into England in 1812, immoral. Both poems emphasize the arousal of sexual feelings and the immodesty encouraged by the waltz. "Round all the confines of the yielded waist," Byron exclaims, "The strangest hand may wander undisplaced;/The lady's in return may grasp as much/As princely paunches offer to her touch" (ll. 192-95). Sheridan contrasts the "timid, downcast glance" of "our first Parents" with the modern couple, led out of Eden by the devil, who "taught them how to *Walse*" (ll. 1-6). The most exact parallel is Byron's "Pleased round the chalky floor how well they trip,/One hand reposing on the royal hip" (ll. 196-97) and Sheridan's couplet, "One hand grasps hers, the other holds her hip —/For so the Law's laid down by Baron Trip" (ll. 7-8). The moral commentary in both poems is sharpened by the suggestive verb "grasp" and the piquant rhyming of "hip" and "trip."

In his longer and more famous poems, Byron inherited from Sheridan and his tradition the ability to concentrate "on isolated scenes or groups of scenes" that succeed "by reason of incongruities and surprises conveyed visually as well as verbally."[36] The discovery scene in Donna Julia's bedroom is a case in point. Moreover, while an ardent theatergoer like Byron would have seen many bedroom farces (one recalls his fondness for Fielding), this scene's kinship with Sheridan's screen scene is further emphasized by both Lady Teazle and Donna Julia being desirable young women married to men three times their age. One or two other useful parallels may be drawn between *Don Juan* and *The School for Scandal.* Bottrall observes that in "*Don Juan,* the natural man who acts according to impulse is contrasted with the hypocrite, or the hypocritical society, which acts according to convention";[37] the same is equally true of Charles Surface's role. Charles's merits are, of course, finally recognized, while Juan's fate is open-ended. Also, the gossipy, drawing-room flavor of Sheridan's comedy is frequently evident in the narrative voice of *Don Juan* as well as that of *Beppo.*

Don Juan also includes two specific references to Sheridan's plays and a line lifted as neatly as Sir Fretful Plagiary himself might have done. Describing Juan's virtue succumbing to Gulbeyaz's tears after having withstood her rage, the narrator reports that "As through his palms Bob Acres' valour oozed,/So Juan's virtue ebb'd" (V.cxlii). Readers of Byron's day — and since — would have recognized the allusion here to *The Rivals,* and when the poet borrows a line from Tilburina's final speech in *The Critic* ("'An oyster may be cross'd in love,' — and why?/Because he mopeth idly in his shell" [*D.J.* XIV.lxxxi; *The Critic* III.i]), he acknowledges the original by using quotation marks. But whatever Byron's intent, in one of his better-known borrowings (one, by the way, which most readers today would probably attribute to him rather than Sheridan), he does not acknowledge Sheridan: the lines, "For my part I say nothing — nothing — but/*This* I will say" (I.lii), accord perfectly with the narrator's character, but they were first spoken by, of all people, Sir Fretful Plagiary: "I say nothing — I take away from no man's merit — am hurt at no man's good fortune — I say nothing — But this I will say" (I.i). Byron must have smiled as he wrote them.

However, the most significant parallels in the works of Byron and Sheridan, who both delighted in the burlesque, are those in *The Vision of Judgment* and *The Critic.* Unquestionably the play was one of Byron's favorites, and the evidence is overwhelming that, consciously or unconsciously, he had it in mind when he sat down to parody Southey's extravaganza.[38] Of similarities of a general nature, one, as Claude Fuess has shown, is that in this poem Byron "chose a method largely ... dramatic." The most conspicuous dramatic devices he employs, besides his having "placed Southey in a ridiculous situation and made him the sport of other characters,"[39] are extensive use of dialogue, the confrontation scene between Satan and Michael, and the emphasis on visual effects notable at such instances as Asmodeus staggering under the weight of Southey's books or St. Peter knocking Southey into the lake with his keys.

The Critic and *The Vision of Judgment* do, of course, diverge in many respects, even beyond the fact that one is a poem and the other a play. *The Critic* contains none of the theological satire of *The Vision of Judgment,* and — with the possible exception of Satan and his angelic caravan arriving like "a rush of mighty wind" (xxiii) — there is no burlesque of theater conventions in the poem. And yet in some ways they are remarkably alike. From a technical standpoint, Byron's having his narrator watch the proceedings at the gates of Heaven through a telescope roughly approximates Sneer, Puff, and Dangle's viewing Puff's tragedy *The Spanish Armada* on a rehearsal stage. Then, too, each employs both burlesque and parody to annihilate a popular but pretentious work of its day, as in Sheridan's re-creation of Cumberland's blank verse in *The Battle of Hastings* and Byron's satire on the "spavin'd dactyls" (xci) in Southey's *Vision of Judgment.* Even the elaborate masque that concludes the play anticipates Southey's reading of his own *Vision of Judgment* with a "'melodious twang'" (cii), scattering angels and devils alike.

The two works are closely related in theme as well. Perhaps better than any of the other writings, these two reflect their authors' interest in both art and politics. *The Critic* was written in 1779, the juncture of Sheridan's theatrical and political careers, *The Vision of Judgment* during Byron's days of political intrigue in Italy; both works were inspired by historical events. In eighteenth-century fashion both, first of all, excoriate hack writers, particularly their readiness to write anything for a price. Puff, who describes himself as "a Practitioner in Panegyric," informs Sneer that he is "at your service — or any body else's" (I.ii). Southey, having told Satan that he has written Wesley's life, adds, "'Sir, I'm ready to write yours,/In two octavo volumes, nicely bound,/With notes and preface, all that most allures/The pious purchaser'" (xcix). Both Puff and Southey choose their own reviewers or, more likely, write their own reviews. But most deplorable of all is their wrapping such practices in the cloak of patriotism. Eulogizing a blind, mad old king and his blinder policies or exploiting a nation's fears of invasion is both regrettable and dangerous. Like Byron, Sheridan had "emphasized the correlation between bad art and bad humanity, especially as expressed through flawed patriotism."[40] Finally, for all their devastating effectiveness, these two brilliant satires remain, like most of the authors' other works, essentially free of malice. Puff is generally recognized as one of the most delightful villains in English literature, and even Southey is more comical than malicious.[41] With a kind of healthy and good-natured tolerance in their satires, both Sheridan and Byron attempt to redeem man from his folly.

Whatever Sheridan's and Byron's own follies, their brilliance as artists who shared common interests makes them worthy of comparison. One can only regret that Sheridan's desire, that Byron be his biographer, was not fulfilled. Nevertheless, we can look to Byron for "sympathetic lightning sketches of Sheridan, and for some slight but accurate knowledge of his last three years on earth."[42] We can also look to Sheridan to find the themes, wit, and humanity that gave Byron's art its peculiar character, particularly in *Don Juan* and *The Vision of Judgment*. The last lines of the "Monody" serve exceptionally well as an epitaph for Sheridan:

> While Eloquence, Wit, Poesy, and Mirth,
> That humbler Harmonist of care on Earth,
> Survive within our souls — while lives our sense
> Of pride in Merit's proud pre-eminence,
> Long shall we seek his likeness — long in vain,
> And turn to all of him which may remain,
> Sighing that Nature form'd but one such man,
> And broke the die — in moulding Sheridan!

Another poet might easily have written these lines about Byron.

NOTES

1. Leslie A. Marchand (*Byron: A Biography* [New York: Alfred A. Knopf, 1957],1:401) observes that "Byron had no doubt met him at a London assembly soon after *Childe Harold* was published, but they reached intimacy at a dinner at the home of Rogers in the spring of 1813."

2. E. M. Butler, *Sheridan: A Ghost Story* (London: Constable and Co., 1931), p. 65.

3. *BL&J*, 9:16. It is worth noting also that, a few months before his death, Sheridan requested from Murray a copy of "Lord Byron's last verses" (*The Letters of Richard Brinsley Sheridan,* ed. Cecil Price [Oxford: Clarendon Press, 1966], 3:245).

4. The other members were Lord Essex, Douglas Kinnaird, George Lamb, and Peter Moore.

5. Thomas Moore, *Memoirs of the Life of the Right Honourable Richard Brinsley Sheridan* (London: Longman, Hurst, Rees, Orme, Brown, and Green, 1825), p. 683.

6. *Medwin's Conversations of Lord Byron,* ed. Ernest J. Lovell, Jr. (Princeton, N.J.: Princeton University Press, 1966), p. 192.

7. Walter Sichel, *Sheridan* (Boston: Houghton Mifflin, 1909), 1:122.

8. *The Speeches of the Right Honourable Richard Brinsley Sheridan, With a Sketch of His Life,* ed. by a Constitutional Friend (1842; reprint ed., New York: Russell and Russell, 1969), 1:v. The editor reports that "the house heard him with particular attention, but his success does not appear to have equalled the expectation of his friends." Told afterward by the reporter Woodfall that "Oratory is not in your line; you had better cleave to your literary pursuits," Sheridan was temporarily "dumb-foundered," then replied vehemently, "It is in me, however, Woodfall, and by Heaven I'll have it out."

9. Jack D. Durant, *Richard Brinsley Sheridan* (Boston: Twayne Publishers, 1975), p. 28.

10. Sheridan, *Speeches,* 1:vii. Unfortunately this speech was badly reported and does not exist in accurate form. The one that is usually anthologized is the longer Westminster Hall speech, delivered over a four-day period between June 3 and 13, 1788.

11. Quoted by Margot Strickland, *The Byron Women* (New York: St. Martin's Press, 1974), p. 102.

12. R.C. Dallas, *Recollections of the Life of Lord Byron from the Year 1808 to the End of 1814* (London: Charles Knight, 1824), pp. 203-4.

13. Quoted by Leslie A. Marchand, *Byron: A Portrait* (New York: Alfred A. Knopf, 1970), p. 114; Dallas, *Recollections,* p. 203.

14. Marchand, *Byron: A Portrait,* p. 114.

15. Sheridan, for example, compared Sir Elijah Impey's role to the ghost's in *Hamlet*, popping up in every quarter exclaiming "Swear!" Byron comically portrayed the regiment sent out to arrest the frame breakers as marching ridiculously up and down, arriving after the culprits fled, and being hooted at by women and children.

16. Durant, *Richard Brinsley Sheridan,* p. 30.

17. Jerome Landfield, "The Triumph and Failure of Sheridan's Speeches Against Hastings," *Speech Monographs* 28 (1961): 144.

18. *BL&J*, 1:113. Robert F. Gleckner (*Byron and the Ruins of Paradise* [Baltimore, Md.: The Johns Hopkins Press, 1967], p. 119n), in quoting this passage, distinguishes "Byron's public-private voice from his private-public voice." He also cites two other studies that have treated, directly or implicitly, declamatory or "histrionic" qualities in some Byron poems: Ernest de Selincourt, "Byron," in *Wordsworthian and Other Studies* (Oxford, 1947); and W.W. Robson, "Byron as Poet," *Proceedings of the British Academy* 43 (1957).

19. Quoted by Jack D. Durant, "R. B. Sheridan's 'Verses to the Memory of Garrick': Poetic Reading As Formal Theatre," *Southern Speech Journal* 35 (1969): 120.

20. Ibid., p. 122.

21. Durant, *Richard Brinsley Sheridan,* p. 60.

22. These include, in particular, several references to "tears" and "time" and the use of oxymoron: "splendid sorrows" and "patient woe" (ll. 12, 106) in Sheridan's "Address"; "tenderer woe" and "sweet dejection" (ll. 13, 16) in the "Monody." Quotations from Sheridan are from *The Plays and Poems of Richard Brinsley Sheridan,* ed. R. Crompton Rhodes, 3 vols. (Oxford: Basil Blackwell, 1928).

23. Marchand, *Byron: A Portrait,* p. 164.

24. John Clubbe, "Byron in His Letters," *South Atlantic Quarterly* 74 (1975): 510, 512.

25. For example, both objected to the rampant abuses of the contemporary theater: excessive sentimentalism, lack of consistency, hackneyed conventions, spectacular stage effects, and escapism (see in particular Sheridan's *The Critic* and Byron's *English Bards* and *Hints from Horace*).

26. Marchand, *Byron: A Biography,* 1:401.

27. Sichel, *Sheridan,* 1:5.

28. John Loftis, Introduction to Richard Brinsley Sheridan, *The School for Scandal* (New York: Appleton-Century-Crofts, 1966), p. v.

29. Lane Cooper, *An Aristotelian Theory of Comedy* (New York: Harcourt, Brace and Co., 1922), p. 131.

30. A. B. England, *Byron's Don Juan and Eighteenth-Century Literature: A Study of Some Rhetorical Continuities and Discontinuities* (Lewisburg, Pa.: Bucknell University Press, 1975), pp. 80-147; John Loftis, *Sheridan and the Drama of Georgian England* (Cambridge, Mass.: Harvard University Press, 1977), p. 6.

31. England, *Byron's Don Juan,* p. 89.

32. W. W. Robson, "Byron as Poet," *Proceedings of the British Academy* 43 (1957); reprinted in W. W. Robson, *Critical Essays* (Routledge and Kegan Paul, 1966), pp. 178-80.

33. Sheridan appears in the role of improviser in some of his satiric poems as well, as in the concluding couplet from "Lines by a Lady on the Loss of Her Trunk": "But my rhymes are all out; — for I dare not use st——k;/'Twould shock Sheridan more than the loss of my *Trunk*" (*Plays and Poems,* 3:254). And Byron, although he may simply have been anticipating criticism, appears to be poking fun at himself by choosing as an epigraph for *The Two Foscari* these lines spoken by the governor

of Tilbury Fort in Puff's *Spanish Armada*: "The *father* softens — but the *governor*/Is fix'd!''; Byron — and the playgoers of the time — were well aware that the next line was Dangle's ironic reminder that "that antithesis of persons — is a most establish'd figure" (II.ii).

34. Ronald Bottrall, "Byron and the Colloquial Tradition in English Poetry," *Criterion* 18 (1939): 209.

35. England, *Byron's Don Juan,* pp. 21-79.

36. Loftis, *Sheridan and the Drama of Georgian England,* p. 6.

37. Bottrall, "Byron and the Colloquial Tradition in English Poetry," p. 216.

38. While no direct reference to the play is to be found in *The Vision of Judgment,* allusions to two other works suggest that Byron was thinking of Sheridan. E. H. Coleridge (*Poetry,* 4:511n) speculates that Satan's remark about John Wilkes's having "turned to half a courtier ere [he] died" (lxxii) might have been partly inspired by a political pasquinade of Sheridan's rebuking "Johnny Wilkes, Johnny Wilkes,/Thou greatest of bilks" for his "blasphemy, 'God save the King.' " The phrase "Three gentlemen at once" (lxxix), used to describe the protean Junius, was originally spoken by Mrs. Malaprop in *The Rivals* (IV.ii).

39. Claude M. Fuess, *Lord Byron as a Satirist in Verse* (1912; reprint ed., New York: Russell and Russell, 1964), pp. 194-95.

40. Durant, *Richard Brinsley Sheridan,* p. 121. Compare the opening lines of Sheridan's satiric poem, "A Familiar Epistle":

> Of all the ways a man can choose
> To introduce a youthful muse,
> There is not one so sure to raise
> A sudden burst of public praise,
> As feigning well a *Patriot's* call,
> To dip the pen in party gall.
>
> [*Plays and Poems,* 3:177]

41. Leslie A. Marchand remarks in *Byron's Poetry: A Critical Introduction* (Cambridge, Mass.: Harvard University Press, 1968), p. 238, that "Byron's triumph throughout is in lighting Southey's solemnities with a human and a humorous touch."

42. Butler, *Sheridan,* p. 65.

Byron and Grillparzer

ERWIN A. STÜRZL

Perhaps for some whose German is not very good the very name *Franz Grillparzer* will summon up phonetic nightmares. If so, they are in good company, for Lord Byron, after reading Grillparzer's drama *Sappho,* confessed his bewilderment in trying to stammer it out: "Grillparzer — a devil of a name, to be sure, for posterity; but they *must* learn to pronounce it" (*BL&J,* 8:25). That the reproduction of the Austrian writer's strange-sounding name created certain problems for Byron's fellow countrymen can be gauged from a report in the *New Monthly Magazine* concerning a performance of *Sappho* in Vienna in 1818:

> Its success is almost without a parallel. At the close of the third act, the author was so loudly called for, that he was under the necessity of appearing on the stage. ... He is a young man, named Gripalzer [*sic*].[1]

Surprisingly, Grillparzer himself displayed a certain aversion to hearing his own name spoken[2] and pretended to be highly embarrassed when someone called him by it or asked him for it. While reading a French translation of Byron's *Letters and Diaries,*[3] he seems to have come across Byron's remark quoted above and to have been touched by melancholy at finding himself mentioned in the letters of a dead man, but the self-abasement that he shows on seeing the cursed name that had always vexed him has something almost psychopathic about it, for he broke out: "Written, I can't bear it, printed it infuriates me. Such names are not remembered by posterity, Lord Byron can say what he likes."[4] Grillparzer was forty years old when this *cri de coeur* escaped him, but fate has dealt more kindly with him than he prophesied. In the present century there has been a marked interest in the works of the Austrian writer, particularly in the United States and in England, where Arthur Burkhard's translations of a number of his dramas have helped to make him more widely known. While it is true that even so he has not achieved sensational popularity, this is no more than Grillparzer himself would have expected.

Although *Sappho,* which has always been a favorite with translators, was already available in an English version by 1820 — probably due to the pen of John Bramsen[5] — Byron did not see this rendering, for in his Italian exile the number of new publications he received from England was inevitably limited. Furthermore, he was incapable of reading the text in the original, for he had forgotten the little German he had learned in his youth.[6] He admitted freely that he understood nothing of the language, "except oaths learned from postillions and officers in a squabble" (*BL&J,* 8:26). Byron therefore had to content himself with Guido Sorelli's Italian translation of *Sappho,* published in 1819. He suffered no illusions about its probable fidelity to Grillparzer's text, for he concurred in the judgment of Lessing, who had once consoled German translators by asserting that their Italian colleagues were, on the whole, a good deal worse than they.[7] Byron summed up his own views on the question by declaring that one had to make allowances for the Italians, for they were "the very worst of translators, except from the Classics"; for there "they ape their fathers' tongue" (*BL&J,* 8:25).

In spite of the unsatisfactory nature of the available

version, Byron nevertheless found *Sappho* "superb and sublime." He particularly singled out for praise the intellectual qualities of the Austrian, whom, he stressed, he did not know personally, but whom future generations would certainly hold in honor. He noted especially the simplicity of Grillparzer's diction, though he admitted that it did not quite bear comparison with that employed by the ancient classical authors. The only negative criticism that he offered of *Sappho* was that it was "too Madame de Stael-*ish*" (*BL&J,* 8:25, 26).

Not only was Byron attracted by the blending of the ancient and modern spirit in the play — a cultural ideal that he himself had advocated — but he was fascinated by the motif of conflict between art and life, which was embodied in the character of the Greek poetess, who yearned to turn back from the world of the spirit and beautiful ideals to the realities of human existence. Through her failure to unify artistic creation with human happiness, Sappho was unable to perceive that the passionate longing of young Phaon was directed toward the youthful Melitta, and she mistook it as an erotic desire for her own person. The piece ends with Sappho's farewell to life when she ceremoniously casts herself into the sea from a rocky promontory.

Byron was clearly enthralled by Grillparzer's portrayal of the tension between the spirit and the forces of nature, between the longing for all the enjoyments of life and aversion to existence as such, between thought and deed, that the Austrian, drawing on his own inner psyche, so powerfully etched. The proud English lord, who abhorred and loathed the Austrians and all that they stood for and who could not "find words for [his] hate of them" (*BL&J,* 8:26), must have been deeply moved; otherwise he certainly would not have praised the Austrian writer so unreservedly. There were a number of grounds for Byron's hatred of everything Austrian. The legalism of Metternich's system of government must have seemed an inhuman atrocity to Byron's liberal view of the human lot. It is surely ironic that Prince Metternich himself was an enthusiastic admirer of Byron's poetry and that he even intervened personally to restrain the excessive zeal of those officials of his administration who were anxious to curtail the activities of the famous foreign nobleman by irksome restrictions.[8] Nonetheless the poet felt himself to be constantly under the surveillance of the Austrian secret police, and indeed such spying was not altogether unjustified, given Byron's sympathy for the Irridenta movement. When Count Goes was replaced by Count Inzaghi as governor of Venice, the petty irritations became almost insupportable; later, when the Gamba family — and thereby Teresa Guiccioli, his mistress — were banished from the Austrian dominions on account of their political activities, Byron did not hesitate to follow them into exile of his own free will.

Byron was grievously offended when Michele Lioni's Italian translation of *Childe Harold's Pilgrimage* was prohibited by Count Sedlnitzky, the president of the imperial police, on account of its seditious tendencies. Medwin records that the poet voiced his indignation about such treatment: "The Austrian Government, too, partly contributed to drive me away. They interrupted my book and papers, opened my letters, and proscribed my works."[9]

However, the hatred that such measures aroused in the poet's heart did not poison his admiration for Grillparzer's genius. While still under the influence of *Sappho,* Byron began his drama *Sardanapalus.* He had given the Italian translation of Grillparzer's play to Teresa, and after reading it she urged her cavalier servente to "put more love into 'Sardanapalus' " (*BL&J,* 8:26). Her advice was followed, for the Countess Guiccioli herself is portrayed in the character of the beautiful Ionian slave girl, Myrrha — one of the most touching creations of Byron's poetic art.

Quite apart from this indirect influence, Leopold Brandl has pointed out that Grillparzer provided Byron with some important elements for his tragedy.[10] He underlines the similarity between the two pairs of characters, Sardanapalus and Myrrha and Phaon and Melitta, and shows that the renunciation of the queen in Byron's play is very close in concept to Sappho's renunciation of the man she loved. Another indication of Grillparzer's influence can be detected in the banquet scene at the beginning of Act III of *Sardanapalus,* when the hero, seeking to restore the mirth of the party, shattered by the sudden terror of a thunderstorm, begs his Greek slave girl to play to him on her lyre:

> Sing me a song of Sappho, her, thou know'st,
> Who in thy country threw —
>
> [III.i.67-68]

One should not trouble oneself too much about the anachronism involved in Byron's referring to Sappho at this point, although the Greek poetess's lifetime in fact can scarcely be fixed to correspond with the historic time of *Sardanapalus,* but it suggests that Grillparzer's drama was very much on his mind.

Byron's influence on Grillparzer was, however, more extensive than Grillparzer's on Byron, for as far as we know the English poet's acquaintance with his Austrian colleague's works was limited to *Sappho,* while Grillparzer became something of a Byron devotee. At any rate, during the first half of his life he was deeply fascinated by the psychological problems that the noble Englishman's character posed, and his interest in his literary productions continued up to his death. Although the political climate was less favorable for a Byron vogue in Austria than in Germany, in the winter of 1818 his poetry was in mode in cultivated circles of the capital of the Hapsburgs.[11] He was promoted by Caroline Pichler, whose literary salon constituted a focal point of old Viennese culture. There the educated read Byron's lyric poetry and his verse tales, while their hostess herself tried her hand at translating *The Corsair* — a task that she called a work of

Hercules in a letter to Grillparzer dated 19 May 1819.[12] Translations of three of Byron's poems by the hand of Caroline Pichler were indeed printed in the periodical *Aglaja*,[13] but more significant for the present investigation is the fact that Grillparzer appears to have heard Byron's "Fare thee well" read in the original at one of the meetings of her salon before he left for Italy.[14] Presumably Grillparzer became acquainted with other poems by Byron around this time. In a notebook begun in October 1819, he copied out passages drawn from *Childe Harold*,[15] *Mazeppa*,[16] and later *Don Juan*,[17] following his practice of collecting the fruits of his reading.

Unfortunately it is not possible to establish with certainty which edition of the various poems he used, for the *Collected Works* cataloged in his library is the 1833 edition prepared by Thomas Moore.[18] In any event, Grillparzer read a good deal of Byron's poetry in 1818 and 1819 and the Austrian was deeply impressed not only by the power of the language and the brilliance of the pictures depicted in the verse, but also by the magic of the poet's personality. Grillparzer was certainly a neurotic who suffered repeatedly from periods of nervous depression, during which he wallowed in exaggerated introspection that often led to painful self-mockery. He frequently doubted his vocation as a writer and "the spark of his poetical talent was all too often submerged by his unprofitable musings."[19] Thus the conflict between his intellect and his fantasy was never fully resolved, and he found a macabre consolation in the profession of Byronic weariness. His tendency to carp at his own shortcomings assumed such proportions that in his mania he began to observe abnormal symptoms in others and follow their development as if they were reflections of his own sufferings. Thus through his fantastic subjectivity he imposed his own characteristics on the figures he created for his works, and furthermore he feverishly sought to discover traits of persons whom he admired in his own psychological makeup. The result was that, in his fantasy, reality and the longed-for dream world melted into one another.

Hans Roselieb has perceptively remarked that Grillparzer admired "nothing so much as strength and power, and yet saw himself condemned to weakness and ineffectuality; he strove for nothing so much as completeness and perfection, and yet was destined to see his powers dissipated in so many unrelated and often unfinished works and mere projects."[20] With his strikingly handsome appearance and his man-of-the-world aplomb, with his demonstration of courage and bodily strength (in spite of his deformity) — all qualities that Grillparzer so sadly lacked but admired so much — Byron was predestined to be an ideal figure for the Austrian writer, who in his trauma managed to persuade himself that he indeed had traits in common with the noble lord.

The principal of these shared characteristics that Grillparzer imagined he perceived was a certain *taedium vitae,* such as he found displayed in the figure of Manfred, that somber Byronic hero with whom Grillparzer thought he felt a certain spiritual affinity. He also flattered himself that he participated in the fascination that Byron reputedly exercised over the weaker sex, although Grillparzer's record in obtaining the ultimate favors was by no means so impressive as that of the noble lord. Nevertheless, he conceived that there was a certain parallel, and in 1827 he noted in his diary that he had never tried to establish intimacy with a woman who had not herself taken the initiative[21] — an observation that was certainly true of his relationship with Charlotte von Paumgartten. Grillparzer surmised that with Byron a similar state of affairs prevailed, for he recorded in his diary an anecdote about his famous contemporary that refers precisely to this characteristic: "One relates of Lord Byron that as he finally obliged a woman who had pursued him with passion for a long time, he seized her and shouted: 'Now for it! You are mine! But remember you surrender your being to me, as one gives oneself to the devil. You should have no feelings, no thoughts that are not mine! I shall watch over you like a treasure and plague you as I do myself.' — I have often reflected on similar characters and scenes for a tragedy.''[22]

Maybe Grillparzer also conceived similarities between the circumstances that led to his own journey to Italy in 1819 and those that motivated Byron's flight from the wrath of English society in 1816. The serious illness of his mother, accompanied by fits of lunacy, undermined Grillparzer's somewhat labile constitution, and to this tribulation was added the imagined guilt that he conceived he had incurred towards his cousin through his relationship to Charlotte von Paumgartten. His stricken conscience also led him to make a morbid confession on her death some years later.[23] In any event, life became too much for him when his mother committed suicide during a bout of insanity in February 1819. He felt he had to free himself from his surroundings,[24] so he traveled to Italy in the company of Count Deym, hoping not only to escape from the torment of his unsatisfying relations with others, but also seeking flight from himself under new skies.

When Grillparzer arrived in Venice, Byron was perhaps the most notorious inhabitant of the city of lagoons. His reputation was on all lips, and it is clear from Grillparzer's autobiography that the Austrian felt a powerful urge to make his acquaintance.[25] There was no need for Caroline Pichler to suggest such a step to him, as she did in her letter, cited above[26] — a letter which, incidentally, only reached Grillparzer in Naples, and thus far too late for him to act upon. Count Goes, the governor of Venice, received Count Deym and his traveling companion most cordially, and he was anxious to oblige Grillparzer by inviting Byron to supper so that the two writers might meet. In his autobiography Grillparzer gives a curious account of the circumstances surrounding this invitation. He declares that in the normal course of events Byron would have scorned the governor's suggestion that he should visit him, but just at that moment he was greatly obliged to him for protecting him from the wrath of the mob during the introductory phase of his affair with the baker's wife — a fact that is not mentioned in any other source.[27]

However, it was an unfortunate dispensation of providence that during Grillparzer's stay in Venice, several official receptions had been arranged, so that Byron could not be invited before the third evening. As Count Deym was not inclined to miss the Easter celebrations in Rome for the doubtful pleasure of seeing an English poet, he insisted on departing, and so the meeting of the literary giants did not take place. Surprisingly, Grillparzer first refers to these unfortunate circumstances that prevented the meeting in his autobiography, written at the request of the Imperial Academy of Arts in Vienna as late as 1853. He also mentioned there that he had indeed caught sight of Byron in the theater at Venice, but regretted that the poet had deliberately seated himself in the shadow of the wall of his box to protect himself from the gaze of the curious, even those armed with opera glasses. Byron, however, struck Grillparzer as being more corpulent than he had imagined him.[28] In his *Diary of the Journey to Italy,* Grillparzer noted that the first act of *The Barber of Seville* and the second act of *Capriciosa* were on the program at the San Simone Theatre that evening. Although he praised the highly accomplished performance of Madam Fodor,[29] he made no allusion to the fact that he had cast eyes on Byron in the theater. Perhaps here is an instance of Grillparzer's phobia about personal meetings with the great of this world.[30] Maybe at heart the notorious temporizer, who hated to open his soul to others, was content that the encounter with the famous lord did not in fact take place.

Yet even if Grillparzer only glimpsed Byron in the flesh across the auditorium of a Venetian theater, the influence of Byron's intellectual qualities on him was both considerable and lasting. He was well acquainted with *Childe Harold's Pilgrimage*, particularly with Canto IV, before he left for Italy. This can be proved from the Byronic echoes in Grillparzer's poem "Kennst du das Land?" [Dost thou know the land?], which he wrote on 8 March 1819. The urge to embark on a pilgrimage, the journeying to view the famous sites of ancient cultures, the dream of bringing back a portrait of Venus or a sparklet of divine Apollo's wreath, all clearly stem from Canto IV (see particulary xlix ff. and clxi ff., as well as *Manfred* III.iv.10 ff.). Even verbal parallels[31] can be found in Grillparzer's "Kolosseum" and "Die Ruinen des Campo Vaccino," composed in Rome on 14 and 20 April 1819. The full beauty and power of *Childe Harold* IV were to receive added emphasis during the Austrian writer's sojourn in Naples.

Grillparzer had the chance to travel in Count Wurmbrand's coach and four from Rome to Naples, and once they arrived in the Neapolitan city the count's spacious suite in the Albergo Reale was at his disposition. All formalities were waived as the count, being a member of the Imperial retinue, had obtained an official pass for Grillparzer. He records that while he was there he received an invitation from Prince Metternich, and after the meal, as they sat over coffee, the prince recited by heart and with great enthusiasm the newly printed and, Grillparzer maintains, for him largely unknown *Childe Harold* IV from beginning to end. A memorable feat, even if Grillparzer does concede that Metternich's daughter, the Countess Joseph Esterhazy, occasionally prompted him — though it should be noted that she did not use the text either![32]

As Grillparzer wrote his reminiscences thirty-four years after the event, it is more than possible that his recollection of the actual facts had become rather vague. Metternich was certainly a Byron enthusiast, a fact that Grillparzer also stressed in his essay, "Meine Erinnerungen aus dem Revolutionsjahr 1848"[33] [My Recollections of the Year of

Revolutions, 1848], but it seems a rather tall story to expect us to believe that the prince was capable of reciting all the 186 Spenserian stanzas of Canto IV, even with the aid of his charming daughter. The doubt is reinforced by the fact that Grillparzer told Ludwig August Frankl in 1865 that Metternich had recited from memory, with the most perfect nuances, the famous apostrophe to the ocean, a passage of around a hundred lines[34] — a performance that surely seems more credible. In any case, Grillparzer was wrong in maintaining that he first became acquainted with Canto IV in Naples, for the poems he wrote in Rome fully demonstrate his familiarity with it.

The impression created by the princely recitation — however long it might have been — was so overwhelming that Grillparzer promptly began to translate the *Childe Harold* IV, a fact that is all the more remarkable when one recalls that Grillparzer, like a good many famous authors, staunchly maintained "that one could not translate the works of a poet."[35] His undertaking was favored by a fortuitous circumstance: the journey he was planning to Sicily fell through, owing to an unfortunate accident that happened to Count Wurmbrand while he was visiting the English flagship in the harbor of Naples along with the imperial court. He was doomed to a boring convalescence in Naples and begged Grillparzer not to leave him on his own. The Austrian poet occupied his leisure in rendering the first eleven stanzas of *Childe Harold* IV into German. The famous glorification of Venice, the erstwhile proud city that had ruled the seas, forms the opening to the canto. Byron compared her to the earth goddess Cybele, and indeed the city still retained much of the magic of the days of her former supremacy. Grillparzer must have experienced much the same sentiments as Byron did during his stay in the Venetian metropolis, for he declared that there was no other place in the world where the relics of ancient culture remained so vital in the impression they left on contemporary humanity, commenting that "he who does not feel his heart beating faster when he stands in the square of St. Mark, should call for the undertaker, for he is dead, dead beyond recall."[36]

In the opening stanzas of *Childe Harold* IV, Grillparzer found and translated precisely what had left so lasting an impression on his own mind. Together with the evocation of the magic atmosphere of the lagoon city, Grillparzer was particularly moved by the fifth stanza, in which Byron recalls the happier lot of "beings of the mind" that "are not of clay" and enjoy a higher kind of existence than that accorded to mere mortals. Though Grillparzer is on the whole very faithful to the original, following it line-by-line and sometimes even reproducing little plays on words, he did allow himself the liberty of an addition to the sixth line of the seventh stanza. Byron wrote:

> I saw or dream'd of such, — but let them go, —
> They came like truth, and disappear'd like dreams;
> And whatsoe'er they were — are now but so:
> I could replace them if I would; still teems
> My mind with many a form which aptly seems
> Such as I sought for, and at moments found;
> Let these too go.

Grillparzer's rendering runs:

> Ich sah dergleichen oder träumt es; — Fort!
> Es kam wie Wahrheit und verging wie Traum —
> Und was es war, jetzt gilt das letzte Wort,
> Ersetzen könnt' ich's noch; des Herzens Raum
> Hegt noch Gestalten minder lieblich kaum,
> Als ich einst sucht' und fand — nun lange nicht
> Doch fort auch damit —[37]

Perhaps the words "nun lange nicht" ["not for a long time"] betray Grillparzer's reluctant admission that his work on the Golden Fleece had been at a standstill for a considerable period of time, a recollection that he wished to banish with the powerful "fort" ["away"], "Doch fort auch damit" ["Nevertheless away with that too"]. The heartrending cry of bitterness and melancholy that escaped Byron in stanzas 9 and 10 must have spoken to Grillparzer's own soul, for he, far more than Byron, was constantly obsessed by fears that his reputation would not live on after him and that "dull Oblivion" might eradicate his name all too quickly from the book of those who "Are honour'd by the nations."

Why did Grillparzer break off his translation after the eleventh stanza? Certainly not through incapacity to do justice to the original, for his version is one of distinction. Maybe the reason is to be found in the fact that stanza 12 alludes to the chains that the Austrians had laid on the former city of the Doges. Grillparzer was not a front-rank fighter for Amnesty International.

If Grillparzer did not attempt any further translations of Byron's poetry after 1819, his interest in Byron's works nevertheless remained keen. Ferdinand Hübner maintains that he seized with particular eagerness on those passages that he suspected contained personal confessions of the lord,[38] and by a process of assimilation turned them to account in his own poetic creations. As an example Hübner cites Grillparzer's "Napoleon," a poem composed in 1821, in which one finds reminiscences of Byron's "Ode to Napoleon" and stanzas 9 and 42 of *Childe Harold* III. Another possibility, one that seems less convincing, is to be found in his epigram "Kuβ" ["Kiss"], in which the proposition "respect kisses the hand ... blissful love the mouth"[39] echoes "A hand may first, and then a lip be kist" (*Don Juan* I.lxxx). Whether Grillparzer, the son of the country in which the kissing of female hands was, and still is, practiced with more fervid devotion than anywhere else in the world, was tributary to Byron for this thought must surely remain a very open question.

With the correspondences between Grillparzer's "Incubus," written in 1821, and passages in *Childe Harold's*

Pilgrimage and *Manfred* one is on surer ground. The torments of mind that Manfred undergoes during his sojourn in the isolated fortress, typical symptoms of the Byronic hero, reappear in Grillparzer's poem. In the conflict between art and life, in which art finally retains the upper hand, the poet is tormented by a gloomy spirit that renders him mournful and pallid, granting him no rest, but searing relentlessly in his breast. We know that the Austrian poet culled such pessimistic thoughts from *Childe Harold* when he was collecting Byronic utterances in his notebook, and as time passed he felt himself more and more related to the English lord both by feelings and fate. As we have seen, he copied out stanzas 33 and 34 of *Childe Harold* IV, in which Byron speaks of the "demons" who "seek their prey/In melancholy bosoms," and those gloomy spirits who disfigure heaven and earth and do not even respect the peace of the dead:

> Making the sun like blood, the earth a tomb,
> The tomb a hell, and hell itself a murkier gloom.

Grillparzer, who, like Manfred, longed for "Forgetfulness . . . Of that which is within" him (I.i.136-37) but could never attain such bliss, concludes the poem with the terrible and highly significant discovery that it is his own being that revolts against himself and that this supposed dichotomy will never grant him peace. If he wishes himself and all his works in the grave, the incubus would surely follow him there.

These same evil spirits in Grillparzer's breast were to poison his relationship with Katharina Fröhlich, whom he got to know in the period after his mother's death, a time during which he felt an overpowering emotional need for a loving heart that might understand and sustain him. Although he soon became engaged to this highly refined but very personable young lady, whose deep dark-brown eyes and handsome appearance he had so admired on the very first day of their acquaintance, he soon came to realize that he was utterly incapable of that complete self-surrender and renunciation that a real relationship with his beloved would have implied. He regarded himself as a heroic martyr to his art, a devotee who must sacrifice all at the altar of poetry. Though he might strive for human happiness for a brief interval, he felt himself doomed never to establish a permanent relationship with any being other than his muse. As misunderstandings and jealous disputes with Katharina multiplied, Grillparzer's eye lighted on the lines in *Manfred* in which the hero speaks of his "deadliest sin," his love for his sister Astarte:

> She had the same lone thoughts and wanderings,
> The quest of hidden knowledge, and a mind
> To comprehend the universe: nor these
> Alone, but with them gentler powers than mine,
> Pity, and smiles, and tears — which I had not;
> And tenderness — but that I had for her;
> Humility — and that I never had.
> Her faults were mine — her virtues were her own —
> I loved her, and destroy'd her!
>
> [II.ii.109-17]

Manfred's words struck him with a peculiar force, and Grillparzer took them as a terrible warning. Under these very lines he wrote: "I have just read this passage in Byron's gruesome *Manfred*. They fit her and me in a terrible way. But the last line does not fit, will not, and shall never fit."[40]

It is clear that the Austrian poet saw a reflection of his personal fate. The parallel "called to mind in a terrible way his own beloved, whose failings he indeed shared, but whose virtues he could not aspire to."[41] Perhaps fortunately, Grillparzer realized that he was not made for matrimony. His egocentric tendency toward solitude made true married life for him an impossibility. The unhappy development of his relations with Katharina Fröhlich caused him to see in a passage of *Don Juan* that he carefully copied into his diary in

1824[42] a clear confirmation of his own experience:

> 'Tis melancholy, and a fearful sign
> Of human frailty, folly, also crime,
> That love and marriage rarely can combine,
> Although they both are born in the same clime;
> Marriage from love, like vinegar from wine.
>
> [III.v]

Byron had condemned marriage after he failed to find the happiness he had hoped for within the bonds of matrimony; Grillparzer, on the other hand, drew back from marriage because he did not believe he was capable of finding happiness in such a union. He feared that he might "destroy" the young lady, and, with a whimsical morosity, refrained from draining the chalice of love even in the form of a free relationship. While the poet in Grillparzer indulged in aesthetic panegyrics to the immaculate purity of Katharina, the man in him found her jealous, violent, and quarrelsome, and attributed these vexing defects to an unsatisfying sex life.[43] As the artist in him maintained the upper hand over the man, he was condemned to remain a prisoner of the constant strife between the desires that his feelings stimulated and the renunciation that his reason dictated.

Perhaps Grillparzer's affirmation that the Byronic "I loved her, and destroy'd her" must not be allowed to fit his case is a first indication of a slight change in the relationship of the Austrian writer to the English poet that can be perceived during the 1830s. That Byron remained, however, at any rate for the moment, the poet par excellence in Grillparzer's eyes — a genius who deserved the highest veneration — can be deduced from his poem "Beethoven," written in late March 1827 after the famous composer's death. Grillparzer imagines the soul of the great musician soaring through space to the fields of paradise, where famous musicians and poets are gathered to welcome him. It falls to the lot of Mozart, "gleich den Besten" ["equal to any"], to receive the new arrival into the ranks of the undying. As curiosity declines and the crowd of those who wish to greet the new arrival thins, Byron, "der Feind der Knechte" ["the sworn foe of oppression"], who has been standing pensively alone apart from the crowd, steps up to Beethoven and asks him:

Are you happy in the crowd?
Do you like to be always surrounded by masses of people?
See those shady beech avenues,
Let's take a stroll there![44]

Grillparzer could hardly pay Byron greater homage than to single him out from the crowd of immortals and to put him on a pedestal with Beethoven, who was universally recognized as one of the greatest geniuses of the age.

How highly Grillparzer esteemed Byron's gifts can also be seen from an entry in his diary, in which he holds up Byron as a measure for judging Southey's poetical achievements and declares: "Even when he makes a mistake, Byron is greater than Southey, when the latter is in the right."[45] In another passage of his diary, dealing with the recently published letters of the Swiss essayist Karl Victor von Bonstetten to the lyric poet Friedrich von Matthison, whose poem "Adelaide" the recently deceased Beethoven had set to music, Grillparzer jotted down Bonstetten's highly perceptive judgment: "There is no one who can be compared to Byron. His voice rings like music, and his features are those of an angel. But a little devil of fine mockery flashes through, yet even he is half devout."[46]

Grillparzer devoted considerable critical attention to the works of European authors throughout his life. He allotted Byron a special place in English literature, maintaining that after a close scrutiny of the literary scene in the British Isles, "since Byron's death he cannot recognise a single truly original spirit."[47] In an essay on Sir Walter Scott, he recalls the answer that Scott had given to someone who asked him why he had given up writing poetry. Scott had declared that the reason was "because Lord Byron threw me out of the saddle, surpassed me in the description of heart-rending suffering and in deep knowledge of the human heart."[48] This last quality, which Byron shared with Shakespeare, was specially stressed by Grillparzer, who no doubt made Scott's opinion his own, for he also quoted the famous novelist's judgment of Byron "as the only poet of exceptional gifts that England had had since Dryden, and who had possessed more endearing qualities than the world in general gave him credit for."[49]

Despite Grillparzer's undoubted enthusiasm and general admiration for Byron's works, he did not hesitate to criticize the English poet on points of technique and the use of source material. Thus he did not conceal his opinion that the character of the Doge in Byron's *Marino Faliero* was too fluid and lacked the firm lines that the plot of the drama demanded. He himself had conceived a play on the same subject; he described it as among his earliest projects. Grillparzer admitted that such a character as Byron's Doge might have a place in a tragedy and could even be highly effective, but only when there was another firm center of interest in the play, one that constituted the focus of the whole dramatic development. Byron had failed, in Grillparzer's opinion, "to make Venice and its system of government such a focal point."[50]

While Byron conceived his play as primarily a political one, and not without relevance to the movement for the liberation of Italy, for Grillparzer the springboards of the action would have been the insult offered by Steno to Faliero's wife and the implied assault on the honor of the Doge. The Austrian writer declared that when he depicted Marino Falieri (he used the form Falieri and not Faliero), he would characterize him as a hero not unduly suspicious, superbly confident in the virtue of his wife, but who, nevertheless, in defending his wife would avenge his own honor without realizing it. To achieve his aims, he would devote a whole act to Steno's slander, presenting it before the eyes of the audience so that the illusion might be created that many might have believed it, thus arousing Falieri's hatred through "fear of being thought an old foolish cuckold, cheated by a much younger wife."[51] Yet in Grillparzer's concept, all this had to be portrayed as though the Doge did not understand his true motivations, and much of it was to be left to the intelligent perception of the audience, being only hinted at implicitly.

In accordance with such a conception, Grillparzer also viewed the Doge's relationship to the common people and to his fellow-conspirators differently. He maintained that "one must portray Marino Falieri in such a way that he counts less on the power of the other conspirators than on his belief that the masses would rise with joy at the first call to cast off the humiliating chains that the nobles had bound them in."[52] When he realizes after the eruption of the conspiracy that he has made a mistake, that the masses have been so deeply degraded that they are incapable of rising to liberate themselves, then he goes calmly to his death. Grillparzer unfortunately never wrote the play, but a number of its themes, such as the confident relationship of the old man to his much younger wife and the role of Steno, were utilized in his tragedy *Ein treuer Diener seines Herrn* [*A Faithful Servant of His Master*].[53]

It would be surprising if Grillparzer, who constantly returned to Shakespeare in his critical writings, had failed to discuss Byron's attitude towards the bard. In a short essay compiled in 1839, Grillparzer held that "the relatively slight respect that Byron showed Shakespeare"[54] was remarkable. He was not content, however, like Tieck and others — whom Grillparzer dubbed mere drivelers — to explain the phenomenon by the simple fact "that the lesser spirit had failed to understand the greater." Grillparzer sees the real explanation in the independence of Byron's superior spirit that only allowed him to fully appreciate what had emanated from his own mind. Nothing that was not closely related to his own convictions could be truly valued by the poet. Grillparzer supported his view on the basis of Byron's attitude toward the classical authors, on which point Byron showed himself a true Englishman. For him it was unimportant to find out the ways in which the ancients differed from modern men, a field in which the Germans excel in treating art history and related topics; what was needed was to show what ancients and moderns have in common. As Byron followed a "very modern line,"[55] Grillparzer maintained that he had no particular objection to Alexander Pope's rather cavalier treatment of Homer in the translations he did from the ancient Greek writer. On the contrary, Byron had great admiration for Pope. The Austrian saw in Byron's modernity, which he tried to relate to what he called the English poet's "pedantry," another reason why Byron did not praise Shakespeare in the customary tones of idolatry. Grillparzer identified this modernity in the fact that Byron was a poet of perception, a category apart from the poets of feeling. While feelings involve sympathy and are related to the faculty of volition, Grillparzer understood "perception" to be the total expression of the soul, both in its spiritual and sensual aspects, a monopathic principle related to the power of cognition. Grillparzer was all the more inclined to see Byron as a poet of perception, since he felt that he fell into this enviable category himself.

In his essay on Shakespeare's *Othello,* written in 1849, Grillparzer again indicated that "Byron was not fully convinced of the excellent qualities of his great fellow countryman."[56] The sense of truth to nature that Shakespeare had possessed in such ample measure was by no means lacking in Byron. Nor had his reserve vis-à-vis England's greatest poet in any way diminished Grillparzer's respect for the noble lord's own poetic achievements. What impressed the Austrian writer, who stood on the Rubicon between classicism and romanticism and who demanded from a poet "originality and individualism as regards his outlook on life,"[57] was the creative originality that Lord Byron had manifested from the very beginning — a creativity that had been sustained by a blazing fantasy. The Austrian, who had become a pessimist through his sad experience of the deceit and falsehood of the world, felt a certain spiritual affinity with Byron, who so outspokenly condemned all sham, hypocrisy, and make-believe, and who was so uncompromising in his stand for the victory of truth. Grillparzer places these forces in direct opposition in his play *Ein Bruderzwist in Habsburg,* when he has Don Caesar cry out:

> Then as there is only one virtue, Truth,
> There is also only one vice, hypocrisy.[58]

The advocacy of right and truth cannot remain confined in empty words, but must find its realization in deeds. In 1844, Grillparzer cited Byron in support of his own attitude during the debates on censorship in Austria: "'True words are things,' Byron said. Words are things, and I think he was right."[59] Byron's words in Grillparzer's case did in fact become deeds. From the poems of his famous English contemporary, whom he acclaimed "England's second greatest poet"[60] in his essay on Shakespeare's *Othello,* Grillparzer drew numerous impulses that were to lead to his own independent and original artistic creations. His achievements make him, if not the greatest, at least the second greatest Austrian writer.

NOTES

1. *New Monthly Magazine* 10 (1818): 68-69.
2. Franz Grillparzer, *Sämtliche Werke. Historisch-Kritische Gesamtausgabe*, ed. August Sauer and Reinold Backmann, section I, vols. 1-21; section II, vols. 1-13;

section III, vols. 1-6 (Vienna, 1909 ff), II, 8:322: "Widerwillen gegen den Klang seines Namens."

3. This translation was entitled *Mémoires de Lord Byron, publiés par T. Moore,* translated into English by Mme. L. S. Belloc (Paris, 1830). Byron's texts, Grillparzer holds, often became almost unrecognizable in French dress, owing to the difficulty in rendering the frequently colloquial English into acceptable French. Nevertheless Grillparzer declared: "Ich muß froh seyn, nur die Übersetzung gelehnt bekommen zu haben." *Tagebücher und literarische Skizzenhefte* III, *Sämtliche Werke* II, 9:12.

4. *Sämtliche Werke* II, 9:49-50: "Geschrieben kann ich ihn nicht sehen, gedruckt entsetzt er mich. Derlei Namen kommen nicht auf die Nachwelt, Lord Byron mag sagen was er will."

5. Cf. Arthur Burkhard, *Franz Grillparzer in England and America* (Vienna, 1961), pp. 45 ff.

6. See *BL&J,* 8:25-26.

7. *Hamburgische Dramaturgie, Achtes Stück, Lessings Werke,* ed. Franz Bornmüller, 5 vols. (Leipzig and Vienna, n.d.), 4:38.

8. Cf. Karl Brunner, "Byron und die österreichische Polizei," *Archiv für das Studium der neueren Sprachen und Literaturen* 148 (1925):32.

9. *Medwin's Conversations of Lord Byron,* ed. Ernest J. Lovell, Jr. (Princeton, N.J.: Princeton University Press, 1966), pp. 75-76.

10. Cf. *Deutsche Literaturzeitung* 4.4 (1891):499.

11. Cf. Wilhelm Ochsenbein, *Die Aufnahme Lord Byrons in Deutschland und sein Einfluß auf den jungen Heine* (Bonn, 1905), p. 21.

12. *Sämtliche Werke* III, 1:189.

13. "Lebewohl. Nach dem Englischen des Lord Byron." *Aglaja.* Ein Taschenbuch auf das Jahr 1820, 6:186 ff; "Auf ein weißes Blatt. Aus dem Englischen des Lord Byron," *Aglaja* 7 (1821): 19; "Tassos Klage," *Aglaja* 7 (1821): 124 ff.

14. *Sämtliche Werke* III, 1:189.

15. The last four lines of stanza 33, stanza 34, and stanza 122 of Canto IV, *Sämtliche Werke* II, 7:258 and 259.

16. Lines 137-42, *Sämtliche Werke* II, 7:260.

17. Canto I, stanza 103, and lines 1-2 of stanza 132, lines 3-4 of stanza 133, lines 7-8 of stanza 196. Canto II, stanza 22, and lines 1-6 of stanza 23, *Sämtliche Werke* I, 7:261 and 262.

18. *The Works of Lord Byron, with his Letters and Journals and his Life,* ed. Thomas Moore, 17 volumes (London: John Murray, 1833). No. 108 in Grillparzer's library.

19. *Diary 1808/10, Sämtliche Werke* II, 7:29: "Aufblitzen des dichterischen Talentes von unnützen Grübeleien niedergedrükt."

20. "Grillparzers Weltanschauung," in *Grillparzer-Studien,* ed. Oskar Katann (Vienna, 1924), p. 45: Grillparzer verehrte "nichts so wie Stärke und Kraft und sah sich zur Schwäche und Zerbrechlichkeit verurteilt; er strebte nach nichts so eifrig wie nach Ganzheit und Vollkommenheit und sah seine Kraft in so viele einzelne, nie ganz vollendete Arbeiten und Pläne zersplittern."

21. *Sämtliche Werke* II, 8:291.

22. Entry probably from late March 1819 in Venice, *Sämtliche Werke* II, 7:231:

"Man erzählt vom Lord Byron, er habe, als er einem Frauenzimmer, das ihm lange mit Liebe gefolgt, endlich entgegen gekommen, sie angefaßt und gerufen: 'Wohlan! Du bist mein! Aber denk, daß du dich mir übergibst, wie man sich dem Höllenfeind übergibt. Keinen Gedanken, keine Empfindung sollst du haben, die nicht mein wäre, mein! Ich will dich bewachen wie einen Schatz und quälen wie mich selbst.' — Ähnliche Charaktere und Lagen habe ich mir oft für ein Trauerspiel gedacht."

23. On 16 September 1827, the day of the death of Charlotte, *Sämtliche Werke* II, 8:290.

24. Cf. *Selbstbiographie, Sämtliche Werke* I, 16:138.

25. Ibid., I, 16:141.

26. *Sämtliche Werke* III, 1:189. Caroline Pichler writes in the same letter that there were rumors that Byron would come to Vienna, and she was indeed anxious to make his acquaintance, although no one could really say he knew this "chameleon."

27. *Sämtliche Werke* I, 16:140.

28. *Selbstbiographie, Sämtliche Werke* I, 16:141.

29. Entry under 31 March 1819 in *Tagebuch auf der Reise nach Italien, Sämtliche Werke* II, 7:160.

30. When Grillparzer visited Goethe in 1816, the planned intimate discussion between two writers also fell through because of Grillparzer's reluctance to place himself in a position where his inner thoughts might be revealed.

31. Cf. Ferdinand Hübner, "Grillparzer und Lord Byron," Ph.D. diss., University of Vienna, 1945, p. 89.

32. *Selbstbiographie, Sämtliche Werke* I, 16:148.

33. *Sämtliche Werke* I, 16:40. Christian von Zedlitz, knowing of Metternich's partiality for Byron's poetry, sought permission to dedicate his translation of *Childe Harold's Pilgrimage, Childe Harolds Pilgerfahrt* (Stuttgart and Tübingen, 1836) to the prince. As Zedlitz was obviously seeking to curry favor by such a move and must have hoped for some post as a reward — he was habitually an opponent of the aristocracy — Grillparzer was decidedly nettled. He regarded it as undignified to try to gain personal profit from Byron in this way and in 1836 expressed his contempt in an epigram:

> *Lord Byron an seinen Übersetzer*
> Was nennst du Meister mich und Herrn?
> Wie ist dein Kuß gemeint?
> Der du für dreißig Silberling
> Mich lieferst an meinen Feind?

When Zedlitz deserted the liberals to join the party in power in 1840, Grillparzer let fly with another epigram:

> *Der bekehrte Dichter*
> Gewohnheit bleibt der Meister doch zuletzt,
> Was Einer treibt, lehrt ihn die Übung schätzen,
> Kaum hatte er Lord Byron übersetzt,
> Kam ihm die Lust sich selbst zu übersetzen.
> [*Sämtliche Werke*, I, 12/1: 115]

34. August Sauer, ed., *Grillparzers Gespräche und die Charakteristiken seiner Persönlichkeit durch die Zeitgenossen*, 7 vols. (Vienna, 1904 ff), 6:143.

35. *Selbstbiographie, Sämtliche Werke* I, 16:114: "daß man einen Dichter nicht übersetzen könne."

36. *Tagebuch auf der Reise nach Italien, Sämtliche Werke* II, 7:158: "Wer nicht sein Herz stärker klopfen fühlt, wenn er auf dem Markusplatz steht, der lasse sich begraben, denn er ist tod, unwiderbringlich tod."

37. *Sämtliche Werke* I, 11:22.

38. Hübner, "Grillparzer und Lord Byron," p. 106: "in denen er persönliche Bekenntnisse des Lord vermutete."

39. *Sämtliche Werke* I, 10:27: "Auf die Hände Küßt die Achtung, . . . Sel'ge Liebe auf den Mund."

40. *Sämtliche Werke* II, 7:362: "Eben habe ich diese Stelle in Byrons gräßlichen *Manfred* gelesen. Sie passen auf eine furchtbare Art auf mich und sie. Aber der letzte Vers paßt nicht, wird, soll nie passen."

41. Grillparzer's *Sämtliche Werke,* 5th edition in 20 vols., ed. August Sauer (Stuttgart, 1892), I, 61: Sie "erinnert ihn auf furchtbare Weise an die eigene Geliebte, deren Fehler er zwar besaß, deren Tugenden er aber nicht teilen konnte."

42. *Sämtliche Werke* II, 8:145.

43. *Tagebücher,* May 1827, *Sämtliche Werke* II, 8:204: "Wirkungen der unbefriedigten Geschlechtsliebe."

44. "Beethoven," lines 124-27, *Sämtliche Werke* I, 10:89:

> Bist du gern in dem Gedränge?
> Magst du gern bei Vielen stehn?
> Sieh dort dunkle Buchengänge,
> Laß uns mit einander gehn!

45. *Tagebücher,* Summer 1830, *Sämtliche Werke* II, 8:365: "Byron wo er irrt ist größer als South[e]y wo er Recht hat."

46. *Tagebücher,* late 1827, *Sämtliche Werke* II, 8:321: "Ich kann kein Geschöpf mit Byron vergleichen. Seine Stimme tönt wie Musik, und seine Züge sind die eines Engels. Nur blitzt ein kleiner Satan feinen Spottes durch, der aber doch halb fromm ist." *Bonstettens Briefe an Matthison,* p. 33.

47. *Tagebücher,* Spring 1837, *Sämtliche Werke* II, 10:182: er "seit Byrons Tode keinen einzigen eigentlich selbstständigen Geist kenne."

48. *Tagebücher,* Summer 1838, *Sämtliche Werke* II, 10:241: "Weil Lord Byron mich aus dem Sattel hob, mich übertraf in Beschreibungen starker Leidenschaften und in tiefer Kenntnis des menschlichen Herzens."

49. Ibid.: "als den einzigen Dichter von ausgezeichneten Gaben, den England seit Dryden gehabt, und der dabei mehr liebenswerthe Eigenschaften besessen als die Welt im allgemeinen glaube."

50. From a diary dated 1821, *Sämtliche Werke* II, 7:354: Byron habe es versäumt, "den Staat von Venedig und sein Verfaßungssystem als einen solchen Mittelpunkt hinzustellen."

51. Ibid.: "als der betrogene Alte, der hintergangene Gatte einer weit Jüngern dastehen zu müssen."

52. From a diary dated 1821, *Sämtliche Werke* II, 7:352-53: "Man müßte den Marino Falieri so schildern, daß er weniger auf die Macht der mit ihm Verschwornen zählt, als vielmehr glaubt, das von den Edlen gedrückte Volk werde mit Freuden den

ersten Aufruf benützen, seine schimpflichen Fesselün abzuwerfen."

53. Cf. Ludwig Wyplel, *Grillparzer und Byron. Zur Entstehungsgeschichte des Trauerspiels "Ein treuer Diener seines Herrn," Euphorion* 9-10 (1902-3). Wyplel also endeavored to demonstrate Byron's influence on *Die Ahnfrau,* Grillparzer's earliest tragedy, written in 1817, in his study "Byron und Grillparzer. Ein Beitrag zur Entstehungsgeschichte der *Ahnfrau," Jahrbuch der Grillparzer-Gesellschaft* 14 (1904): 26-59. Wyplel claims that Grillparzer borrowed a number of motifs and also character traits from figures that appear in Byron's verse tales. On the question of verbal parallels, he seems on occasion to exaggerate Grillparzer's dependence on Byron.

54. *Tagebücher und literarische Skizzenhefte* IV, *Sämtliche Werke* II, 10:284: "die verhältnismäßig geringe Achtung Lord Byrons für Shakspear."

55. Ibid., p. 285: "moderne Richtung."

56. *Tagebücher und literarische Skizzenhefte* V, *Sämtliche Werke* II, 11:204: "von den Vorzügen seines großen Landsmannes nicht weniger als durchdrungen war."

57. *Tagebücher und literarische Skizzenhefte* II, *Sämtliche Werke* II, 8:365: "Originalität, Eigenthümlichkeit der Weltanschauung."

58. *Ein Bruderzwist in Habsburg,* IV.1931-32:

> Denn wie's nur eine Tugend gibt: die Wahrheit,
> Gibt's auch ein Laster nur: die Heuchelei.

59. *Sämtliche Werke* I, 13:186: "'True words are things' sagt Byron. 'Worte sind Dinge' und ich glaube er hat Recht." Grillparzer had already noted in his diary for 1821: "True *words* are *things*" (*Marino Faliero* V.i.289), *Sämtliche Werke* II, 7:353.

60. *Sämtliche Werke* II, 11:204: "zweitgröße [sic] Dichter Englands."

Byron and Napoleon in Polish Romantic Myth*

STEFAN TREUGUTT

While paying a visit in 1979 to the Institute of Russian Literature in Leningrad, I unexpectedly discovered a copy of *The Works of Lord Byron, Complete in One Volume,* published in Frankfurt am Main in 1826, and which came to the Institute from Pushkin's library. On the title page is this dedication in Polish: "Bajrona Puszkinowi poświęca wielbiciel obudwóch — A. Michiewicz" ("Here is Byron dedicated to Pushkin by an admirer of both of them — Adam Mickiewicz"). What impressed me was not the elegance of the dedication but the sign of a community transcending national boundaries: a volume of a great English author published in Germany had been presented to the foremost poet of Russia by a Polish poet in exile. This volume commemorates an internationalism of free spirits in which Byron's name, evoking an entire range of feelings and ideas, serves as the symbol of freedom.

"There was Byronism before Byron," says William Rose in his study on the origins and development of the notion of *Weltschmerz* in German literature, and he continues:

*The editor wishes to thank Professor Hubert F. Babinski (Columbia University) for his assistance in preparing this essay.

"Weltschmerz was epidemic in German literature for the forty years or more which preceded the publication of *Childe Harold*. . . . There is no doubt equal scope for an enquiry into the symptoms of 'le mal du siècle' in France before Chateaubriand, while a study on the same lines of the precursors of Byron in England should yield fruitful results."[1]

No doubt there was "Byronism before Byron" in Poland, whose artists also distrusted "reality" and lost confidence in the ideas of the Age of Reason. The Enlightenment was expected to bring the Poles a reform of their state, a constitution, democracy, and prosperity, but no such transformations occurred. Hopes ran high again during the Napoleonic wars, but the conqueror of Europe did not restore Poland. The feeling of bitterness, especially among young people, was even stronger than that of the preceding generation.

> Poland! o'er which the avenging angel pass'd,
> But left thee as he found thee, still a waste,
> Forgetting all thy still enduring claim,
> Thy lotted people and extinguish'd name,
> Thy sigh for freedom, thy long-flowing tear.

These words of Byron, dedicated to Poland after the fall of Napoleon and uttered with pathos in *The Age of Bronze* (ll. 161-65), were not known to Adam Mickiewicz as a young man. Yet the Polish poet found other reasons for admiring Byron when he wrote to a friend in 1822: "It is only Byron I am reading now. I push away books written in any other spirit, as I have no liking for lies."[2] The point here is that for the young Polish poet, who was then affected by private grief, Byron was not a teacher of pessimism. What Mickiewicz found in his lines was the truth of his own feelings and a critique and condemnation of hypocrisy. There was surely Byronism before Byron, but for Mickiewicz and for the entire generation born as the eighteenth century succeeded to the nineteenth, the name of the English poet became a symbol, a token of an adopted attitude, a declaration of community.

We all know how great was Shakespeare's authority in Europe during the Romantic period. It is, consequently, very significant that the volume that proclaimed the triumph of Romanticism in Poland — the *Ballads and Romances* of Mickiewicz — contains in the discourse on Romantic poetry preceding the poems a rather unusual comparison: "In the descriptive genre and in the tale Byron is what Shakespeare was in the dramatic genre." What Mickiewicz has in mind is of course not prose fiction, but the Byronic poetic tale: perhaps the Turkish tales; or perhaps *Beppo* and the opening cantos of *Don Juan,* which the Polish author might have known at that time. According to Mickiewicz, Byron created "a new kind of poetry," a new and feeling expression of "the passionate soul."[3] To some scholars, the equal footing conceded to Byron and to Shakespeare may seem extravagant, but Mickiewicz was right in finding certain common elements in both poets, such as pathos side by side with raw realism, sublimity with irony, lofty ideals with the grotesque. Both writers told him truths about the nature of man, but of the two Byron stood for unrestrained individualism, for revolt, for cult of genius and worship of freedom. Besides, he was a contemporary, still living and working when Mickiewicz was placing him in the gallery of patron spirits of the new Romantic literature.

Searching for genealogies and adducing great examples from the past were characteristic of all the new literary trends until the twentieth century. The futurists and other radical avant-garde groups were the first to proclaim that they had neither ancestors nor family archives. But the Romantics, though in revolt against tradition and the classroom brand of classicism, were very anxious to have a good pedigree, and in this very respect they were legitimists. When Victor Hugo wanted to point to the ancient roots of Romantic poetry and attitudes, the names that appeared the most frequently in his manifesto were those of Homer, Dante, Cervantes, and Shakespeare, plus the Bible and — Byron. A comparative study of proclamations and manifestoes of the Romantic movement in Europe (from Italy to Scandinavia and from Madrid to Saint Petersburg) would reveal, undoubtedly, a similar and select assortment of the patrons of the new writing, with Byron's name among the predecessors and patrons of the new literature: he was the youngest, the closest to the new generation, and the most intelligible. He was also the most adaptable to the spiritual needs and experiences of differing societies, of various writers and their readers. H. G. Schenk says in *The Mind of the European Romantics*: "Although the enthusiasm for Byron's personality caught on all over Europe, the appeal of the poet whom Goethe hailed as the herald of world literature varied from nation to nation, in that each picked out that part of Byron's *œuvre* most congenial to itself."[4] Byron's language became in an incredibly short time an international language of the generation in revolt, of the spiritual and social outcasts alienated from the conventional rules of living and thinking.

The practice of adducing literary patrons is as old as literature itself. For a number of centuries, the writers of ancient Greece and Rome played this part for most European artists. The eighteenth century chose the patronage of Voltaire, but Byron's impact was something of a different quality. Voltaire's influence was traditionally unifying: it raised the representatives of different traditions to the level of French intellectual culture. But Byron's individualism offered no ready-made doctrine and thus could become a stimulus within the bodies of various national literatures. Voltaire provided a national lesson to be learned; Byron provided an international inspiration that respected individuality. That is why the cult of Byron contributed in so many literatures, and quite certainly in Polish literature, to an increase of originality. It also stimulated literary invention and favored personal features in poetic expression. All this is valid, of course, only for a certain period: with the formation of clichés and rigid patterns, the poets whom literary history posthumously honors as leaders of their age outgrew the fashion of Byronism. It was then cultivated only by belated followers. Still, Byron's name, even more glorious after his death in Greece in 1824, continued to inspire and enthuse. This enthusiasm is eloquently documented in the Paris lectures on Slavonic literatures given by Adam Mickiewicz in Collège de France in 1840-44. According to Mickiewicz, Byron was a spokesman for collective feelings:

> Avec lord Byron commence l'époque nouvelle de la littérature, de la poésie. Cette littérature et cette poésie se rapprochent d'un côté de la philosophie, et d'un autre côté de la vie réelle. Personne n'a mieux que lui représenté les tourments de ces existences anormales qui ont marque le passage entre le XVIIIe et le XIXe siècle, ce voyage sans but, cette recherche des aventures extraordinaires, ces élans vers un avenir dont on n'avait encore aucune idée. Tout cela remplissait les âmes des jeunes gens de notre génération; tout cela a été représenté par lord Byron avec une grande fidélité. Sous ce point de vue, c'est un poëte de réalité.[5]

Mickiewicz held Byron to be equally important as a harbinger of political ideas ("On connait aussi la hauteur et la sûreté de son coup d'oeil lorsqu'il jugeait les questions politiques") and as a metaphysical poet ("son désir incessant de sonder et de connaître les mystères de l'existence"). He ranked the English poet among the great who could express a whole age and at the same time point a way to the future:

> Ainsi, dans la politique, comme dans l'art, il y a toujours des individus qui conduisent les époques. ... il faut suivre leurs traces, comme les navigateurs qui parcourent les mers sont obligés de suivre le chemin de ceux qui ont fait les premières découvertes, sauf ensuite à compléter leurs observations.

Yet, to follow such predecessors does not mean to imitate

them, to counterfeit their literary form or their heroes. What should be followed is their spirit ("c'est s'inspirer de leurs esprit"). Mickiewicz's verdict is categorical:

> et nous sommes convaincu que ceux-là seulement qui ont saisi ce qu'il y avait de fort, de vrai, de sincère et de profond dans lord Byron, ont été appelés à prendre le devant dans la marche littéraire de notre siècle.

Mickiewicz further explains that many of his contemporaries did not see Byron's works but that they grasped a few lines, a few sounds that were sufficient to inspire them: "La force de cet homme était si grande qu'elle se faisait sentir même dans quelques paroles, et que ces paroles suffisaient pour remuer les âmes et leur faire découvrir le secret de leur propre existence." Byron, something much more than a distant literary authority, addressed his contemporaries without intermediaries and simply spoke their language.

Juliusz Słowacki, another Polish Romantic poet who antagonized and competed with Mickiewicz, still agreed with him on Byron's position in world literature when he wrote in April 1833:

> Dante wrote about Hell at a time when people believed in Hell; Voltaire was in agreement with a materialistic age; Byron while despairing about the future and its uncertainty opened the nineteenth century. These three people represent the epochs in which they lived, their spiritual countenances reflect the faces of their age. If one could put together one single monument of thought out of the thoughts of many people in those days, the statues on the monument would be those of Dante, Voltaire, and Byron.[6]

In short, Byron's contemporaries agreed that he was a personification of the spirit of the age, a voice of the Romantic Zeitgeist. He was, paradoxically, the leader of an international community of solitaries, of egocentrics, of individualists in revolt. Because of the universal appeal of the Byron cult, Romantic individualism did not mean the breaking of communication between people or an expression of doubt about such communication. Byron's language could be used for communication and mutual comprehension by all those who understood it, by those "Byronists before Byron" who experienced painfully the widening gap between their inner experience and the outer world. To them and on their behalf, the poet spoke a language of solitude and despair that at the same time was a language of pride and energy.

Because Byronism was a Continental more than a British phenomenon, the question arises why Byron's works, read in translation or in the original by people who were not native speakers of English, proved so much more interesting abroad than to his own countrymen. Perhaps the answer could be found in the quicker pace of literary developments in the British Isles, where Romanticism was no longer a revelation at the time of Byron's appearance upon the literary stage. In Germany, on the other hand, where the campaign for a national literature had already been successfully carried on by the Storm and Stress movement, where Byron's works could not inaugurate Romanticism, his prestige was very considerable, if not overwhelming as in Central or Southern Europe. Although Germany was as rich as Britain in Romantic inspirations of its own, the German peoples were fascinated with the personality of the English lord and poet. One could perhaps formulate the following principle: the further from Britain, from English literature, and from the actual biography of Byron, the stronger were the impact of the myth of his personality and the influence of his poetical works.

Slavonic literatures and the Polish writers in particular were indeed far away from Britain at that time, but they nevertheless recognized a kinship with Byron. The Polish Romantic artist discovered in him what he wished to be — a non-conformist, a solitary, and a man of magnanimity, a hero of freedom, an incarnation of creative genius. From the protean character and works of the man, Polish Romantics abstracted and formed their own ideal and pattern of an active poet who did not draw limits between literature and life, between his words and his deeds.

Byron's death in Greece played an important part in the shaping of his legend. For contemporary young enthusiasts of political freedom and of Romantic poetry, it was not an accident but the logical outcome of a certain attitude. Moreover, it refuted tales about the dissolute and perverted fiend. Continental poets exalted his death in a crusade for freedom, and Cyprian Norwid, the last of the great Polish poets bred in the Romantic tradition, concluded an evaluation of Byron as follows:

> How serious, indeed, is the poet's service and vocation! And yet this truth began to dawn only at the threshold of the present age upon which Byron lies with the lyre of Homer and the sword of Leonidas — a man who might have said about himself: *veni, cantavi, vici.*[7]

Norwid's parallel, taken from ancient history, illustrates his conviction that Byron's death in a war for the sake of mankind confirms the truth of the poet's works, and that the two symbols of sword and lyre are the attributes of "serious" poetry. A poem is an actual deed, and there can be no boundary between poetry and action. This view is very characteristic for the Polish Romantics, especially after the failure of the uprising in 1830-31. The desperate national situation induced people to think of every possible means of struggle, both ideological and political. For creative artists, action and deed became a category that overshadowed the opposition of the spiritual and the real. One could speak here, perhaps, of a suppression and uplifting of the clash between the ideal and reality. Byron — the poet of freedom rushing to the battle of liberation — provided a sign: he prefigured the future role of poetry, that which would abolish the distinction between word and action.

In order to stress the importance of Byron's mission,

Norwid identifies Byron's ancestors as the crusaders for the recovery of the Holy Land. Envisioning Byron's death as the beginning of a new era, Norwid writes about himself in his autobiography: "He saw the world ... in the patrimonial estate a few miles away from Warsaw, at the time when Noel Byron was just dying in Greece." One could treat this reference as a simple stylistic ornament opening an auto-biography, but Norwid actually postpones the date of his birth for three years (he was really born in 1821) in order to make it symbolically agree with the date of Byron's death. The beginning of his own life is to be connected with the end of the life of Byron.

Adam Mickiewicz, in his lectures at the Collège de France, best sums up the part Byron played in shaping the ideal of a poet both in Poland and in other Slavonic countries:

> Ce qui a élevé, ce qui a facilité la marche des poètes slaves, et ce qui en général pourra rendre plus claire l'idée qu'ils se font de la poésie, c'est la carrière politique de lord Byron. Lord Byron commence l'ère de la poésie nouvelle; lui, le premier, a fait sentir aux hommes tout le sérieux de la poésie; on a vu qu'il fallait vivre d'après ce qu'on écrit; que le désir, que la parole, ne suffisent pas; on a vu ce poëte riche et élevé dans un pays aristocratique quitter le parlement et sa patrie pour servir la cause des Grecs. Ce besoin profondément senti de rendre la vie poétique, de rapprocher ainsi l'idéal du réel, constitue tout le mérite poétique de Byron. Or, tous les grands poëtes slaves ont passé par là. Byron, c'est l'anneau mystérieux qui attache la grande littérature slave à celle de l'Occident.

It does not matter that Byron's biography has been simplified here. It is important to observe that this is how Mickiewicz wants to see, to interpret, and to understand Byron. He really saw in the English poet an example of the principle that "one should live according to what one is writing," proving that it is possible to bring an ideal close to reality. Such an interpretation was possible, and even natural, in the circum-stances in which Polish literature had to operate in the period under discussion. The leading Romantics were involved in political activities; they were looking for effective ways and means of working for their nation. The art of beautiful speech consequently seemed unimportant and a secondary matter. Mickiewicz stopped his literary activities in the very middle of his dazzling career to become a politician, a prophet of a new religion, and finally a soldier. Juliusz Słowacki, the most Romantic of the Polish writers and a Byronist at the beginning of his career, suddenly at the age of thirty-three changed his views of poetry, stopped producing literature, and devoted himself to penetrating the mysteries of Nature and the ways of Creation. He went on writing feverishly, but his later works are visions put down in verse or prose, fragments of a mystical system of the Great Chain of Being and Universal Evolution that would free Poland and all mankind. Like Byron and Mickiewicz, Słowacki finally hurried to the battlefield. At the end of his life he went to the German part of Poland, which was then caught by the fire of the revolution in 1848. He did not die in the campaign like the other two poets, but succumbed a few months later after his return to Paris.

The life of Juliusz Słowacki is an exemplary Romantic biography in the history of Polish literature. It began with solitude and alienation from the world and ended in the mystical communion with an all-embracing creative evolution. Słowacki is so typically Byronic that his period of Childe Haroldism, of the youthful cult of one's own personality, is followed at maturity by a phase of romantic irony and satire in which Byron served as master and example. Słowacki's *Podróz na Wschód* (*Journey to the East*) in six-line stanzas and the digressive poetic tale *Beniowski* in ottava rima are the best Polish equivalents of Byron's style in *Don Juan*.

Byron's pattern was followed by young Romantics, by young people searching for their own identity. But he still provided an example of how to render life poetic, how to bring about a close union between poetry and life, when the youthful solitaries grew up to become patriotic leaders, prophets, and spiritual commanders in the war "for our freedom and for yours." The years 1831 and 1863 were those of tragic Polish national uprisings, but were also the dates of the triumph and the end of great Romantic poetry in Poland. For the Polish Romantic poets who lived during these years, Byron was not a hero of the past. On the contrary, they looked upon him as their forerunner, a John the Baptist of the future, a prefiguration and a mythical impulse that was calling for fulfillment.

There is a striking parallel here with the myth of Napoleon: Byron died on his mission of a liberator, Napoleon did not accomplish his mission. The latter's genius had been tempted by egoism, which made him replace the sword of Europe's liberator and creator of a new order with the imperial crown of dynastic ambitions. In his case, as in that of Byron, the mission had to be taken up and the mystical impulse had to be brought to fruition. In the preface to his translation of *The Giaour,* Mickiewicz thus establishes a connection between the two geniuses as forerunners of the future: "The voice of the general has called Byron the Napoleon of the poets, while Napoleon has been acknowledged as the only poet of France."[8] It is difficult to imagine a more striking declaration of unity between word and deed, between poetry and life. Byron himself had certain reservations about the subject when he treated the parallel between Napoleon and his own person with the irony of a grand seigneur:

> Even I — albeit I'm sure I did not know it,
> Nor sought of foolscap subjects to be king, —
> Was reckon'd, a considerable time,
> The grand Napoleon of the realms of rhyme.
> [*Don Juan* XI.1v]

For Mickiewicz and other Romantics, equating Byron and Napoleon was not a mere compliment paid to the poet. Mickiewicz was deeply convinced, and Byron and Napoleon served him as examples, that "il y a des signes de parenté entre toutes ces créations, malgré l'indépendance et l'originalité des créateurs." Characteristically, Mickiewicz stresses the affinity of poetry and practical action produced by a poet and a military leader, and not the links between different arts or between poetry and other kinds of intellectual creativeness. Also Norwid's praise of Byron (*"veni, cantavi, vici"*) paraphrases the famous words of Julius Caesar — a genius of poetry and a genius of energy and action are again put on the same level. The common denominator between Byron and Napoleon is their moral force that changes people and may shape life itself. This is exactly what, according to Mickiewicz, Byron saw and understood in Napoleon:

> C'est le seul des écrivains anglais qui ait compris quelque chose à Napoléon. Il est vrai qu'il l'a réduit aux proportions d'un corsaire. Il comprennait seulement la force que Napoléon exerçait sur ses semblables, force toute morale; il sentait aussi où elle résidait: Napoléon a dominé parce que son âme était toujours en travail; son sentiment ne pouvait dormir. *I suoi pensieri in lui dormir non ponno,* c'est la devise qu'a choisie lord Byron. Cette âme en travail dévelopait la force qui lui donnait le pouvoir sur ses semblables.

What is mentioned here is energy, but not energy for its own sake: energy must actively influence other people. Napoleon began the work of Europe's reconstruction and demonstrated man's creative scope and power; a poet should do likewise. Practical influence becomes the norm and canon of poetry. The anticlassical revolution had indeed come to its ultimate limit. By appealing to the memory of Napoleon as a poet of action and to Byron as the leader of souls of a generation, Polish Romantics raised poetry to such a high position that it stopped being what is called an art of language. In their view, poetry was a prediction, an expectation of the fulfillment of a prophecy — *"ut sermo ... prophetae impleretur,"* as John 12:38 states. Poetry was no longer merely literary.

The historical explanation of this strangely utopian and anachronistic view of poetry is to be found in the situation of the Poles and in the situation of Europe on the eve of the revolution of 1848. The lack of real power made men's minds more heated and ecstatic. Words were plentiful and stood for the deeds and actions that were sadly lacking. Here are the sources of the phenomenon of heroizing poetry, of the cult of genius, of the posthumous career and activeness of the spirit of Napoleon. Here is also the explanation of the power of Byronism treated as a source of inspiration and energy. One must always keep in mind that, through Byronism, the poet's work and person were transformed into myth. Only in recent decades has critical examination of Byron's poetic work begun to prevail over biographical studies, over studies of the Byron legend and of the myth of a superman. The turning point was T. S. Eliot's essay on Byron's poetry in 1937. It is certainly important to strip Byron of the Byron mythology, to examine his poems in a critical way by using all the equipment of modern literary criticism. But one must not, in the process, overlook Byronism, a mythic force as real to nineteenth-century Europe as were Byron's poems.

Byronism is an important component of the history of ideas and of the history of literary consciousness. In Poland, the reading public actually acquaints itself with Byron's works through the tradition of Byronism. There is a very good translation of *Don Juan,* which was quite the rage with schoolboys of my generation. This translation was published in 1883 and is clearly modeled in its style upon Juliusz Słowacki's tale *Beniowski,* which, in turn, is a Polish replica of *Don Juan.* Byron's text in Polish was decisively influenced by Byronism as understood by an eminent Polish Romantic poet some forty years before the actual date of translation.

There are, however, reasons of much greater importance for this interest in Byronism and the Byron myth. The presence of Byronism in simple and naive forms — or in complicated and sophisticated shapes — is strong in the works of Polish Romantic literature, as well as in much contemporary literature. One may believe or not in the power of the word to change people's minds or to stir them to action, but in any case Polish readers expect poetry to offer more than linguistic delights or expressions of impotence. The ideal of effective poetry may be a utopia, and it is perhaps wrong to confuse poetry or literature in general with any sphere of activity. But poetry that abandons in advance its claim to the *energy* of despair and the *energy* of enthusiasm is not worth reading at all.

In any case, it is certainly worthwhile to continue research on Byronism as a community of the lonely, as a movement from narrow, personal truth to the larger truth of mankind. Sheer curiosity should be sufficient reason — a curiosity to learn something about the exceedingly high tasks that art undertook 150 years ago. By such research, one may observe an international exchange of ideas that still exert their influence on contemporary poetry and politics.

NOTES

1. William Rose, *From Goethe to Byron: The Development of "Weltschmerz" in German Literature* (London: George Routledge & Sons, 1924), pp. 1-2.
2. Letter to Francziszek Malewski, 22 November 1822, in Adam Mickiewicz, *Dzieła* (Warsaw: Czytelnik, 1955), 14:207.
3. Mickiewicz, *Dzieła*, 5:198.
4. H. G. Schenk, *The Mind of the European Romantics* (London: Constable, 1966), p. 147.
5. Adam Mickiewicz, *Les Slaves. cours professé au Collège de France (1842-1844)* (Paris: Musée Adam Mickiewicz, 1914), pp. 19-20. All subsequent quotations from these lectures are from these same pages.
6. Juliusz Słowacki, *Dzieła Wszystkie,* ed. Juliusz Kleiner (Wrocław: Ossoleneum, 1954), 2:12.
7. Cyrpian Norwid, *Wszystkie Pisma* (Warsaw: Przesmycki, 1938), 6:147.
8. Mickiewicz, *Dzieła,* 2:156.

Byron and Lermontov: Notes on Pechorin's "Journal"*

NINA ÎA. D'ÎAKONOVA

Pechorin's "Journal" constitutes the principal part of the novel *A Hero of Our Time* (1840), in which Lermontov has recourse to a device much favored in early-nineteenth-century literature and fairly familiar to readers of Pushkin's prose: the story is supposed to have been written by an unknown Russian officer who died young. But the story is not a straightforward narrative, as is so often the case with Pushkin or Walter Scott: it acquires the shape of a journal, a diary of unassuming everyday happenings whose sequence seems to be formed by chance and to break off independently of the will of the so-called author.

While painting the portrait of a person "made up of the vices ... of an entire generation,"[1] Lermontov could not fail to think of the Byronic heroes that for many years had for European readers served as an embodiment of the "spirit of the age" (and its maladies) and had given birth to innumerable imitations not only in literature but in life. It goes without saying that Russian Byronism was born out of

*This essay is a translation and adaptation by Professor D'îakonova of her article, "Iz nablîudeniĭ nad Zhurnalom Pechorina," *Russkaiîa literatura; istoriko-literaturnyĭ zhurnal,* no. 4 (1969): 115-25.

conditions specifically Russian, and that it differed radically from English Byronism in developing later and in expressing the suffering and the doubts besetting the advanced part of Russian men and women, as well as their disgust with political reaction. But such differences should not obscure the tremendous influence of Byron's life and works on Russian literature. The legend of his Satanic nature spread widely in the 1820s and, eloquently voiced in Lamartine's poem, exercised a certain influence upon the central concept of Lermontov's *The Demon.*[2] Therefore, when Lermontov set out to depict a hero of his time (a period of Byronic woe, skepticism, and negation), he could hardly miss the book wherein the mind and life of the poet so congenial to him were displayed with the utmost sincerity and completeness. That book was Thomas Moore's edition of Byron's *Letters and Journals: With Notices of His Life.*[3]

Historians of literature are well aware of the fact that Lermontov was an enthusiastic reader not only of Byron's poetry but also of his prose. His most important prose work — the Memoirs — had been burned on the decision of his relatives and friends, who feared they might injure his reputation. Fortunately, Byron's letters and portions of his diaries became part of Byron's *Life,* written by his friend Thomas Moore. Lermontov carefully read that book. In one of his autobiographical notes, he refers to Byron's *Life* as a book he has read and adds that he too, like the English poet, early started collecting and copying his own poems; in another of the same notes he states that, like Byron, he had been foretold a great future; in a third note, the story of the great love of his childhood has obvious affinities with Byron's reminiscences of his early love for Mary Duff (*Works,* 6:385-87). The inner connection between these two confessions is confirmed by Lermontov's quotation from Byron's entry in his 1813 journal concerning Mary (see *Works,* 6:386 and Moore, p. 7).

These references were made by Lermontov in 1830 and

concern only the first chapters of Moore's *Life*. But since the complete edition of that work was published in Paris (and London) at the beginning of 1830, it is inconceivable that Lermontov, who cared so much for Byron's poetry, should not have read his life to the end. This seems all the more likely, for next to the title of Lermontov's poem "To***" ("Do not think I deserve to be grieved for"), the poet wrote: "On having read Byron's Life by Moore, 1830" (*Works*, 1:407). And yet, numerous students of Lermontov have not thought of Byron's *Letters and Journals* as a possible source of Pechorin's "Journal." Some of them have emphasized the influence of Chateaubriand, Constant, Senancour, and Musset (and their respective novels *René* [1802], *Adolphe* [1810-16], *Obermann* [1814], *Confessions of a Son of the Age* [1836]), but they never considered these influences as interacting with that of Byron's prose, which deserves a more detailed study than it has so far enjoyed.[4]

The history of Byron's mind as told by himself is, no doubt, a very striking composition. Written by a poet who had a stronger hold on his contemporaries than any other poet of his time, it presents a self-portrait of extraordinary power and penetration. Readers are baffled by the personality of one who is so much possessed by world problems that they have become part of his innermost self, so much so that he feels ready to give up his own life in a fight for the triumph of liberty. And yet he is a fatalist fully convinced of the hopelessness of struggling with fate — though he finds it difficult to care for anything else. He detests and loathes all things established, and his journals are brimful of protest and universal negation.

The unspiritual god of circumstance and Byron's own inner instability prey on his mind and make him unbalanced, inconsistent, and ever changeable. Byron himself confessed that he could not understand his own nature, and Moore stated that in him several distinctly different personalities were fantastically intertwined (Moore, p. 497). Byron is really consistent only in wrath, grief, and doubt: he wavers between skepticism and longing for faith, between a scornful and ironical attitude to feelings as they really are (despite their common poetic presentation) and very high demands on feelings as they should be. He is a cold, mistrustful observer of Vanity Fair and the passions agitating it — and is at the same time deeply involved in them. He is capable of sentiments that he never expected to share, of regrets concerning actions that he but recently justified. He can rise to true heroism, to self-sacrifice, to thought that can appeal to thousands — and then sink to the extremes of pettiness, childishness, and vanity. He speaks ill of himself and of others, for he is obsessed with the notion of the vast difference between what is and what should be; he carelessly plays with the highest flights of philosophy and culture — both because he felt very much at home among them and because he realized their inadequacy to account for the complexities of modern existence and therefore mocked their pseudo-universality and irrefutability.[5]

The personality of the author, whose features naturally coincided with those of the Byronic hero but are at the same time considerably more complex and profound, could not fail to impress young Lermontov. His Pechorin goes as far beyond Izmail-Bei, Khadži-Abrek, and Arseni as Byron himself goes beyond the Giaour, Selim, and Conrad.

This is not merely the result of the influence of the senior poet upon his junior: Byron's self-portrait served Lermontov in delineating "contemporary man as he conceived him" (*Works,* 6:203). While drawing a disillusioned and disappointed man, Lermontov found his prototype in the personality of Byron as reflected in his confessions. For that reason, Byron, as the author of the *Letters and Journals,* and Pechorin — particularly Pechorin as the author of a journal — have a great deal in common. Both are remarkable for their pessimistic appraisal of human nature, for subtle critical observation, for caustic wit, for scorn of sentimentality and highflown phrase, and for sensitivity to beauty, particularly the beauty of nature. Both are self-centered and given to ruthless analysis of self, both perfectly realize their own weaknesses and do not hesitate to state them (this is particulary true of Pechorin), both seek fearlessly for the motives of other people's actions as well as their own, both feel torn by inner contradictions and have a sense of being not one person but at least two — and very different from each other at that. Both are shy of revealing their minds to other people; both love mystifications of all sorts; both tend to inflict suffering upon themselves and to understand how dangerous they are to others; both are haunted by unaccountable sadness, by melancholy, spleen, and boredom (ennui), by a bitter feeling of recklessly wasted energy.

It goes without saying that neither Pechorin nor Lermontov himself was able to write or do many of the things Byron wrote and did. But dissatisfaction with the sphere of action open to him and a longing for higher activity (so typical of the English poet) are obvious in Pechorin's journal and raise him above his actual doings: he too could have become one of the Carbonari and a leader of the Greek insurgents.[6]

The psychological affinity between Byron as the hero of his own letters and journals and Pechorin as the author of his journal finds a natural expression in the stylistic affinities of their diaries. The influence of Byron's prose style upon Lermontov's *A Hero of Our Time* is no less obvious than the influence of French novelists (of Benjamin Constant in particular) and even the influence of Pushkin's novel in verse, *Eugene Onegin*. The journals of Byron and Pechorin are equally characterized by an abstract philosophical style whose experimental and analytical tendencies are there to reveal the illogicality of the inner life of man and to anatomize the very mechanism of thought, the very nature of remembrance. In both journals there is the same striving for self-knowledge, the same questioning of self, the same alternation of concrete fact with generalizing and often cynical utterances, a leaning to aphorism and epigram, frequent and unexpected transitions from subjective and lyrical to objective and ironical narrative and back again. In both journals, personal confessions go with general reflections, numerous well-conceived scenes of everyday life go with true-to-life portraits, plain speaking goes with parody of poetic clichés and stylistic beauties, prosaic details go with abstract considerations about the influence of digestion and food on morals and intellect. Thus both journals have really a great deal in common.

The most characteristic feature of Byron's prose is its wide stylistic range, from the low colloquial to the highest flights of metaphorical language, from irony and antithesis to the sphere of emotion and lyricism, from a style philosophically abstract to that of ordinary narrative. Deeply felt doubts are expressed in a style where the vocabularly of emotion, the syntactic structures of oral speech, and the sententiousness of abstract truths alternate with bleak avowals unexpectedly turning into a joke: see Byron's entry of 31 January 1821 in his Ravenna Journal (Moore, p. 372). Elsewhere, in his 1813 journal, Byron can switch from lyrical reminiscences of his early attachment (along with surprise at a mere child's capability for such intense feeling) to reflections on the state of his stomach, and from descriptions of a wicked beauty to thoughts on the sufferings of parting — leading up to a maxim on the intensity of the feelings of lovers when reduced to brief moments together ("yet we live ages in moments, *when met,*" Moore, p. 155).[7]

The 1816 journal that Byron wrote for his sister Augusta is an alloy of narrative, of description of nature and customs, and of lyrical effusions; in his London journal of 1813-14, self-analytical entries accompany ironical observations of high life and highly connected acquaintances, lively scenes of drawing-room life, and anecdotes about friends and great men. Lofty subjects (such as mankind, politics, and literature) jostle with low ones (for example, the funny tale of a very drunken bachelor party). An amusing combination of styles — lyrical and meditative on the one hand and low colloquial on the other hand — is characteristic of most of Byron's letters and the greater part of the entries made in his journals.

The structure of the entries in both Byron's and Pechorin's journals is worth examining. In an entry for 20 March 1814, Byron expresses disgust for high life, proceeds to say that he must, willy-nilly, go out a great deal, and winds up with stating a general rule: "it is better to do as other people do, confound them!" After rendering his impressions of a recent review of his poems, Byron aphoristically comments: "Many a man will retract praise; none but a high-spirited mind will revoke its censure, or *can* praise the man it has once attacked." An analysis of the character of the critic Jeffrey and their mutual relations is followed by a statement of utter indifference to any critical opinion whatsoever; a discussion of the political opinions of an acquaintance, Lord Erskine, is preceded by a tale of his own success in boxing and followed (without the least logic and to the surpise of Byron himself) by a description of six eagles he once happened to see in Greece and of the young eagle he wounded (Moore, p. 173). Inconsistency, violent shifts in mood, subject, style, and even genre — these are the characteristics of Byron's journal. No less so are they typical of Pechorin's.

Pechorin's journal begins with a description of the spa Pyatigorsk, its nature and society. Facts are accompanied by their emotional treatment and philosophical reflections: "How gay life is in a land like that. A joyous feeling seems to flow in all my veins. The air is as pure and fresh as the kiss of a child; the sun is bright, the sky very blue — what more could I wish? Why indulge in passions, longings, and regrets?" (*Works,* 6:261). References to the spa society include epigrams with sudden *pointes*: the local dandies profess a great contempt for provincial houses and sigh for aristocratic drawing-rooms where they are really not allowed. The description is followed by a dialogue with Grushnitsky and an analysis of his nature, interrupted by a narrative (of the first meeting with Princess Mary) and lyrical self-critical digressions: "I have an innate passion to contradiction; my whole life has been a chain of sad and unlucky contradictions to my heart and reason" (*Works,* 6:262, 267).

In another and later entry Pechorin begins with self-analysis, passes on to general philosophical considerations, and thence to narrative and dialogue interrupted by generalizations: "compassion, a feeling to which women yield so easily, thrusts its claws in her inexperienced heart . . . ; we often deceive ourselves into thinking that women love us for our physical or moral merits . . . but it is really the first touch that settles everything" (*Works,* 6:297-98). The structure of the entries in Pechorin's journal is thus similar to that of Byron's, both being based on similar combinations of elements representing different genres and styles. The difference, however, lies in the interrelation of those elements, in the obvious predominance of narrative and plot in Lermontov's work.

Both authors are given to aphoristic generalizations, as often as not paradoxical in their nature. The paradox is the result of a juxtaposition of ideas or notions rarely considered together. It is only gradually that a judgment based on such a juxtaposition is found to be shrewd, even if not absolutely true; and its paradoxical nature comes to be felt as caused by unexpectedness. Such are often Byron's utterances on women. In his journal for 10 March 1814, he describes a friend: "If *he* holds out and keeps to my instructions of affected indifference, she will lower her colours. . . . But the poor lad is in love — if that is the case, she will win. When they once discover their power *finita è la musica.*" Guided by a similar train of thought, Byron three months earlier quotes Madame de Staël's opinion of him — "C'est un démon" — and adds: "True enough, but rather premature, for *she* could not have found it out, and so — she wants me to dine there next Sunday" (Moore, pp. 172, 159). An invitation to dinner resulting from the lady's notion of the demoniac nature of her future guest exactly renders Byron's notion of the paradoxical structure of the female mind.

Paradoxes of a very similar nature also abound in Pechorin's journal. True constancy, he believes, can only be brought about by unrequited love; he can account for Vera's love of himself only by stating that he has made her suffer very much: "Perhaps ... that is just why you loved me: joys are forgotten, sorrows never are!" Or else: "Women only love those they do not know" (*Works,* 6:293, 278, 276).

These aphorisms contribute a great deal toward characterizing Pechorin as a man who has good knowledge both of women and of his own powers over them. "I never became the slave of the woman I loved," he says; "on the contrary, I always acquired an invincible power over their heart, without in the least trying to do so" (*Works,* 6:279). Byron in his journal speaks of his relations with women in words that are very nearly the same: "It is odd I never set myself seriously to wishing without attaining it — and repenting" (Moore, p. 149). Lermontov does not repeat Byron's words; rather, he reproduces the way of feeling and thinking peculiar to the author of *Letters and Journals.* He does not adhere to any definite maxim, but to the English poet's predilection for it, to the aphoristic cast of mind.

Characteristically, with both Lermontov and Byron maxims always result from concrete observations of the facts of life. Thus Byron in November 1813 says that he would have made a fool of himself about Lady Melbourne had she been younger and thus would have lost a very good friend: "Mem. — a mistress never is nor can be a friend. While you agree, you are lovers; and, when it is over, any thing but friends" (Moore, p. 154). On a different occasion Lermontov says (about Doctor Werner): "We understood each other very well, and became friendly, though real friendship is something I am incapable of: of the two friends one is always the other's slave, though they won't admit it" (*Works,* 6:269). In both cases there is generalized experience, emotions leading up to a logically drawn conclusion.

Lermontov makes use of the structure of Byron's aphoristic formulae: Pechorin writes: "What is happiness? Satisfied pride." In Byron one finds: "What is Poetry? — The feeling of a Former world and Future. ... *what* predominates in memory? — *Hope baffled*"; "what is Hope? nothing but the paint on the face of Existence" (Moore, pp. 371, 214). Byron ironically observes that Italian women "exact fidelity from a lover as a debt of honour, while they pay the husband as a tradesman, that is, not at all" (Moore, p. 331). Pechorin says about Vera: "She respects him as her father! and will deceive him as her husband" (*Works,* 6:279). The ideas are different, but their ironical coloring and antithetical structure are similar.

Many of the entries in Byron's journal would be quite appropriate in Pechorin's. Here is one from Byron's "Detached Thoughts": "If I were to live over again, I do not know what I would change in my life, unless it were *for — not to have lived at all.* All history, and experience, and the rest, teaches us that the good and evil are pretty equally balanced in this existence, and that what is most to be desired is an easy passage out of it. What can it give us but years? and those have little of good but their ending" (Moore, p. 503). This reasoning is not unlike the dialogue between Pechorin and Werner, the latter saying: "'As far as I am concerned I am only convinced ... that sooner or later one fine morning I'll die.' — 'I am richer than you,' I answered, 'I have one more conviction — namely, that one nasty evening I had the misfortune to be born'" (*Works,* 6:269-70).

Numerous parallels between the novel of Lermontov and the prose of Byron could be pointed out. The English poet repeatedly stresses the peculiarities of his memory that enabled him to remember things past with such power that the memory is in no way weaker than the experience itself (see Moore, pp. 170-71, entry for 20 February 1814). Pechorin in his turn discusses the quirks of his own memory: "no man on earth felt so much the power of the past; every memory of past sorrows and joys strikes my soul so as to force similar sounds out of them; I have been made so foolishly I can never, never forget anything" (*Works,* 6:273). Pechorin's discussions of the paradoxical nature of woman's mind and logic, especially in their ingenuity to justify passion and sin, also have several analogies in Byron's letters.[8]

Byron is proud to tell his mother (and other correspondents) that Ali Pasha recognized him for a nobleman as soon as he saw his small hands (Moore, p. 71; see also *Don Juan* IV.xlv). Lermontov also mentions in particular Pechorin's small, aristocratic hands (*Works,* 6:243).

Byron quotes an episode in the life of his friend Edward Noel Long. "Although a cheerful companion, he had strange melancholy thoughts sometimes. ... he told me that, the night before, he 'had taken up a pistol — not knowing or examining whether it was loaded or no — and had snapped it at his head, leaving it to chance whether it might, or might not, be charged'" (Moore, p. 23). A similar situation is the subject of Lermontov's *A Fatalist.* V. A. Manuïlov, a well-known Lermontov scholar, does not accept the arguments of I. M. Bondakov, who was the first to notice the likeness, and counters them by saying that the Russian writer could well have made use of an authentic fact.[9] But I cannot help thinking that life and literature are here at one. Byron, by the way, repeatedly called himself a "fatalist" in his journals.

Byron confessed he loved power over the minds of men (Moore, p. 293); the same sort of admission is made by Pechorin (*Works,* 6:294). Both are prone to give an unceremonious and rather prosaic analysis of female beauty and learning (Moore, p. 444; *Works*, 6:265-66). Byron complained that all his life he had been *ennuyé,* and supposed this to have been innate with him: "my heart and head have stood many a crash, and what should ail them now? They prey upon themselves, and I am sick — sick. ... Six-and-twenty years, as they call them — why, I might and should have been a Pasha by this time. 'I 'gin to be weary of the sun'" (Moore, p. 171; see also pp. 364, 372-73). Such complaints are frequent: "I ... am grown as tired as Solomon of every thing, and of myself more than any thing"; "I am in such a state of sameness and stagnation"; "The worst of it is, I feel quite enervated and indifferent"; "What matters it what I do? or what becomes of me. ... I wish I could settle to reading again, — my life is monotonous, and yet desultory. I take up books, and fling them down again. I began a comedy, and burnt it because the scene ran into *reality*; — a novel, for the same reason" (Moore, pp. 181, 206, 194, 150).

Complaints of boredom, of idleness, and of indifference to everything including self, as well as disgust with inactivity, are equally characteristic of Byron's and Pechorin's journals. Both scorn man and higher society; both argue that life is nothing but a poor show. "I had my share of high life," Pechorin writes, "and was soon bored with it"; in another entry he says he is "sick of the world of fashion" (*Works,* 6:231, 275). Similar confessions are very frequent with Byron: "I am *ennuyé* beyond my usual tense of that yawning verb, which I am always conjugating; and I don't find that society much mends the matter"; "after all, what is the higher society of England? According to my own experience ... (and I have lived there in the very highest ...), no way of life can be more corrupt" (Moore, pp. 159, 392). Pechorin reflects: "I sometimes despise myself ... is that not the reason of my contempt for others?" (*Works,* 6:319). Byron is possessed by a similar mood: "The more I see of men, the less I like them." In fact, he frequently confesses great contempt for his species and for himself (Moore, p. 170; see also pp. 175, 414).

In 1813, Byron states: "Past events have unnerved me: and

all I can now do is to make life an amusement, and look on while others play" (Moore, p. 153). "Well," Pechorin writes, "if I must die I will; the world will not be a great loser; and I have really had enough of it. I am like one who yawns at a ball and does not go to bed only because his carriage has not yet arrived" (*Works,* 6:321). Lermontov half-humorously associates his hero's state of mind with a fashion introduced by the English and by Byron. Pechorin also compares himself to a vampire (*Works,* 6:311) — the hero of the novel that was ascribed to Byron, though written by his young physician, Polidori.

The English poet's reflections on the value of doubt ("I cannot and will not give the lie to my own thoughts and doubts. ... If I am a fool, it is, at least, a doubting one" [Moore, p. 155]) are paralleled by Pechorin's declaration: "I like to put everything to the doubt" (*Works,* 6:347). In recollecting his early — too early — passions, Byron writes: "Perhaps this was one of the reasons which caused the anticipated melancholy of my thoughts, — having anticipated life" (Moore, p. 63). Pechorin similarly accounts for his precocity: his early devotion to dreams was the reason why he "entered life, having lived it before in his thoughts" (*Works,* 6:343). Byron's sorrowful comments on the senselessness of his existence, especially when compared to what it was in his power to do, are akin to Pechorin's thoughts before the duel: "why did I live? Why was I born? ... there must have been a purpose and it must have been high, for I feel that powers immeasurable are mine" (*Works,* 6:321).

In *A Hero of Our Time*, some echoes of Byron's poetry can also be heard. As has been pointed out before, Lermontov's words on the air being "as pure and fresh as a child's kiss" are very close to Byron's line in *The Bride of Abydos*: "Pure, as the prayer which Childhood wafts above" (I.167); so are the descriptions of the eyes of Pechorin and Lara: Pechorin's eyes, Lermontov writes, did not laugh when he laughed. Neither did Lara's: "That smile might reach his lip, but pass'd not by,/None e'er could trace its laughter to his eye" (*Lara* 1.301-2). It might also be added that Lermontov says of Pechorin that he who has seen him once can never forget him. So does Byron say of Lara. The lyrical outburst at the end of "Princess Mary" comparing Pechorin to a restless sailor used to storms and battles seems to have been inspired by the celebrated lines of *Childe Harold* on eternal wanderers (II.lxx). These and other echoes are probably unconscious, such as can also be found in Lermontov's later poetry when he had already freed himself from deliberate imitation of Byron's poems.[10] In the well-known lines of the lyric where the sounds of song melt like kisses on the lips, Lermontov echoes Byron's words in *Beppo* about the Italian language that "melts like kisses from a female mouth" (xliv).

A distant memory of an impression conceived in early youth can be traced in the following entry by Pechorin: "When I was a child an old woman told my fortune to my mother and foretold that my wicked wife would be the death of me." This confession has a bearing upon one of the autobiographical notes of 1830: having read Moore's *Life,* Lermontov says that an old woman had assured Byron's mother that her son "would be a great man and marry twice; the same forecast was uttered about me to my grandmother when we were in the Caucasus" (6:314, 387).

Parallels like those cited above, never quite exact but too numerous to be considered coincidences, are pointed out here to illustrate the psychological and stylistical affinity between the two journals under examination. And yet the points of difference between the works of Byron and Lermontov are far more suggestive than the points of similarity between them. Though Byron made it quite clear that he intended his letters and journals for posthumous publication and on several occasions asked his correspondents to let mutual friends read them, his letters and journals should be regarded rather as brilliant sketches of future works, as a collection of preliminary studies. The poet is overwhelmed by subjective feeling, which he, in the passion of self-accusation so typical of him, called his egoism (his verdict was supported by that of numerous critics). Byron confessed he was unable to complete either his novel or his comedy, as they turned out to be too personal. The memoirs that have not come down to us were, according to Byron, too full of himself and of nothing else (see Moore, pp. 150, 292, 293).

However hard Byron tries to persuade himself and others that he is past the years of passions and is actuated by reason alone, he is, of course, ruled by feeling and mood. In the confessional style he has adopted (his letters hardly differ from his journals in this particular), subjectivism is natural and unavoidable, but Byron cannot go beyond it in his other experiments in prose, as, for example, in the fragment on the young Andalusian included in Moore's *Life*.

Byron is himself the hero of the *Letters and Journals,* while Pechorin, though the author of a journal, is a character introduced by Lermontov. The young writer has a firm grasp over both emotions and facts and creates a generalized portrait of his own generation. Two examples illustrating the difference should suffice. Byron asks himself in January 1821: "Why, at the very height of desire and human pleasure, ... does there mingle a certain sense of doubt and sorrow — a fear of what is to come — a doubt of what is. ... From whatever place we commence, we know where it all must end" (Moore, p. 370). Similar self-questioning thoughts in Pechorin's journal grow into a burning indictment of an entire generation of his contemporaries: "And we, their pitiful descendants, roving all over our earth without the least convictions or pride, without pleasure or fear, except the involuntary dread that fills our heart at the notion of the inevitable end — we indifferently pass from doubt to doubt ... devoid of hope" (*Works,* 6:343).

On another occasion Pechorin voices his sorrow and

remorse at how often he has been the cause of the sufferings of others and especially of the women who loved him (*Works,* 6:321). Byron also admits he has a soul that possessed the art of torturing both himself and others: " 'un âme,' which not only tormented itself but every body else in contact with it" (Moore, p. 372). The difference, however, is that Lermontov takes an objective view of this peculiarity of Pechorin's temperament — just as he takes an objective view of his entire character. Pechorin's confessions can only partly be taken as Lermontov's own confessions, while Byron's are certainly his and reveal if not the truth about himself at least the truth as he saw it.

Deliberately endowing Pechorin with Byronic features and demonstrating their tragic effect both on himself and on those emotionally dependent upon him, Lermontov certainly rises above his hero and goes beyond Byronism. Specific Byronic motifs acquire here a new and different sense. Thus, one of the motifs of the *Letters and Journals* (and of *Don Juan* too, for that matter) — the motif of life as a theatrical show — comes to be structurally relevant in *A Hero of Our Time.* In different contrasting combinations, it dominates the whole of the novel.

From the very beginning, Pechorin has a presentiment that he will take part in a thrilling performance. "'This is the starting-point,' I cried with delight — 'We shall see to the proper *dénouement* of this comedy!'" A theatrical declaration of love and hatred mixing in the hideous farce of life is one of the earliest of Grushnitsky's utterances: "Mon cher, je haïs les hommes pour ne pas les mépriser, car autrement la vie serait une farce trop dégoûtante." An equally theatrical phrase, this time spoken in Russian, turns out to be the last he is destined to speak: "Shoot," he says, "I despise myself and hate you." He dies and Pechorin's final phrase, "Finita la comedia," echoes Grushnitsky's declaration on life as a farce quoted above (*Works,* 6:271, 265, 331).

Characteristically, Grushnitsky used the conditional form ("serait") while Pechorin makes use of the perfect form: the sentence over Grushnitsky has already been passed. Pechorin calls himself an "instrument of the execution," "a hatchet in the hands of fate." His lot is to rouse hatred — not only that of Grushnitsky, but of Mary as well: "I hate you," is her answer to Pechorin's question (*Works,* 6:338). That question ("If you ever loved me, you despise me now, don't you?") echoes two questions that Mary formerly asked Pechorin: "Either you despise me, or you love me very much" and "You don't despise me, do you?" — to which Pechorin had replied: "I do not love you" (*Works,* 6:310, 313). There is also an obvious connection between all of these anxious questions and Pechorin's ironical travesty of Grushnitsky's rhetoric at the beginning of the novel: "Mon cher ... je méprise les femmes pour ne pas les aimer, car autrement la vie serait un mélodrame trop ridicule" (*Works,* 6:266).

Pechorin despises so as to avoid love, and hates so as not to suffer from the absence of love: the antithesis of love and contempt has a parallel in the antithesis of love and hatred in the Byronic speech that Pechorin makes to strike the imagination of Mary: "I was ready to love everybody — nobody understood me, and I learned to hate" (*Works,* 6:297). The science of hatred that he has mastered has caused new waves of hatred whose victim he became, along with those who came in contact with him. Even women's love of Pechorin verges on hate: Mary's feeling for him begins in hate ("the princess positively hates me") and ends in it ("I hate you"); Vera says that she ought to hate him for all the suffering he has brought upon her, but Pechorin realizes that the suffering resulted in love.

Everything that in Byron's journal was a mood, a personal feeling, in Lermontov's book grows into moral judgments embodied in a deliberately contrived system of stylistic devices in persistently repeated parallels and contrasts. In Byron's autobiographical notes the organization of the material was entirely submitted to the subjective mood of auctorial confession. Byron was well aware of the danger of subjectivism and rightly believed that it was easier for him to escape from egoism in poetry where he could avoid all mention of the circumstances of his own life (see Moore, p. 150). But Lermontov's prose is remarkable for its objective nature. Objectivity alloyed with lyricism creates a realistic psychological novel.

Byron also had such a novel in mind: in 1816-17 he proclaimed prose a more respectable genre and expressed the wish to devote himself to prose writings (Moore, pp. 242, 252). His memoirs, his *Letters and Journals,* and *Don Juan* (written in the same vein) were all stepping-stones towards this future novel. Dozens of literal coincidences between *Don Juan* and Byron's correspondence prove how close they are to one another. It is therefore appropriate to compare *A Hero of Our Time* both to *Don Juan* and to *Letters and Journals,* if one is to account for the novelty and the significance of Lermontov's masterpiece.

A Hero of Our Time differs from the *Letters and Journals* by being objective, particularly so with regard to the hero himself; but from *Don Juan* it differs in the method of psychological analysis. Despite the all-European scope of the poem, its satirical power and depth, it lacks some of the important features of realism: there are no dialectics in character-drawing (Byron achieved it only in the self-portrait that emerges from the *Letters and Journals*); there is no consistent development of character as influenced by its milieu. Don Juan, an adventurer *malgré lui*, has only formal connection with this milieu. Byron considered this problem but did not succeed (perhaps did not have the time) in solving it, though the milieu itself is brilliantly and shrewdly described: the very portraits in the Amundeville picture-gallery turn into a sort of milieu (*Don Juan* XIII.lxvii-lxv), betraying a clear sense of the typical features of the most important characters and phenomena, a critical understanding of motives actuating men. It is also obvious that Byron meant to analyze the influence of the world of fashion upon Don Juan who, as the poet says in one of his letters, was to appear *gâté* and *blasé* in the long run, and some elements of this plan have found their way into the last cantos of the poem. But this is rather a tendency than an achievement.

Byron's *Don Juan* is intended as an argument against the optimistic simplification of character in the works of the writers of the Age of Reason, but his hero does not become a fully developed character. Though Byron hoped to demonstrate in the story of Juan the shallowness of the rationalist idea of unchangeable and abstract human nature, the changes in his nature are mentioned but not visualized. The poet deprived his hero of all inner significance when he soared himself far beyond Juan in numerous lyrical digressions. Objectifying the hero led to impoverishing him. The female characters of the poem are either "ideal" (Haidée, Aurora), or primitive (Dudù, the Duchess of Fitz-Fulke), or obviously caricatured (Inez, Gulbeyaz, Catherine), or else combine caricatured and primitive features (Julia). If an interesting, psychologically convincing character does put in an appearance (Lady Adeline), Byron feels the necessity of introducing the angelic Aurora at her side. Lermontov's heroines are incomparably more lifelike and complex.

Pushkin's experience helped Lermontov to create a character that is at one and the same time infinitely subtle and dialectically mobile, and to make him the center of the realistic novel in prose that was to turn over a new leaf in the history of the European novel — just as Stendhal, another admirer of Byron, had done. Lermontov's characters are drawn as part of the reality they belong to; they share in its imperfections and are torn by its contradictions. "Not only does Lermontov oppose an outstanding personality to society as had been done before, he also gives it an objective evaluation from the point of view of the actual problems of his time'';[11] he reveals the social and historical background and function of character. Lermontov does not break away from Byron but, on having learned a great deal from him, adopts a critical attitude to Byron and leaves him far behind. The style of the *Letters and Journals* is the style of Byron; Pechorin's style, though very close to Lermontov's, does not entirely express him. This is obvious in the narrative of Maxim Maximovich.[12]

One of the important manifestations of the independent Lermontov style was a new concept of tragedy, which makes itself felt in the poet's late lyrics and in *A Hero of Our Time*. Byron had treated the tragical in the classicist style. Even if he does introduce tragedy alongside comedy as in *Don Juan,* it is only to emphasize the relativity of both and thus deliberately to weaken the most tragic situations. His serious tragedies are impervious to low and comic elements. The hero becomes the victim of his tragic error; this is what happens in *Manfred* and *Cain* on the one hand, in *Marino Faliero* and *Sardanapalus* on the other.

The tragic collision of Lermontov's novel is based on Shakespearean principles. Circumstances definitely low, such as the conspiracy of Grushnitsky's drunken rowdies and the arrival of the trickster Apfelbaum, not only form the background of the tragedy but in a certain way set events in motion. The tragedy of the hero is further complicated by the fact that in the course of the novel he rouses in the reader controversial feelings ranging from sympathy to antipathy. The latter never prevails, for Pechorin is redeemed by the charm of his bright intelligence, by the clarity of his critical perception of self, and by his full realization of the insecurity of his moral position. He can neither find a way out that could satisfy moral feeling nor rouse enough compassion for the hopelessness of his plight. Fully aware of his moral possibilities, he fearlessly bears his burden with dignity, analyzes it dispassionately, and expects no indulgence on anybody's part. Pechorin's tragedy is not the result of traditional dramatic collisions and is not brought about by the classicist idea of error, but by the relation between the pressure of outward circumstances (forced inactivity, limited possibilities, the moral ugliness of his surroundings) and his personal responsibility for the fact that fate made him a torturer and murderer.

Such a realistic and psychological treatment of the tragic was not and could not be achieved by Byron, but it was achieved by Lermontov and is to be felt in many of his lyrics. Their tragic tone is enhanced by utter simplicity and irony. Lermontov coldly and calmly speaks about his cheerless union with a woman scorned by the many, and he scorns their scorn ("To a Charmer, A Contract"); Byron mourns the "light ... fame" of his love and her "shame" ("When We Two Parted") and describes her in poetic terms. With Lermontov both emotions and phraseology are more simple and prosaic. The quiet tale of the carnage on the river Valerik, utterly devoid of oratorical flights and indignation, is as new a way of exposing war as the "war" cantos of *Don Juan* had been, with their passionate antimilitarist tirades and curses of war as evil and dirty.

Pechorin not only embodies Byronism as a peculiar phase in the development of thought and feeling, but he also represents a treatment of character that differs from Byron's. Thus does Lermontov outgrow the influence of Byron and mark the beginning of a new stage in the development of literature.

NOTES

1. Mikhail IUr'evich Lermontov, *Sochineniia v shesti tomakh* [*Works in Six Volumes*], Academy of Sciences Edition (Moscow-Leningrad, 1957), 6:203. Quotations from Lermontov in this paper will be translated into English from this edition, which will be parenthetically identified as *"Works."*
2. Alphonse Marie Louis de Lamartine, "Meditation seconde: L'Homme: A Lord Byron," in *Méditations poétiques* (Paris, 1820). According to some memoirs,

Lermontov liked to recite this poem. After deliberating on whether Byron should be looked upon as a mortal, an angel, or a demon, Lamartine compares him to Satan, whose glance has measured the depths of a precipice: his home is between night and horror; his soul, equally remote from the light of day and God, has bidden farewell to hope; he glorifies only the God of evil. Such is the fate of man: a fallen God, he clings to his memories of heaven; a slave, he was born to be free. Lamartine therefore calls upon Byron, the bard of hell, to devote his poetry to heaven. The seraphim themselves could not outdo his singing, if he, like a fallen angel, soared on his mighty wings beyond eternal darkness. Lamartine winds up with the hope that Byron will leave doubt and blasphemy to the son of night and will assume his place among the pure children of glory and brightness. The notion of the freedom-loving and proud angel, pining for paradise lost and equally fit to partake of horror and beauty, is repeated by Lermontov in his epic poem *The Demon*. Lamartine's identification of Byron with Satan, of the poet with his creation, may have contributed to the loftiness and humanity of Lermontov's Demon: not only is he a Byronic hero but partly Byron himself.

3. Quotations in this paper from Byron's *Letters and Journals* will be from the 1830 Paris edition, published by A. and W. Galignani, and will be parenthetically identified as "Moore."

4. See Anna Arkad'evna Elistratova, "Byron's Letters and Journals," in *Dnevniki i Pis'ma Bairona*, Academy of Sciences Edition (Moscow, 1963), pp. 341-58.

5. Byron's personality appears to greater advantage in later and fuller editions of his letters and journals. Here, however, I confine myself to the Moore edition that Lermontov knew.

6. In Pechorin's consciousness, Byron's activity is opposed to the nothingness of common existence: "Many are they who start living with the hope of finishing up like Alexander the Great or Lord Byron, and yet never rise above titular councillors" (*Works*, 6:301).

7. Moore gives the greater part of this entry on p. 7.

8. Byron writes to Moore on 24 May 1820: "She says, 'I will stay with him [the husband] if he will let you remain with me. . . . but, if not, I will not live with him; and as for the consequences, love, &c. &c. &c.' — you know how females reason on such matters" (Moore, pp. 338-39). Compare Lermontov's "Nothing is more paradoxical than the mind of woman. . . . the arguments they use to destroy their prejudices are very original, and to study their dialectics you have to forget all school rules of logic" (*Works*, 6:307-8).

9. Viktor Andronikovich Manuĭlov, *Roman M. IU. Lermontova "Geroĭ nashego vremeni"* (Moscow-Leningrad, 1966), p. 261.

10. Compare, for example, *Childe Harold* III.xciv, III.cxiii, and IV.cxxiv with Lermontov's poems (*Works*, 6:153 and 2:190); or *Don Juan* XV.xcix and VIII.lx with *Works*, 4:94.

11. E. N. Mikhaĭlova, "Ideia lichnosti u Lermontova i osobennosti ee khudozhestvennogo voploshcheniia," *Zhizn' i tvorchestvo M. IU. Lermontova* ["The Notion of Individuality in Lermontov's Work"] (Moscow, 1941), p. 162.

12. Lidiia Ginzburg, *Tvorcheskiĭ put' Lermontova* [*The Creative Path of Lermontov*] (Leningrad, 1940), p. 171.

Byron and Madame de Staël

ERNEST GIDDEY

Between 1813 and 1816, Madame de Staël and Byron were regarded by English public opinion as two outstanding figures: he had become famous overnight and was as sincerely admired as he was savagely attacked; her castle at Coppet, near Geneva, for years had been a center that had attracted the intellectual élite of her time. When, in 1812, she had left Coppet secretly and fled to Russia, she had won the sympathetic approval of all who were hostile to the imperialistic tendencies of the French policy; she had been received in England as a personification of liberty.

And yet Byron and "Corinne" (she was often given the name of the heroine of her most popular novel) were openly dissimilar: born twenty years before him, she had long been an established celebrity, whereas he was a rising young genius. He was a poet, and she had gained renown by her prose, an essay on literature in 1800 (*De la littérature*), her novels *Delphine* and *Corinne,* her *De l'Allemagne,* which had been forbidden in France and was now published in London. In 1813, Byron was not yet married; de Staël had abandoned her husband, the Swedish ambassador to France, fifteen years before. He had visited the sun-scorched shores of the Mediterranean; she was fascinated by the mists and fogs of the northern countries. And above all he sincerely admired

Napoleon ("he has been a 'Héros de Roman' of mine," he wrote in his diary in November 1813 [*BL&J,* 3:210]); she was a symbol of anti-Bonapartist resistance, having personally experienced in France the dangers of tyranny based upon military glory. Byron was young enough to believe that only radical views would bring about progress and happiness; Corinne, after playing the part of the rebellious victim, enjoyed the satisfaction of being recognized as a prima donna and accepted homage, even though it came from conservative circles.

When two exceptional beings come face to face, their actions and reactions usually arouse great interest. And in fact the Byron-de Staël relationship has been alluded to or studied several times. Gossips and critics, however, often express preconceived ideas. Byron's admirers appreciate his sarcastic judgments on the *bonne dame de Coppet.* De Staël specialists insist on the influence she had on the English poet. And historians who relish anecdotes and bons mots go through his and her letters for innuendoes, witty remarks, or ironical understatements so as to quench the thirst of scandalmongers. Objectivity, apparently, is impossible. Napoleon — his very name pleased Byron as much as it displeased de Staël — would probably retort that "impossible n'est pas français," a motto that will justify this attempt at historical truth.

In the mass of documents involving both Byron and Madame de Staël, a clear distinction should be made between what they did, what they wrote or said, and what they thought. Facts, words, and opinions may be equally fascinating, but cannot be given the same importance.

Byron first met Madame de Staël at Lady Jersey's on June 20, 1813. Next day, he dined with her at Lady Davy's, Sheridan being one of the other guests. In the following months they often met, both idols of the London season. Samuel Rogers, who was celebrated for his exclusive taste and his literary dinners, invited them several times. We know that on one occasion, at least, Byron declined the invitation, alleging as a reason that "he could not endure to see women eat," however famous they might be.[1] But he was not against exchanging letters, and a few letters or short notes they did write to one another, each using his or her own language. Besides, Byron could not remain indifferent to the charms of Madame de Staël's daughter Albertine,[2] or Libertine, as he later called her.

Dawning "friendship" (the mother and the daughter did not appeal to his feelings in the same manner) was interrupted when Madame de Staël went back to Paris in May 1814. It was resumed two years later, in June 1816, when Byron settled at Villa Diodati near Geneva. The poet was asked to come to Coppet and join the European intelligentsia that surrounded Madame de Staël. He made the acquaintance of Wilhelm von Schlegel, Pellegrino Rossi, Charles-Victor de Bonstetten, and the Abbé de Brême, and he soon became himself a sort of attraction: strangers would come and stare at him as if he were "his Satanic Majesty" or "some outlandish beast in a raree-show"; the novelist Elizabeth Hervey fainted, when she first saw him.[3] "We have many Englishmen here," Madame de Staël wrote in August 1816, "but it is Lord Byron, though he is scarcely seen by anybody except myself, who most occupies the mind of people"; she was simply repeating what her son Auguste had declared a few weeks before: "We have a crowd of Englishmen, but all insignificant, except Lord Byron, who travels with two gay young ladies and an Italian doctor."[4]

Madame de Staël advised Byron to reopen negotiations with his wife and tried to arrange a reconciliation. The attempt was not successful. Byron, however, greatly appreciated her good-natured efforts as well as the congenial atmosphere she had created in her drawing-room: "she has made Coppet as agreeable as society and talent can make any place on earth" (*BL&J*, 5:109). However, Madame de Staël also gave him a copy of *Glenarvon,* Caroline Lamb's novel.

He was not annoyed, apparently, by the caricature-portrait it contained. He greatly enjoyed another novel Madame de Staël lent him, Benjamin Constant's *Adolphe,* and ingenuously asked her if she was supposed to be the heroine, a question "which rendered her furious."[5] Byron's last visit to Coppet took place on October 3, 1816. Two days later, the poet set off to Italy. He was not to see Madame de Staël again. She died in July 1817.

So much for what they did. What they wrote or said falls into three categories: the notes they exchanged; the letters sent to other persons; the table-talks and conversations recorded by friends or relatives who saw them together or separately.

The Byron-de Staël correspondence appears insipid and unconvincing. Byron's excessive politeness is almost unbearable, particularly when he declares that his praise is "only the feeble echo of more powerful voices," that "any attempt at eulogy must be merely repetition," and that all his friends are her admirers (*BL&J,* 3:185). Her letters are even more artificial: his mentioning her name in the footnote of one of his poems gives her the assurance that she will be remembered by posterity; his praise, she adds, has awakened her pride. "Come and have dinner with me next Sunday," she writes in February 1814, "and bring your friends, I shan't say your admirers, because I haven't found anything else."[6] Both writers were conscious that they were guilty of base adulation: "She *flatters* me very prettily in her note; — but I know it," Byron wrote in his journal. "She has written, I dare say, twenty such [billets] this morning to different people, all equally flattering to each. So much the better for her and those who believe all she wishes them, or they wish to believe" (*BL&J,* 3:227, 235).

The mask of obsequiousness is thrown off whenever they write to other persons. She suggests that he is a devil and her daughter Albertine graciously condescends to say that "he has the grace of a cat in all his movements."[7] As if to pay her back, he calls her Mrs. Stale, Staël the Epicene, the immaculate de Staël, the Begun of literature. And again and again he alludes to her quenchless eloquence: she "writes octavos, and *talks* folios." She even managed to bore Monk Lewis, who was reputed to be one of the greatest bores in England. "She always talks of *my*self or *her*self," Byron noted in his journal, "and I am not (except in soliloquy, as now,) much enamoured of either subject." "Her books are very delightful," he wrote to Lady Melbourne, "but in society I see nothing but a very plain woman forcing one to listen & look at her with her pen behind her ear and her mouth full of *ink.*" In another letter, Byron related how Madame de Staël once reproached him for being affected and always shutting his eyes during dinner: "If I really have so ludicrous a habit . . . I will try and break myself of it . . . I have more faults to find with *her* than *'shutting'* her eyes — one of which is opening her mouth too frequently" (*BL&J,* 3:207, 231; 4:19, 33).

"She is frightful as a precipice" (*BL&J,* 4:122), he declared to Henriette d'Ussières, a Swiss correspondent who no doubt was able to visualize what he meant. Her thoughts sometimes do have the depth of unfathomable abysses. With reference to her, the word *metaphysics* is naturally associated with fog. Her essay against suicide will probably "make somebody shoot himself." "I have not read it," Byron comments, "for fear that the love of contradiction might lead me to a practical confutation" (*BL&J,* 3:73, 160). Her politics are "sadly changed." She is no longer an apostle of freedom, but "a vile antithesis of a Methodist and a Tory." She hopes "that God and the government will help her to a pension."[8]

Byron's sarcasms did not spare her when her favorite son, Albert de Staël, was killed in a duel in Germany: "Corinne is doubtless very much affected — yet me thinks — I should conjecture — she will want some spectators to testify how graceful her grief will be — to relate what fine things she can say on a subject where commonplace mourners would be silent." And a few days later: "Made. de Staël Holstein has lost one of her young barons, who has been carbonadoed by a vile Teutonic adjutant, — kilt & killed in a coffee-house at Scrawsenhawsen. Corinne is, of course, what all mothers must be, — but will, I venture to prophesy, do what few mothers could — and write an Essay upon it. She cannot exist without a grievance — and somebody to see, or read, how much grief becomes her" (*BL&J,* 3:86-87, 94).

Byron's cynicism plainly justifies Madame de Staël's accusation of immorality and amoralism. Did Byron realize that he had gone too far? The fact is that he slowly came to respect her. The letters he wrote to John Murray, Samuel Rogers, and Augusta Leigh after his visits to Coppet in the summer months of 1816 are less aggressive: "Me. de Stael has been particularly kind and friendly to me" (*BL&J,* 5:92, see also p. 124).

In Regency England, conversation was freer than correspondence. Conversationalists usually rejected the urbane hypocrisy that was so common in epistolary art. Byron seldom visited Madame de Staël without provoking her. "The Staël last night attacked me most furiously," he wrote to Thomas Moore on July 13, 1813, the cause of her indignation being his treating Caroline Lamb "barbarously" and his being "totally *in*sensible to *la belle passion*" (*BL&J,* 3:76). He took pleasure in telling her that *Delphine* and *Corinne* were "very dangerous productions to be put into the hands of young women,"[9] a statement that never failed to enrage her. And Byron would sometimes add that Benjamin Constant's *Adolphe* ought to be given to every reader of *Corinne,* as an antidote. "Poor De Staël," Byron said to Lady Blessington, "she came down upon me like an avalanche, whenever I told her any of my amiable truths, sweeping every thing before her, with that eloquence that always overwhelmed, but never convinced."[10]

Byron keeps repeating in discussions with friends what he has written in letters: Madame de Staël, though she was one of the cleverest women he had ever known, "declaimed to you instead of conversing with you ... never pausing except to take breath." Her language is "recondite but redundant"; she often loses herself "in philosophical disquisition" or gets "entangled in the mazes of the labyrinth of metaphysics." But other subjects are sometimes broached in conversations: how she had troubles with her corset one day when she was at table with a large party; how with "a total want of tact" she told an English lady that she looked like a parrot: "Ah, mon Dieu, miladi! comme vous ressemblez à un perroquet."[11] Both Byron and de Staël were too famous not to attract public attention and give birth to unconsidered remarks. Some of these appeared in Byron's minor poems. In his "Epistle from Mr. Murray to Dr. Polidori," he wrote, a few weeks after Madame de Staël's death:

> 'T is said she certainly was married
> To Rocca, and had twice miscarried,
> No — not miscarried, I opine, —
> But brought to bed at forty-nine.
> Some say she died a Papist; some
> Are of opinion that's a Hum;
> I don't know that — the fellows Schlegel,
> Are very likely to inveigle
> A dying person in compunction
> To try th'extremity of Unction.
>
> [*Poetry,* 7:50, ll. 67-76]

When Madame de Staël died in 1817, Byron had not yet begun *Beppo*, not to mention *Don Juan*. The poet she had known in England and welcomed at Coppet was the young bard upon whom fame had lighted when he had bewitched public opinion by the publication of *Childe Harold*. Like so many other readers in England and on the Continent, she had accepted him as "the first poet of the century," although — or, perhaps, because — he "did not love mankind."[12] She had read *The Bride of Abydos* and *The Corsair* without changing her opinion of the author. When he had first entered her drawing-room at Coppet, he was still the gloomy wanderer, an uncommon and bewildering figure whose devilish tendencies had been emphasized by his recent matrimonial difficulties. Madame de Staël's perception of Byron's literary genius was superficial and conventional. And Byron's slightly provoking attitudes did not make her change her mind.

Byron was more familiar with de Staël's works than she was with his. His depreciatory remarks about *Corinne* were intended to exasperate Madame de Staël and did not imply that he undervalued the importance of her second novel. He probably discovered some of its interest in his later years, under the influence of Teresa Guiccioli: *Corinne* was a favorite book of hers and Byron had some difficulty in persuading her that his own feelings were more genuine than those of de Staël's heroine — "Without translating so many pages of *Corinne,* or forcing so great a semblance of romance, I assure you that I love you as I always have loved you" (*BL&J,* 8:170).

Byron greatly admired *De l'Allemagne.* "I like it prodigiously," he had declared as early as December 1813 (*BL&J,* 3:231). His annotated copy, which is now preserved in the Houghton Library, Harvard University, proves that he had read de Staël's major work carefully. He had been impressed by what the author had written on the influence of northern and southern virtues and on the analogy between painting and music. He probably realized that, in the history of European literatures, the publication of *De l'Allemagne* had been a turning point. Just as Voltaire, in his *Lettres philosophiques,* had revealed England to French readers, Madame de Staël had focused public interest on a country that so far had been utterly neglected by criticism. She had shown that artistic and literary values were inseparable from their political and sociological background. She had insisted on the fragility of national frontiers, as fixed by kings and governments, an idea that in *Don Juan* is not absent from

Byron's "detestation/Of every despotism in every nation" (*Don Juan* IX.xxiv). In *De l'Allemagne,* Byron had also read pages on Goethe's *Faust* and found supernatural visions that were not fundamentally different from those that later haunted his mind when he wrote *Manfred* or *Cain.*

Byron knew, however, that there were ridiculous statements in Madame de Staël's major work. "But there are fine passages; — and, after all, what is a work — any — or every work — but a desert with fountains and, perhaps, a grove or two, every day's journey? To be sure, in Madame, what we often mistake, and 'pant for,' as the 'cooling stream,' turns out to be the *'mirage'* (criticé *verbiage*); but we do, at last, get to something like the temple of Jove Ammon, and then the waste we have passed is only remembered to gladden the contrast." All things considered, *De l'Allemagne* is a book that will never "act as an opiate"; it prevents insomnia (*BL&J,* 3:211, 218). Though he regretted not to find in it any allusion to Napoleon, he considered *De l'Allemagne* as the masterpiece "of the first female writer of this, perhaps of any age" (fn. to *The Bride of Abydos*).

When the *Considérations sur la Révolution française* was offered to Murray a few weeks before Madame de Staël's death, Byron advised him to accept the proposal: "You should close with Madame de Stael — this will be her best work — & permanently historical — it is on her father — the revolution — & Buonaparte, &c. Bonstetten told me in Switzerland it was *very great.*" Madame de Staël died before an agreement was reached: "She will leave a great gap in society & literature," Byron wrote to Murray in August 1817 (*BL&J,* 5:204-5, 256). In the "Sonnet to Lake Leman," which had been written at Villa Diodati one year before, he had already indicated that he thought highly of her and placed her on the same level as the great eighteenth-century writers:

Rousseau — Voltaire — our Gibbon — and De Staël —

Leman! these names are worthy of thy shore,
Thy shore of names like these!

Five years later, Corinne is still placed on the same level as Rousseau: "The sentimental anatomy of Rousseau and Madᵉ de S[taël]. are far more formidable than any quantity of verse. They are so, because they sap the principles, by *reasoning* upon the *passions*; whereas poetry is in itself passion, and does not systematize" (*L&J,* 5:582). But Byron's best, sincerest, and often overlooked tribute to the memory of Madame de Staël is a note to Canto IV of *Childe Harold's Pilgrimage*:

> Corinna is no more; and with her should expire the fear, the flattery, and the envy, which threw too dazzling or too dark a cloud round the march of genius, and forbad the steady gaze of disinterested criticism. We have her picture embellished or distorted, as friendship or detraction has held the pencil: the impartial portrait was hardly to be expected from a contemporary. ... Corinna has ceased to be a woman — she is only an author; and it may be foreseen that many will repay themselves for former complaisance, by a severity to which the extravagance of previous praises may perhaps give the colour of truth. ... She will enter into that existence in which the great writers of all ages and nations are, as it were, associated in a world of their own, and, from that superior sphere, shed their eternal influence for the control and consolation of mankind. But the individual will gradually disappear as the author is more distinctly seen; some one, therefore, of all those whom the charms of involuntary wit, and of easy hospitality, attracted within the friendly circles of Coppet, should rescue from oblivion those virtues which, although they are said to love the shade, are, in fact, more frequently chilled than excited by the domestic cares of private life. Some one should be found to portray the unaffected graces with which she adorned those dearer relationships, the performance of whose duties is rather discovered amongst the interior secrets, than seen in the outward management, of family intercourse; and which, indeed, it requires the delicacy of genuine affection to qualify for the eye of an indifferent spectator. Some one should be found, not to celebrate, but to describe, the amiable mistress of an open mansion, the centre of a society, ever varied, and always pleased, the creator of which, divested of the ambition and the

arts of public rivalry, shone forth only to give fresh animation to those around her. . . . Her loss will be mourned the most where she was known the best; and, to the sorrows of very many friends, and more dependants, may be offered the disinterested regret of a stranger, who, amidst the sublimer scenes of the Leman lake, received his chief satisfaction from contemplating the engaging qualities of the incomparable Corinna.

What is striking in this note is Byron's seriousness, the delicacy of his homage, and a sort of repressed emotion. As a piece of literary criticism, it is excellent and proves that Byron had perceived Corinne's greatness: he had realized that Madame de Staël's most significant contribution to the intellectual history of Europe had been called "Coppet." Though she was a woman, she had been more influential than many men who had won a good name for themselves in philosophy. Byron always refused to "grow metaphysical" and often made fun of bluestockings or female writers who were not able "To build up common things with common places" (*Don Juan* XIV.vii). He accepted de Staël's intellectual superiority, even if he sometimes found it exasperating. She had been contaminated, no doubt, by the German predilection for theoretical reasoning, but managed to remain, what he himself certainly was, "a tremendous cultural force that was life and literature at once."[13]

So Corinne was an exception: "Madame de Stael, I grant, is a clever woman; but all the other *madams* are no Staels."[14] Modern scholarship has shown that the letter in which Byron's position is so clearly presented is a forgery. I am convinced that Byron, had he known it, would have subscribed to the opinion expressed by the unscrupulous scribbler who borrowed his name.

NOTES

1. *Recollections of the Table-Talk of Samuel Rogers*, ed. Morchard Bishop (Lawrence, Kans.: University of Kansas Press, 1953), p. 192.

2. She married the Duke of Broglie in February 1816. See Elizabeth Nitchie, "Byron, Madame de Staël, and Albertine," *Keats-Shelley Journal* 7 (1958): 7-8; Simone Balayé, *Les carnets de voyage de Madame de Staël: Contribution à la genèse de ses oeuvres* (Geneva: Droz, 1971), particularly ch. 5: "Le séjour en Angleterre (1813-1814)" by Norman King.

3. *Medwin's Conversations of Lord Byron*, ed. Ernest J. Lovell, Jr. (Princeton, N.J.: Princeton University Press, 1966), p. 12; *BL&J*, 6:127

4. *Madame de Staël, ses amis, ses correspondants: Choix de lettres (1788-1817)*, ed. Georges Solovieff (Paris: Klincksieck, 1970), p. 522; "Nous avons ici beaucoup d'Anglais; mais lord Byron, que presque personne, excepté moi, ne voit, est pourtant celui qui occupe le plus tout le monde"; Carlo Pellegrini, *Madame de Staël e il gruppo di Coppet*, 2d ed. (Bologna: Pàtron, 1974), p. 233: "Nous avons une foule d'Anglais, mais tous insignifiants, excepté lord Byron, qui voyage avec deux demoiselles d'allégresse et un médecin italien."

5. *Lady Blessington's Conversations of Lord Byron*, ed. Ernest J. Lovell, Jr. (Princeton, N. J.: Princeton University Press, 1969), p. 27.

6. Solovieff, *Madame de Staël, ses amis, ses correspondants*, p. 473: "Dînez chez moi dimanche avec vos amis, je ne dirai pas vos admirateurs, car je n'ai rencontré que cela de toutes parts."

7. Victor de Pange, *Madame de Staël et le duc de Wellington* (Paris: Gallimard, 1962), p. 73: "Il a la grâce d'un chat dans tous ses mouvements."

8. *BL&J*, 3:66; see also "The Devil's Drive," ll. 195-96 (*Poetry*, 7:32).

9. *Lady Blessington's Conversations*, p. 25.

10. Ibid., pp. 91-92.

11. Ibid., pp. 22, 23, 213.

12. Solovieff, *Madame de Staël, ses amis, ses correspondants*, p. 473: "le premier poète de son siècle"; "le tort de ne pas aimer l'espèce humaine."

13. Northrop Frye, *Fables of Identity: Studies in Poetic Mythology* (New York: Harbinger Book, 1963), p. 174.

14. *Byron: A Self-Portrait*, ed. Peter Quennell (London: John Murray, 1967), 2:527; see *BL&J*, 7:270.

Byron and the Romantic Composer*

ALICE LEVINE

The subject of Byron's influence in music is, from the bibliographical viewpoint alone, an extensive one. I have found approximately 750 musical works related to Byron; among these are song settings of the lyrics, larger instrumental and operatic works based on the long poems, compositions inspired by Byron's life, and music for poems that have been attributed to Byron. The principal western nations are represented, as well as the nineteenth and twentieth centuries. Similar studies for other poets lead me to believe that my findings, restricted as they have been to United States collections and to only those European catalogs available here, are far from exhaustive.[1] My bibliography, however, does incorporate the titles found in John P. Anderson's bibliography of music for Byron's poetry,[2] which seems to have been drawn exclusively from the British Museum holdings as of 1909.

The numbers of settings for the most popular lyrics are as follows:

*Excerpts from the Eulenberg Miniature Scores of Berlioz' *Harold in Italy* (Score 423) and Schumann's *Manfred Overture* (Score 646) are reprinted by permission of C. F. Peters Corporation, sole agents for Edition Eulenberg in the Western Hemisphere.

178

"She walks in beauty" (from *Hebrew Melodies*)	57 (mostly 20th century)
"There be none of Beauty's daughters" ("Stanzas for Music")	55 (19th and 20th centuries)
"When we two parted"	40 (19th and 20th centuries)
"Farewell! if ever fondest prayer"	37 (two-thirds in 19th century)
"I saw thee weep" (from *Hebrew Melodies*)	31 (mostly 19th century)
"So we'll go no more a roving"	30 (mostly 20th century)
"Maid of Athens, ere we part"	25 (mostly 19th century)
"The kiss, dear maid!" ("On Parting")	22 (mostly 19th century)
"Fare thee well!"	17 (mostly 19th century)
"Deep in my soul" (from *The Corsair*)	15 (mostly 19th century)
"Sun of the sleepless!" (from *Hebrew Melodies*)	13 (19th and 20th centuries)
"My soul is dark" (from *Hebrew Melodies*)	12 (mostly 19th century)
"Adieu, adieu! my native shore" (from *Childe Harold's Pilgrimage*)	10 (mostly 19th century)

Several observations can be made regarding the composers' preferences. Poems written as "songs" (such as the *Hebrew Melodies* and Medora's song, "Deep in my soul") or poems about music (such as "There be none of Beauty's daughters" and "My soul is dark") held an obvious appeal for composers. Byron's various farewells also seem to have been popular. At times, however, especially during Byron's lifetime and years of fame, a composer's decision to set a Byron poem may have been made merely to ensure sales of his music.[3] The scandalous, if unmusical, subject of "Fare thee well," Byron's venomous verses to his wife, explains why nine of the eighteen settings of this poem appeared by 1825, with six of those published within two years of the poem's publication. In contrast with this lyric or with "Maid of Athens," both of which suffered a decline in appeal for musicians during the twentieth century, interest in "She walks in beauty" and "So we'll go no more a roving" has increased in the present century, among the new critics and new composers alike. While the sensuous imagery and metric regularity of the first of these poems make it an ideal choice for musical setting, the second poem, with its symbolic images and its subtler rhymes and rhythms, must be something of a challenge to the composer: although a musician's attraction to this poem would be expected, it is more likely that a musical setting would detract from rather than enhance the poem's own strong music. Perhaps this explains why the poem, which Yeats singled out for its lyricism,[4] yields only half as many settings as "She walks in beauty."

Not surprisingly, settings of the *Hebrew Melodies* are among the earliest musical works written for Byron's poetry. The composer Isaac Nathan, who had persuaded Byron to write the poems, published them together with his arrangements of liturgical airs; these appeared in four separate sets, dating from 1815 to 1829.[5] The poems in *Hebrew Melodies* became popular among European composers and inspired Loewe, Schumann, Mendelssohn, Joachim, and Mussorgsky. The early attention these poems received is partly attributable to their association with the widely appreciated *Irish Melodies* by Thomas Moore, lyrics that were on Byron's mind when he wrote his poems. Moreover, Byron's *Hebrew Melodies* and many of his other lyrics appealed, again like the poems of Moore, to the

Romantic musician's penchant for ethnicity and orientalism. The folk-obsessed nineteenth-century composer did not turn for poetic inspiration to the works of Keats, Shelley, or (perhaps surprisingly) Wordsworth, but to Moore, Burns, Ossian, and Scott. Composers responded, if not to the Hebrew, then to the Greek or else the Highland flavor of many of Byron's poems. Beethoven's single Byron setting, "Oh, had my Fate been join'd with thine" (composed 1815-16), appears in his *25 Scottish Songs*[6] alongside poems by Scott and Burns.

Instrumental, symphonic, and operatic works are to be found for most of Byron's tales and plays. *The Corsair* and *Manfred* were particular favorites, the latter appealing especially to German composers. *Childe Harold's Pilgrimage* and *Don Juan* were not treated in music as often as the tales and plays, although song composers extracted lyrics from both works and the Haidée episode from *Don Juan* occasionally formed the subject of an opera or cantata. The present century finds composers as diverse as Arnold Schoenberg, Carlos Chavez, and Ned Rorem setting Byron, and in 1972 Virgil Thomson's opera *Lord Byron* was given its premiere at the Juilliard School of Music in New York.

Still, when one thinks of Byron's influence in music, one thinks of an era that extends roughly from 1830 to 1890 and includes the five major composers: Hector Berlioz, Robert Schumann, Franz Liszt, Giuseppe Verdi, and Peter Ilyich Tchaikovsky. Each of these composers left at least one major work inspired by Byron's poetry. Berlioz, Schumann, and Liszt wrote explicitly — in letters, memoirs, and criticism — of their indebtedness to Byron; indeed, their personalities and aesthetics were often self-consciously "Byronic." There is little doubt that the twentieth-century composer Charles Ives had these three figures clearly in view when, implicitly conceding Byron's part in a coherent intellectual and aesthetic development, he denounced the Romantic composer's aesthetic as "the Byronic fallacy"[7] — an indictment that carried a clearly defined meaning for Ives, to which I will return at the conclusion of this essay.

In his essay "Hector Berlioz and His 'Harold' Symphony" (1855), Franz Liszt repeatedly refers to a type of poem that, suited neither to the stage nor to the purely musically oriented symphony, will precipitate the inevitable union of literary and musical form: "among these Goethe's *Faust* is the colossus, while beside it Byron's *Cain* and *Manfred* ... constitute immortal types."[8] Perhaps the really important question to be considered is, what is there about poems like *Faust, Manfred,* and *Cain* that makes them ideal subjects for the dramatic symphony or symphonic poem? This question, in fact, forms one subject of Liszt's article, and while a full discussion of it is beyond the province of this essay, a partial answer may be found in the type of influence Byron had on those composers who, like Liszt, were attracted to his poems.

To speak of literary influence in music, or of musical interpretation of literature, is indeed problematical. Besides the difficulty in finding a critical vocabulary sufficient to account for the translation of the one medium into the other, and besides our skepticism toward the Romantic composer's ideal of a union of literary and musical form (implying an equal partnership of text and tone), other problems in approaching this subject must be acknowledged. In the first place, the so-called literary preoccupations of the Romantic composers here considered were often not much more than projections onto literature of their own feelings and personalities; and secondly, music, even the music of the Romantic composers, is often seen to be more significantly influenced by other composers than by writers. It could be argued, for instance, that to understand even Berlioz' music — which is the most program-ridden of all — one would be better off looking at Beethoven and Gluck, at the teachers of the Paris Conservatory, and at Berlioz' own purely musical understanding, rather than at his infatuations with Shakespeare and Byron or at his intense poeticized encounters with nature.

In fact, upon turning to Sir Donald Francis Tovey's analysis of Berlioz' *Harold in Italy* — the work of striking conceptual originality that first aroused my interest in the study of Byron's musical influence — I found these opening words: "There are excellent reasons for reading *Childe Harold's Pilgrimage*. But among them I cannot find any that concern Berlioz and this symphony, except for the jejune value of the discovery that no definite elements of Byron's poem have penetrated the impregnable fortress of Berlioz's encyclopaedic inattention."[9] But while rightly informing us that Berlioz' second symphony does not have a program based on Canto IV of *Childe Harold,* Tovey is careful to say that "no *definite* elements" of Byron's poem are to be found in Berlioz' work, thus allowing for the whole range of *in*definite elements that are to be found in any instance of real influence.[10] As will be demonstrated, the influence of Byron on Berlioz' *Harold* Symphony is unmistakable. And if one is to acknowledge at all the connection between the ideas of the composer and the peculiar development of his technique, then the literary thoughts of Berlioz and his fellow Romantic composers ought to be considered if only as a frame, or referential background, for discussions of their music.

Moreover, for the Byron critic and the student of literary or intellectual history, Byron's influence in music is particularly illuminating due to its distinctive coloring, its almost homogeneous quality. Unlike Shakespeare's role in music, which is greater and more diffuse,[11] Byron's helps to isolate and characterize a specific phase of musical aesthetics and aesthetic history. Byron's own limitation and strength, in fact, may be seen to lie in his having presented not an infinite variety but a single, strong impression, which he carried through and developed in all his works: a definite *personality* that may be identified as "Byronic." At least most nineteenth-century Europeans, dismissing *Don Juan* and the other satiric works, chose to regard him in this way, as "le sombre génie" of the nineteenth century, according to George Sand. [12]

Scholars have readily acknowledged Byron's role in the history of European literature, a role that sets him apart from the other major English Romantic poets and that has been attributed to Byron's affinity with the European literary tradition, to his political significance for Europe, and to the equivocal poetic virtue of not suffering much in translation. Books such as *The Romantic Agony* by Praz, Thorslev's *The Byronic Hero,* and Peckham's *Beyond the Tragic Vision* dwell on the relation of Byron's hero (for they all agree there is but one and that he is Byron's only real subject matter) to the *Sturm und Drang* and to later German and French developments of the type. [13] In turning to music, we find that the Romantic composers' interest in Byron also answers to a shared, evolving idea of the hero and to a consciousness of the relationship between the heroic and music. Whether expressing a metaphysical or political argument, an introverted madness (as in Schumann's case), or a calculated pose (as in Berlioz'), the Byron-inspired music of these composers offers interpretations of a heroic type that was popularized by Byron and that to a great extent defines Byron's role in European Romanticism. This essay will consider the examples of Berlioz and Schumann, two contrasting personalities related by their roles as the original arch-Romantics and arch-Byronists of music.

Of special importance is the idea of the "heroic" in Romantic music, which served not merely as a literary theme fancifully tacked on to a piece of music by the composer, but as an essential element in symphonic and operatic content. Perhaps the best definition of what the heroic meant to the Romantic composer is to be found in Richard Wagner's commentary on the *Eroica* Symphony. After asserting that Beethoven's Third Symphony does not depict "historico-

dramatic [episodes] ... by means of pictures in Tone,"
Wagner goes on to say:

> In the first place, the designation "heroic" is to be taken in its
> widest sense, and in nowise to be conceived as relating merely to
> a military hero. If we broadly connote by "hero" (*"Held"*) the
> whole, the full-fledged *man,* in whom are present all the purely-
> human feelings — of love, of grief, of force — in their highest
> fill and strength, then we shall rightly grasp the subject which
> the artist lets appeal to us in the speaking accents of his tone-
> work. The artistic space of this work is filled with all the varied,
> inter-crossing feelings of a strong, a consummate Individuality,
> to which nothing human is a stranger, but which includes within
> itself all truly Human, and utters it in such a fashion that —
> after frankly manifesting every noble passion — it reaches a
> final rounding of its nature, wherein the most feeling softness is
> wedded with the most energetic force. The heroic tendence of
> this artwork is the progress toward that rounding off.[14]

What is striking about Wagner's description of the *Eroica* is
that there is scarcely a Romantic work, from Verdi's operas,
to Wagner's own, to the symphonies of a Tchaikovsky or a
Mahler, that cannot be spoken of in these very terms,
however the particular quality of achievement and the
ostensible arrangement of the subject matters may vary. And
while Wagner rightly rejects a literary-*visual* counterpart to
the music, he identifies the poetic idea of the heroic with the
music proper.

Beethoven himself disdained "tone-painting," while he
discovered in the symphony a dramatic correlative for human
experience; thus, the *Pastoral* Symphony is not a poem about
nature, but about the *impressions* (Beethoven's word) made
upon a human consciousness by the various scenes.[15] The
storm passage and the tranquility that follows, for instance,
like the similar passage in Canto III of *Childe Harold,* do not
derive power from their naturalism but from their
meaningfulness: from the meanings that one man — the poet
— has perceived in them, or imposed on them.

Nor is the parallel between Beethoven and Byron

gratuitous; they are clearly analogous as forces in the evolution of the Romantic consciousness. They were contemporaries, and their innovations predate the later musical and European Romantic movements with which we identify them. In the familiar Danhauser painting of Liszt at the piano surrounded by Marie d'Agoult, George Sand, Dumas *père*, Hugo, Paganini, and Rossini, the entire company is nicely framed by the bust of Beethoven to the right, and above, center, the portrait of Byron (see frontispiece). The kinship between Byron and Beethoven may be epitomized in their similar passionate and tormented attitudes toward a shared heroic figure, Napoleon. Both Byron and Beethoven were ultimately disappointed by the man who, by his own superior will and strength, they hoped would lead Europe into a new humanness. So Byron wrote the *Ode to Napoleon Buonaparte,* denouncing the tyrant for his cowardliness and ordinariness; and Beethoven tore up the dedication to the Third Symphony cursing Napoleon as "ein gewöhnlicher Mensch" (an ordinary man) and renaming the work "Eroica."

After Beethoven, the composer was increasingly to become conscious of ideas suggested by and inseparable from the music. Moreover, these ideas pertained primarily to the inner life, were more feelings than ideas, and introduced the element of self-conscious personality into musical expression. The coincident rise in interest in the heroic, in music as an expression of feeling, and in the interrelation of heroism and sensibility marks the Romantic age and is exemplified repeatedly in the music inspired by Byron.

In spite of Beethoven, however, the development beyond conventional symphonic form was to take place some time after 1826, the year that saw Berlioz admitted to the Paris Conservatory. Byron's role in the development of the Romantic symphony — at least in the psychological development of its composers — is largely clarified in terms of his influence on Hector Berlioz (1803-69). Not only was Berlioz, following Beethoven's lead, the father of the Romantic program symphony (or symphonic poem), and along with it the modern orchestra, but he waged an articulate ideological battle against the old aesthetics, in which he enlisted Byron as an ally. Schumann and Liszt, who also felt called upon to explain and defend the new music, did so primarily in the Beethoven fatherland. But Berlioz was more or less coerced by hostile circumstances into a position of self-conscious Romanticism, which gained strength from contemporary literature, painting, and politics.

The arts in early nineteenth-century France were undergoing a transition, and if Berlioz' emotional banner-waving on behalf of new artistic developments was not entirely self-induced, neither was he in the position of the last, and certainly not the first, angry man. It is true, the French public was conservative: in the theater, Shakespeare was still being hissed. And the rise of instrumental music was yet to take place, coinciding with social and economic changes and the rise of public concerts. Parisian musical tastes were Italianate and theatrical: Rossini was the hero of the day. Even the forward-looking *Conservatoire* was not quite ready to accept the music of Beethoven; upon hearing the C Minor Symphony for the first time and acknowledging its power, Berlioz' professor declared, "All the same, music like that ought not to be written."[16] But in the 1820s and '30s Paris felt revolution in the air. Performances of the revived original versions of Shakespeare's plays and Stendhal's eloquent defense of their energy and dramatic realism; Victor Hugo's *succès de scandale Hernani,* along with his equally *épatant* Preface to *Cromwell,* which attacked the fixtures of French classic drama; the paintings of Delacroix; the growth of Philhellenic societies that had sprung up in the wake of the Greek wars (Byron's death at Missolonghi bringing wide popularity in France to the Greek cause); the July Revolution of 1830: from all these artistic and political developments did

Berlioz gather ammunition for his iconoclastic Romanticism.[17]

The impact of Byron on France at this time was, as is well known, overwhelming. Two of Berlioz' earliest works exemplify the immeasurable indirect influence of Byron's poetry. The first, a cantata, *Heroic Scene: The Greek Revolution,* composed in 1826, is imbued with the rhetoric of liberation and the fierce hatred of tyranny found throughout Byron's poetry. The other work, also a cantata, was *The Death of Sardanapalus,* for which the Conservatory awarded Berlioz the Rome Prize — reluctantly; the subject of the work had been popularized in France by Delacroix' painting after Byron's drama *Sardanapalus.*

One passage from Berlioz' *Memoirs* provides an important insight into his relation to Byron. In Rome during that Italian visit he was later to recollect in tranquility for the composition of *Harold in Italy,* Berlioz explained:

> St. Peter's too always thrilled me. It is so vast, so nobly beautiful, so serene and majestic. . . . I would take a volume of Byron and, settling myself comfortably in a confessional, enjoy the great cool air of the cathedral; and in a religious silence, unbroken by any sound but the murmur of the two fountains in the square outside, wafting in as the wind stirred momentarily, would sit there absorbed in that burning verse. I followed the Corsair across the sea on his audacious journeys. I adored the extraordinary nature of the man, at once ruthless and of extreme tenderness, generous-hearted and without pity, a strange amalgam of feelings seemingly opposed: love of a woman, hatred of his kind.
>
> Occasionally, laying down the book to meditate, I let my gaze wander round. . . . Then, coming down to earth a little, I fancied some palpable imprint of the poet might still linger in the place. He must have stood there, I thought, and looked at those figures of Canova's. His feet trod this marble, his hands explored that bronze. He breathed this air, his words vibrated in this stillness — words, perhaps, of tenderness and love. Of course, for he must have come here with his friend the Countess Guiccioli . . . by whom he was so profoundly loved. Yes, loved, a poet, free, rich — he was all these things. And in the silence of the confessional I ground my teeth till the damned must have heard it and trembled.[18]

Berlioz' untroubled confusion, or fusion, of Byron's heroes with the poet himself was not an unusual nineteenth-century response to Byron; but in this case it also indicates Berlioz' own aptitude for autobiographical art, which his two early symphonies, the *Symphonie fantastique* and *Harold in Italy,* exemplify.

Berlioz composed *Harold* in 1834, under a commission by Paganini, who later refused to play the work on the grounds that it lacked virtuosic opportunities. This, of course, merely testifies to the fact that Berlioz conceived of his "symphony with solo viola" as a dramatic exposition. "My idea," he wrote in the *Memoirs,* "was to write a series of orchestral scenes in which the solo viola would be involved, to a greater or lesser extent, like an actual person, retaining the same character throughout. I decided to give it as a setting the poetic impressions recollected from my wanderings in the Abruzzi, and to make it a kind of melancholy dreamer in the style of Byron's Childe Harold. Hence the title of the symphony, *Harold in Italy.*"[19] The choice of the Byronic title seems almost to be an afterthought on Berlioz' part. But rather than this merely proving Berlioz' "encyclopaedic inattention" to Byron's poem, it suggests the essential, even subconscious closeness between the two artists and between these works.

While *Harold in Italy* has no program per se, each of the movements is assigned a descriptive heading. These movement titles themselves recall not only Berlioz' personal adventures, but the favorite subjects of a Romantic generation: "Harold in the Mountains," the first movement, re-creates Berlioz' joyful impressions during his walks on Mount Posilippo; next, the "March of the Pilgrims" conveys the atmosphere of simple and genuine piety where the complex and skeptical Romantic poet sought temporary relief; the "Serenade of an Abruzzi Mountaineer to His Beloved" combines Berlioz' Italian reminiscence with thoughts of his youth in the South of France — a shepherd's song remembered from his youth is incorporated into the movement; the last movement, "Orgy of Brigands," gives form to the typically Romantic attraction to the outlaw, vigorous and true at least to himself and to his fellow outlaw, if not to an effete and corrupt society.

Uniting the four movements, poetically more so than musically, is the character of Harold, Berlioz' protagonist, or alter ego, who functions as a perceiver and commentator on the surrounding events: an obvious parallel with Byron's poem. Harold has a double representation: both by the viola and by a single theme that relates to one significant aspect of his character or experience. Nor are the viola and the theme restricted to each other, thus allowing Berlioz greater flexibility and subtlety in the expression of his dramatic idea. Berlioz referred to this recurrent, identifying theme, and to its counterparts in many of his other works, as an *ideé fixe*— a term the ex-medical student borrowed from the new psychiatry.[20] Musically the concept may be understood as a kind of leitmotiv, and poetically it is to be understood as something that, in Berlioz' words, "keeps obtruding like an obsessive idea."[21]

The influence of Beethoven upon Berlioz while he was composing this piece is well known and is heard clearly in *Harold in Italy,* which echoes and alludes to the music of Beethoven. Moreover, the differences noticeable in the very points of similarity with Beethoven suggest the development of the Romantic sensibility. At the opening of *Harold in Italy,* for instance, one hears a recitative for basses that recalls the introduction to the last movement of Beethoven's Ninth Symphony. Berlioz' moody introductory recitative, however, instead of leading to a sung explanation, as in the Ninth Symphony, leads to a statement of the *ideé fixe* by the viola:

The quality of the viola sound itself relates to the quality of the theme itself: individually and together, and without the benefit of words, they convey the feeling of a "melancholy dreamer," as Berlioz wanted. Thus, the preceding recitative, as well as the ensuing first statement by the viola of the allegro theme of "Harold in the Mountains," becomes a personalized event that the listener readily identifies with the symphony's protagonist. Similarly, just as the last movement of Beethoven's Ninth Symphony is preceded by reminiscences of the previous movements, so is the last movement of *Harold in Italy*. Again, however, there is this difference: in Berlioz, the recollected themes have been personalized as pertaining to one man's experience — a man whose personality and experience are an integral part of the symphony — and these reminiscences are therefore extramusical and nostalgic in a way that they are not in Beethoven's Ninth Symphony. It is the presence of the viola, or Berlioz' establishing the viola as a specific character and personality, that dominates the effect, as it did the concept, of the work. While finally Beethoven's Sixth (*Pastoral*) Symphony may come to mind upon hearing Berlioz' *impressions* of the countryside (complete with descriptive tags heading each movement, as in the *Pastoral*), one soon discovers a major difference between the works: namely, the more extreme subjectivity in the Berlioz, constantly reinforced by the presence of that "melancholy dreamer."

The imposition, even dominance, of personality in art is unmistakable in the works of Byron and Berlioz and is central to their contribution to aesthetic history. But with this approach to poetry and music came new formal problems for the artist to solve: problems of voice and objective distance. Both the *Symphonie fantastique* and *Harold in Italy* are auto-biographical works, and one can easily observe even formal resemblances between them and Byron's poetry — resemblances that suggest both the composer's and the poet's attempts to deal with personal and artistic problems of objectivity, voice, or control. In a fascinating study, *The Composer's Voice,* Edward Cone discusses Berlioz' symphonies in terms of their personae and protagonists, much as one would discuss a literary work.[22] In the earlier *Symphonie fantastique,* for instance, the entire action is, according to Berlioz' program, a dream of the so-called "poet," Berlioz himself. Berlioz' decision to call the work a "dream" comes in a revision of the program, which, as Cone points out, suggests that the reality Berlioz ascribes to the music is an inner, or psychological, reality. Moreover, the revision also suggests Berlioz' need for distance, or to acknowledge the distance, between the voice in the music and his own voice. By the time he was composing *Harold,* he chose to go a step further: whereas in the *Symphonie fantastique* the consciousness of "the poet" (both protagonist and persona) embraces the entire action, the protagonist Harold (whatever his relation to Berlioz) is created as a character *in* the work, as a character whose voice is distinct and is separate from the embracing voice of the composer. There is a resemblance here with Byron, whose struggle to create a protagonist outside himself in *Childe Harold's Pilgrimage* and whose elegant achievement of the relationship between poet, persona, and protagonist in *Don Juan* foreshadow this similar development in Berlioz.

Berlioz' own personality, psychology, childhood experience, and social relationships, all of which may have made him particularly susceptible to the rebellious, hyperemotional Byronic spirit that invaded Paris in the

1820s, are revealed in the *Memoirs* and are scrutinized by Jacques Barzun in his two-volume *Berlioz and the Romantic Century*. Briefly, we may note that in their early compositions both Berlioz and Byron were motivated to vent the hurt feelings of adolescence; they both rejected and felt rejected by their world, one result of their dissatisfaction being their penchant for satire and the satanic; they suffered through precocious, unrequited loves that they idealized and wrote into their poetry; and, most important, they defined their hero as the man of sensibility and power, or, if not actual power, at least independence of mind. Perhaps Berlioz, in contrast to Byron, was more conscious from the beginning that he, or "the poet," was this hero; but Byron's contempt for "scribblers" antedates his own creation of the poet as man of action, power, and, not to be underrated by Berlioz, charisma.

Generally acknowledged to be the most genuinely literary of the Romantic composers, Robert Schumann (1810-56) perceived in literary and musical expression a profound, even formal, kinship. He admired E. T. A. Hoffmann, and about Jean Paul Richter he wrote: "I learned more counterpoint from him than from my music master."[23] Even when we come to see that Schumann's literary interests and interpretations are often limited by his own subjectivity and by the private musical idiom through which he communicated, we are moved by the intensity and nuance of his poetic feeling, which developed steadily from early years. One may no doubt credit his early literary background to his father, August Schumann, a prominent German publisher, in fact the first to produce Byron's collected poetry in German translation.[24]

Schumann's understanding of Byron's poetry is reflected in his somewhat impressionistic music criticism. At one point, for instance, he characterizes Chopin's B-flat minor Scherzo as "a highly attractive piece, so overflowing with tenderness, boldness, love, and contempt, that it may be

compared, not inappropriately, to a poem by Byron."[25]
Berlioz similarly generalized about the poet and hero of *The
Corsair,* a poem that Schumann admired and attempted to
work into an opera. But Schumann also refers to Byron in a
way that displays a more critical appreciation both of Byron's
poetry and of poetry in general. Defending Berlioz in the
Symphonie fantastique, he writes: "And if we were to take
umbrage at the taste of the day which tolerated a burlesque of
the *Dies Irae,* we would only be repeating what for years has
been written and said against Byron, Heine, Victor Hugo,
Grabbe, and others. For a few moments in an eternity,
Poetry has veiled herself in irony in order to hide her grief-
stricken countenance."[26] Despite the difference between
Berlioz' dynamic and Schumann's introspective Byronism,
the line of connection here between the two composers and
the poet is apparent, as is Schumann's understanding of the
paradoxical mixture of sentiment and satanism that
comprises the Byronic/Berliozian character.

Schumann's earliest music for Byron's poetry appears in
his song cycle *Myrthen,* Op. 25, composed in 1840 as a
wedding present for Clara. The song, "My soul is dark"
(translated by Julius Körner as "Mein Herz ist schwer"), is
not consistent with the happier mood of this cycle and,
rather, foreshadows the later Schumann; a melancholy atmosphere pervades the music as it hovers between major and
minor modes. Nonetheless, the generally buoyant spirits of
Schumann at the time probably induced his resolving the
song with the E major chords that imply an optimistic answer
to the question raised in Byron's closing lines: that is, will
Saul's heart "break at once — or yield to song"?[27] The piano
accompaniment appropriately suggests a harplike instrument; in Schumann's later settings of "Jephtha's
Daughter," "Sun of the sleepless," and "Thy days are
done" (*Drei Gesänge,* Op. 95), the accompaniment may be
played on the piano or the harp.

Schumann's Byronism, however, is best represented in his

Overture and Incidental Music to *Manfred,* composed in 1848. The Overture to *Manfred* has been recognized since the time of its first performance as among the best of Schumann's orchestral pieces, an opinion shared by the composer. Unfortunately, the rest of the work may be said to have the honor of failing in attempting to do the impossible: namely, to realize quasi-dramatically what was intended by Byron to be private, read experience. Schumann, wisely, did not attempt a staged, operatic work, but composed an orchestral setting for a dramatic reading of the poem, in which spoken parts of Byron's text (primarily the speeches of Manfred) alternate with sung passages (primarily the utterances of the various spirits).[28] The result is inevitably melodramatic, and although one appreciates Schumann's impulse to realize Byron's drama with music, he probably should have kept to the orchestra for his dramatic medium, as he had done so effectively in the Overture.

"Never before," wrote Schumann, "have I devoted myself with such love and outlay of force to any composition as to that of *Manfred,*" and friends recall Schumann's having given an impassioned reading of the play during which he wept. Critics point to the personal reasons for Schumann's strong feelings about the poem: his own encroaching madness; suicidal thoughts; and the death of Mendelssohn in 1847, which preoccupied and depressed him.[29] Although the *Manfred* Overture — its power as a musical work and its significance as a moment of interaction between music and literature — gains little from an analysis of its subjective content, the ending of Part III, where Schumann has inter- polated an angelic chorus of "Requiem aeternam," might suggest a personalized reading of the poem. In fact this ending, the only instance of Schumann's tampering with Byron's text by way of addition, may reflect the composer's attachment to *Faust*: Schumann was composing his *Scenes from Faust* between 1844 and 1853. But Tovey justifies the composer, reconciling his version with Byron's in the following way:

Schumann's interpretation of *Manfred* in music has a strength and impressiveness nearer to Byron's intentions than the effect of any possible performance of a play in which, as a matter of fact, the hero almost always appears in a state of complete nervous breakdown. ... Schumann has gone beyond Byron's text in accompanying the death-scene of Manfred with the sounds of a requiem sung from the neighbouring monastery, but I see no ... substantial contradiction to Byron in thus heightening the effect of the close. Schumann's reasons are not sentimental. The monastery is in the neighbourhood of the scene; and it is the essence of Byronism to admit the existence of what it so ostentatiously defies.[30]

Thus Berlioz admits the march of the pilgrims into a symphony that ends in an orgy of brigands; in fact, that last nostalgic reference heard, before the brigands take over, is not the *idée fixe* but the pilgrims' march. No doubt Nietzsche, however, who claimed to have composed his *"Manfred*-Meditation" out of anger against Schumann's all-too-human version (referring to the composer as "this sugary Saxon"),[31] would have found Schumann's pious coda objectionable.

Of all Byron's works, *Manfred* may be singled out for its place in the German Romantic tradition, often being compared with *Faust*. Both Nietzsche and Hippolyte Taine agree that, with respect to the development of their heroes, Byron's poem is superior to Goethe's;[32] Franz Liszt, holding both poems as ideal subjects for music and having composed a number of pieces for *Faust,* judged Goethe's hero, when compared to Byron's, "a decidedly bourgeois character."[33] Schumann's Overture is largely an expression of the character Manfred and, as such, essentially contains the whole drama. Like Berlioz' Harold and the protagonist of the *Symphonie fantastique,* Schumann's Manfred represents a type of the Byronic hero that was to dominate the Romantic imagination: he was solitary, intellectually liberated, strongly internalized, and tragic. The "virility of soul"[34] so important to Byron and successfully achieved in the characterization of Manfred is realized in the rhythmic force and thematic originality of Schumann's music. The famous three abrupt opening chords are intense and precipitous; Schumann's beginning the music off the beat following an eighth-note rest reinforces the quality of precipitousness and the thrust forward:

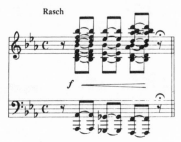

But instead of plunging off the mountain, we are halted by sorrowful, vaguely reminiscent tones; indeed they are a reminiscence, or a premonition, containing themes from the main section that is about to reveal them meaningfully to us. Manfred's *Sehnsucht nach dem Unendliche* is contrapuntally related to his earthly wanderings:

Bursting forth "in a passionate tempo," Manfred's identifying theme, while driven, remains intelligent and controlled, or at least self-willed:

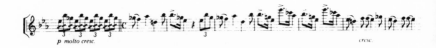

The recurrent tremor of violas in the second subject continues to recall Manfred's feverish psychology:

Moments of madness, sentiment, even resolution, enter and interplay, and they are all finally absorbed into Manfred's overwhelming energy. At last, through Schumann's rhythmic ingenuity, this energy seems to explode within itself and die away, unrepentant. A coda, in which the tentatively understood reminiscences from the beginning of the piece are recalled, contains and balances musically the dangerous and unresolvable subject matter of Byron's poem, which has found temporary resolution in musical expression.

It is worth noting again that in the course of Schumann's setting of the text, Manfred does not sing; thus the musical representation of Manfred's mind, feelings, and tragic situation is restricted to the purely instrumental overture, once more exemplifying the ever-increasing association of symphonic form with dramatic exposition of character that developed during the nineteenth century. Manfred, in his quest for absolutes beyond the delusions of his own mind, is involved with the mysterious and the inexpressible. Where words must fail, realism must fail, and the impossibility of staging *Manfred* successfully (in any traditional way) is inextricable from its power. Manfred's private experience, half tied to this world, half involved with another more permanent, more abstract, asks to be completed in music; his drama, as Franz Liszt perceived, is of the essence of symphonic poetry.

Charles Ives's attack on the Byronic fallacies of Berlioz, Schumann, Liszt, et al. was not merely an attack on the poetry these composers read and enjoyed but a rejection of the influence this kind of poetry had on music. The phrase "the Byronic fallacy," by which Ives meant the fallacy of self-expression, the fallacy of egotism, was directed at once toward ethics, since it was antisocial, and toward aesthetics, since it resulted in a mannered art. The art that was possessed of what Ives called "a common sense" was democratic and was universal in its beauty.

But Ives's criticism indulges in the luxury of passing judgment on one point in history from a later point, without due regard for historic, social, or political context. Actually, Ives's attack points to the curious ambiguity in the Byronic hero and poet of simultaneous egocentricity and human tenderness, or aloofness and social concern: that "strange amalgam" observed by Berlioz, Schumann, and the others. It is true, Berlioz and Liszt found in Byron their own wish-fulfilling, self-aggrandizing image of the hero-as-poet;[35] at the same time, through this self-heroism, they wished to liberate sensibility and genius from an oppressive and repressive, or at the very least increasingly bourgeois, society, and to liberate, or humanize, musical form as well. While Schumann, and later Tchaikovsky, identified with Manfred's quest for absolutes in love, knowledge, and being, Nietzsche surely perceived in Manfred the political implications of Byron's metaphysics. As he once wrote, "Of anyone who denied the gods one expected anything: he was automatically the most fearsome human being, whom no community could suffer because he tore out the roots of fear on which the community had grown."[36] In Giuseppe Verdi's two Byron operas,[37] written during the turbulent period of Risorgimento, the Byronic hero is transplanted to the community and serves in the case of Jacopo Foscari and Corrado the Corsair, explicit and implicit political functions, opposing those very "roots of fear on which the community had grown."

Byron created a heroic type and a consciousness of heroism that inspired later generations of composers. "I want a hero," he finally declared in *Don Juan,* expressing, perhaps, the modern predicament of being unable to find one as well as the Romantic desire to do so; the same cry was heard in music, in pieces dating from the *Eroica* to Richard Strauss's *Ein Heldenleben.* By the time of Charles Ives, Byronism, as a way of being and creating, had accrued all sorts of vague and negative meanings; and the poetry of Byron does not figure as prominently in the imagination of the twentieth-century composer as it did in that of the nineteenth-century composer.[38] But interest has continued, among Romanticists and avowed anti-Romanticists alike, in Byron's personality and life (which formed the subject of Virgil Thomson's opera *Lord Byron*), in his politics (Arnold Schoenberg setting the *Ode to Napoleon Buonaparte* in 1942 as a statement against Hitler), and in his lyrics: among the twentieth-century song settings one cannot help noticing that there are two, one from *Childe Harold* and one from *Manfred,* by Charles Ives.[39]

NOTES

1 .More than a thousand works, for instance, are listed in Burton R. Pollin's *Music for Shelley's Poetry: An Annotated Bibliography of Musical Settings of Shelley's Poetry* (New York: Da Capo Press, 1974).

2. John P. Anderson, comp., "Bibliography," in Roden Noel, *Life of Lord Byron* (London: Walter Scott, 1890), pp. xxv-xxix.

3. F.W. Brownlow, "Byron and the Musicians of His Time," *The Byron Journal* 6 (1978): 102-4.

4. William Butler Yeats, as quoted in Stephen Spender, "The Romanticism of a Daemonic Temperament," *The Daily Telegraph Magazine*, 19 April 1974, p. 37.

5. For the complete history of *Hebrew Melodies*, see Thomas L. Ashton, *Byron's Hebrew Melodies* (London: Routledge & Kegan Paul, 1972).

6. No 12 in *25 Scottish Songs*, for voice, piano, violin and cello, with English and German texts, Op. 108; originally published in *A Select Collection of Original Scottish Airs . . . by Haydn & Beethoven* (London: G. Thomson, 1818).

7. Charles Ives, *Essays before a Sonata* (privately printed, 1920); reprint ed. *Essays before a Sonata, The Majority, and Other Writings,* ed. Howard Boatwright (New York: W. W. Norton & Co., 1970), p. 91.

8. "Berlioz and His 'Harold' Symphony," in *Source Readings in Music History: The Romantic Era*, ed. Oliver Strunk (New York: W. W. Norton, 1965), p. 125.

9. Donald Francis Tovey, *Essays in Musical Analysis* (London: Oxford University Press, 1937), 4:74.

10. In *Berlioz and the Romantic Century*, 3d ed. (New York: Columbia University Press, 1969), 1:254, Jacques Barzun takes issue with Tovey and others who misperceive the nature of literary influence on Berlioz' music: "No doubt the unimaginative fail to grasp how associations *cluster*. . . . To the artist . . . the task of creation is in part the discovery of symbols at once sharp and ambiguous enough for infinite reference."

11. See Phyllis Hartnoll, ed., *Shakespeare in Music: Essays by John Stevens, Charles Cudworth, Winton Dean, Roger Fiske, with a Catalogue of Musical Works* (London: Macmillan & Co., 1964).

12. George Sand, "Essai sur le drame fantastique," as quoted in Edmond Estève, *Byron et le romantisme français,* 2d ed. (Paris: Boivin, 1929), epigraph.

13. Mario Praz, *The Romantic Agony,* trans. Angus Davison, with a foreword by Frank Kermode, 2d ed. (London: Oxford University Press, 1970); Peter L. Thorslev, Jr., *The Byronic Hero: Types and Prototypes* (Minneapolis, Minn.: University of Minnesota Press, 1962); Morse Peckham, *Beyond the Tragic Vision: The Quest for Identity in the Nineteenth Century* (New York: George Braziller, 1962).

14. *Richard Wagner's Prose Works*, trans. William Ashton Ellis (1894; reprint ed. New York: Broude Brothers, 1966), 3:221-22.

15. On the title page of the *Pastoral* Symphony Beethoven wrote: "Mehr Ausdruck der Empfindung als Malerey."

16. Hector Berlioz, *Memoirs of Hector Berlioz, Member of the French Institute, Including His Travels in Italy, Germany, Russia and England, 1803-1865,* ed. and trans. David Cairns (New York: Alfred A. Knopf, 1969), p. 106.

17. Barzun, *Berlioz and the Romantic Century*, 1:46-83 passim.

18. Berlioz, *Memoirs*, p. 166.

19. Ibid., p. 225.

20. Barzun, *Berlioz and the Romantic Century*, 1:164n.

21. Berlioz, *Memoirs*, p. 225.

22. Edward T. Cone, *The Composer's Voice* (Berkeley, Calif.: University of California Press, 1974), pp. 81-114.

23. Robert Schumann, letter to Simonin de Sire, 15 March 1839, as quoted in *On Music and Musicians,* ed. Konrad Wolff, trans. Paul Rosenfeld (New York: Pantheon, 1946), p. 259.

24. *Lord Byron's Poesien,* 31 vols. (Zwickau: Brothers Schumann, 1821-28).

25. Schumann, as quoted in *On Music and Musicians,* ed. Wolff, p. 138.

26. Ibid., p. 182.

27. Eric Sams, *The Songs of Robert Schumann,* 2d ed. (London: Methuen and Co., 1969), p. 65.

28. Liszt admired the work and gave it its premiere at Weimer in 1852.

29. Frank Cooper, "Operatic and Dramatic Music," in *Robert Schumann: The Man and His Music,* ed. Alan Walker (London: Barrie & Jenkins, 1972), p. 339; see also Marcel Brion, *Schumann & the Romantic Age,* trans. Geoffrey Sainsbury (New York: The Macmillan Company, 1956), p. 297.

30. Tovey, *Essays in Musical Analysis,* 4:112-13.

31. Friedrich Nietzsche, *Ecce Homo,* in *On the Genealogy of Morals; Ecce Homo,* ed. Walter Kaufmann, trans. Walter Kaufmann and R. J. Hollingdale (New York: Vintage Books-Random House, 1969), pp. 245-46.

32. Ibid., p. 245; H. A. Taine, *History of English Literature,* trans. H. van Laun (New York: Henry Holt and Company, 1900), 2:354.

33. Franz Liszt, letter of 1869, as quoted in Humphrey Searle, "The Orchestral Works," in *Franz Liszt: The Man and His Music,* ed. Alan Walker (New York: Taplinger Publishing Co., 1970), p. 304.

34. Teresa Guiccioli, in her unpublished *Life of Byron,* as quoted in Jerome J. McGann, *Fiery Dust: Byron's Poetic Development* (Chicago: University of Chicago Press, 1968), p. 243.

35. Franz Liszt, *Tasso: lamento e trionfo,* Symphonic Poem (Leipzig: Breitkopf & Härtel, [score] 1856, [parts] 1865); composed 1849; first performance: Weimar, under Liszt, as overture to Goethe's *Torquato Tasso* given as part of the Goethe Centenary celebration, 1849. In a preface to the Symphonic Poem (a revision of the overture), Liszt states that Byron's poem, rather than Goethe's drama, had been the principal inspiration for the work. In 1866 Liszt composed another work based on themes from *Tasso: lamento e trionfo*: "Le triomphe funèbre de Tasse," No. 3 in *Trois odes funèbres* (Leipzig: Breitkopf & Härtel, 1877).

36. Friedrich Nietzsche, *Notes* (1880-81), in *The Portable Nietzsche,* ed. and trans. Walter Kaufmann (New York: Viking Press, 1954), pp. 74-75.

37. Giuseppe Verdi, *I due Foscari, melodramma lirico,* 3 acts, libretto by Francesco Maria Piave (Milan: Giovanni Ricordi, 1844); first performance: Rome, Teatro Argentina, 1844. *Il corsaro, melodramma tragico,* 3 acts, libretto by Francesco Maria Piave (Milan: Presso F. Lucca, 1849); first performance: Trieste, Teatro Grande, 1848.

38. This contrasts with Shelley's poetry, for which many more twentieth-century musical settings than nineteenth-century settings are to be found; see Pollin, *Music for Shelley's Poetry,* pp. 170-74.

39. Charles Ives, "Incantation" ("When the moon is on the wave," from *Manfred*), for instrumental septet and voice (New York: Peer International Corp., 1958); for voice and piano, in *114 Songs* (Redding, Conn.: Charles E. Ives, 1922); composed 1908, revised for voice and piano 1921. "A Farewell to Land" ("Adieu, adieu! my native shore," from *Childe Harold's Pilgrimage*), for voice and piano, in "Eighteen Songs," *New Music, A Quarterly of Modern Compositions* 9 (October 1935); composed 1909, revised 1925.

Contemporary Portraits of Byron*

SUZANNE K. HYMAN

In a conversation with Lady Blessington, Byron discusses with some delight the difficulties for his future biographers:

> "People take for gospel all I say, and go away continually with false impressions. . . . One will represent me as a sort of sublime misanthrope, with moments of kind feeling. This *par exemple*, is my favourite *rôle*. Another will portray me as a modern Don Juan; and a third . . . will . . . represent me as an *amiable*, ill-used gentleman, 'more sinned against than sinning.' Now, if I know myself, I should say, that I have no character at all. . . . But, joking apart, what I think of myself is, that I am so changeable, being every thing by turns and nothing long, — I am such a strange *mélange* of good and evil, that it would be difficult to describe me."[1]

Byron's delight in role-playing is evident in this quotation. Lady Blessington refers to him as "a perfect chameleon,"[2] and many others who knew him also comment on this aspect of his personality. Byron's need to create roles through literary means is familiar, and the astonishing number and variety of Byron portraits testify to Byron's need to create

*I wish to acknowledge Professors William Keach and Jack Spector of Rutgers University and Professor Charles E. Robinson of the University of Delaware for their assistance in the preparation of this paper. I also thank Mr. Leonard Dore, who assisted me with the accompanying illustrations.

roles through other means as well. This role-playing helps to make a discussion of Byron's portraits both fascinating and problematical.

Byron portraiture is a fertile and relatively untouched field of study. Three articles on the subject appeared in art periodicals in 1894,[3] 1911,[4] and 1924.[5] More recently Doris Langley Moore[6] has written on Byron portraits, but her concern is primarily with costume. For a complete study of the portraits, a *catalogue raisonné* is an essential first task, since the attribution and provenance of many of the portraits are murky matters at this point. The study I envision would be along the lines of W. K. Wimsatt's *The Portraits of Alexander Pope,*[7] starting with the *catalogue raisonné* and then going on to discuss aspects of Byron portraiture in relation to Byron's life and work as well as to Romantic portraiture in general. This type of study would be particularly valuable in the case of Byron, since role-creating and role-playing figure as prominently in his life as in his poetry. Indeed it is often impossible to keep this (and other) aspects of his life separate from his writing. Notice how he himself encourages this confusion in the opening quotation: "Another will portray me as a modern Don Juan." Certainly the portraits represent yet another attempt on Byron's part to create a public identity for himself.

This essay, then, is by way of a modest initial study of Byron portraiture. I will look at a representative group of portraits executed during the poet's lifetime in order to ascertain as nearly as possible what Byron looked like. I will also discuss his contemporaries' views of Byron and his portraits, Byron's judgments on the portraits, and the painters' judgments about Byron.

What, to begin with, are the lineaments of the Byron face? We can partially answer this question by piecing together a verbal description from what people who knew the poet said he looked like. Most say Byron was handsome, and several contemporaries, including Medwin, Moore, and Galt, refer to the "Grecian" quality of his face.[8] He is compared to the Apollo Belvedere, thus suggesting the crisp, chiseled look of his features and his full, downturned lips, an element of Greek sculpture since Phidias's reliefs for the Parthenon. But Byron also swung between extremes of obesity and thinness. He was 5′8″, and his adult weight varied between 149 and 210 pounds.

Medwin mentions Byron's high forehead and receding hairline, and Thomas Moore states that Byron shaved the hair off his temples.[9] Some of the later portraits, however, show him affecting a somewhat different style, with his hair combed forward over his forehead. Byron's curly hair is mentioned by both Trelawny and Lady Blessington.[10] His hair was dark auburn, turning gray toward the end of his life. His very pale skin was considered an attractive attribute, and he often chose the colors of his clothing to accentuate his pallor.

Byron's eyes were close together, as attested to by Marianne Hunt,[11] Medwin,[12] and Lady Hester Stanhope.[13] According to Newton Hanson and Lady Blessington, the left eye was slightly larger than the right.[14] This trait is visible in a drawing of Byron as a young boy at Harrow and also in the 1805 portrait by the French painter Vigée-Lebrun. In viewing Byron's corpse on its arrival in England, Newton Hanson remarked an abnormality of the ear.[15] Most of the portraits show that Byron lacked the rounded, pendant earlobes that most people have. Lady Blessington notes that Byron's nose was broad when seen from the front,[16] as is clearly visible in the portrait busts.

The full, rounded lips are visible in all of the portraits, though more insisted upon in some than in others. Medwin says that Byron had beautiful regular white teeth that the poet "took great pains to preserve." Lady Blessington also mentions his "white and even teeth" and says that "in speaking, he shows his teeth very much." Yet one will not see so much as a single tooth in any of the portraits. This omission is an aspect of the conventions of portraiture in general. Formal portraits seldom show the sitter smiling, but if the sitter does smile, his teeth will rarely be visible. Byron's thick, columnar neck, on which Medwin says he prided himself, is, however, generally evident. In fact, it is because Byron was deemed to have a "fine throat" that he is so often seen in his portraits without a cravat, in an open-necked shirt. The full, rounded chin, which Medwin says "distinguishes Grecian beauty," is mentioned by others as well. His prominent cleft chin is a common distinguishing feature in the portraits.[17]

The various and frequently dissimilar portraits of Byron do, however, present what may be called the Byron pose. The positioning of the head facing towards the right in profile or three-quarter view is strikingly consistent throughout. The pose is not a convention of Romantic portraiture as can be seen by even a cursory study of that genre. This pose cuts across style and convention to imprint itself on nearly every representation of the poet. It is quite clear in a plate of six portraits (see Plate 1), starting with a view of Byron as a child and ending with the Thorvaldsen bust. Here the tendency to carry forth the turn to the right is so strong that the engraver has even rotated the bust, by its nature a frontal work, to the right to bring it into conformity with the other representations.

Several of the features of Byron's face already mentioned would predispose an artist to avoid a frontal view. These would include the broad nose (which Lady Blessington explicitly states looks better in profile[18]), the closeness of the eyes to each other, and their disparity in size. On the other hand, the lack of earlobes would argue against the profile or three-quarter presentation. Evidently this trait did not bother Byron since, vain and sensitive as he was, he seems never to have mentioned it. And he was perfectly willing to have it shown in his portraits. But the particular asymmetry of Byron's face apparently made the artists choose to represent more of his left side. In any case, here is a tradition of representation that began very early in Byron's life, and later portraits seem to imitate the Byronic pose of the earlier ones.

The portraits I have chosen to discuss in some detail were for the most part commissioned by Byron himself. Often he made gifts of them to his friends. For instance, the full-length portrait by George Sanders (see Plate 2) was supposed to have been sent to Byron's mother, but it ended up in the possession of John Cam Hobhouse, who allowed it to be engraved for Moore's biography in 1830. Sanders, a Scottish painter of miniatures who became a fashionable and highly paid portrait painter in London, painted Byron between 1807 and 1809 and shows him at the age of nineteen or twenty. Sanders also painted a miniature of Byron in 1812, which is in many ways quite different from the larger portrait. (One of the anomalies of Byron portraiture is the degree to which the portraits differ, even, as in this case, when they are painted by the same artist.)

The Sanders full-length portrait is remarkable for its pre-figuring of the role of Byron as romantic wanderer, a role Byron himself was to create a few years hence in *Childe Harold*. Lord Byron stands on a promontory of windswept shore. Behind him are rugged cliffs and a lowering sky with heavy dark clouds. The wind blows across the picture from left to right, whipping the water, the flag, the sails on the boat, and the clothing and hair of both Byron and the boy beside the boat. While the boy (perhaps Byron's page Robert Rushton) looks up from below towards Byron, the poet's eyes look out to the right as if he sees in the distance the solitary adventurous path he is to follow. All of nature seems to participate in reflecting Byron's stormy temperament. The use of nature to reflect and proclaim the emotions of the individual is, of course, a typical strategy of Romantic portrait painting.

As Doris Langley Moore notes in her article on Byronic dress, this picture "was begun in 1807, soon enough after the victories of Nelson for nautical styles to have a strong appeal."[19] This is doubtless the way Byron dressed for his boating expeditions in any case. The boating suit here combines aspects of costume and everyday dress, or rather, everyday dress becomes costume in much the same way the open-necked shirt and cape become costume in later Byron portraits. There is, however, nothing particularly arresting about the way Byron himself is portrayed. Bereft of this romantic setting, as in the engraving of the head and shoulders made by Finden from the Sanders portrait, Byron seems only an average young man with windblown hair. The mood and the role, then, come from the placing of the figure in a particular context.

In 1813 after his return from his Eastern tour, Byron had his portrait painted by Richard Westall (see Plate 3), a member of the Royal Academy who started his career as an apprentice to an heraldic engraver. Westall remained a book engraver as well as a painter all of his life, and he illustrated several of Byron's Oriental tales much to the poet's liking.

Byron's view of this portrait is another matter. He went to some trouble to procure the portrait for Lady Frances Webster. The difficulty arose from the fact that the picture had been in the possession of Lady Caroline Lamb, who did not want to relinquish it. Byron writes in his journal that Lady Frances Webster

> has received the portrait safe; and, in answer, the only remark she makes upon it is, "indeed it is like" — and again, "indeed it is like." **** With her the likeness "covered a multitude of sins," for I happen to know this portrait was not a flatterer, but dark and stern, — even black as the mood in which my mind was scorching last July, when I sat for it. All the others of me — like most portraits whatsoever — are, of course, more agreeable than nature. [*BL&J,* 3:224]

In the Westall portrait (there were originally two Westall portraits, one of which is now lost), there is neither costume nor scenery to convey mood. The emotional tone comes from the facial expression as Byron sits staring into space with a dark Hamlet-like gaze. Byron's friend, R. C. Dallas, liked this portrait the most:

> it is Westall's picture that I contemplate at times wth calm delight, and at times with rapture. It is the picture of emanating genius, of Byron's genius. ... I have seen him in the very position represented in Mr. Westall's picture. ... It brings him completely to my mind.[20]

However, when the painting was exhibited at the Royal Academy shortly after Byron's death, the *New Monthly Magazine* remarked:

> The features, the general expression, the hair of the head and even the colour of the eyes, are all Mr. Westall's and none of them Lord Byron's.[21]

These four differing reactions to the Westall portrait suggest the problems involved in studying Byron portraiture, which is further complicated by the fact that the portraits differ so much among themselves. Evidently, Byron was exceedingly difficult to pin down both in person and in recollection.

The most famous portrait of Byron in costume is, of course, the Phillips portrait in Albanian dress, given to John Murray (see Plate 4). Thomas Phillips, another member of the Royal Academy and a well-known prolific portrait painter, executed two, or possibly three, portraits of Byron in 1814. Hazlitt comments ironically and perceptively about these pictures:

> They are said to be the portrait of Lord Byron, though in that case we do not see why they should be incognito. They are too smooth, and seem, as it were, "barbered ten times o'er." There is, however, much that conveys the softness and the wildness of character of the popular poet of the East.[22]

In addition to this reaction by Hazlitt, there is the word of Hobhouse, Byron's close friend and traveling companion, that the Phillips portraits are not faithful to Byron's appearance at the time.[23] Nevertheless, the smoothness of the presentation and the beauty of the man in Albanian dress are part of the paraphernalia of the role of "poet of the East." There is a strong emphasis on the rounded modeling of the face. The hands are sketchily done, and the details of the costume are not precisely rendered, thus calling further attention to the sensual rendering of the face. Shadow falls on the face to give us the soft, rounded contours of the chin and eyes. The thin line of the moustache, which Phillips seems to have added to go with the costume, repeats the slight upturn of the lip. Because the moustache is only a narrow line, it accentuates the full, round, sensual quality of the mouth. Hazlitt's "poet of the East" combines the role of poet, a highly charged Romantic concept, with additional associations long conjured up by the idea of the East. Here is an assent to the idea of a particular role on the part of both the sitter and the artist. Byron is depicted as one of the heroes of his own literary creation in a rather more overt manner than he is in the Sanders full-length portrait, which was, after all, painted in advance of *Childe Harold*. This particular portrait points in the direction of the confusion in the mind of Byron's contemporaries between Byron the man, Byron the poet, and the literary creations of Byron.

James Holmes, a favorite artist of George IV and essentially a painter of watercolors and miniatures, painted a miniature of Byron in 1815. Many copies were made of the portrait and, at this point, it is impossible to tell just which is the original (see Plate 5). The Holmes miniature is oddly innocent and youthful, considering that Byron was twenty-seven at the time. What is more curious is Byron's decided preference for this miniature. Writing to Holmes for copies in 1823, Byron said, "I prefer that likeness to any which has been done of me by any artist whatever" (*L&J*, 6:213). Earlier, in 1818, he asked Murray for a "half a dozen of the coloured prints" of this miniature to distribute to his friends

(*BL&J,* 6:26). In 1821 Byron asked Murray to arrange for Holmes to visit him in Italy to paint pictures of Byron's daughter Allegra and the Countess Guiccioli. "It must be *Holmes,*" Byron says. "I like him because he takes such inveterate likenesses" (*BL&J,* 8:95). Byron repeated this request two more times, but Holmes never went.

It is difficult to conceive in what way this picture could be termed an "inveterate likeness." Byron's preference is an exceedingly odd one for a man of his self-dramatizing propensities. But perhaps we can understand it better when we know that he referred to this portrait as "a picture of my upright self." So perhaps Byron is here in yet another, albeit more subtle role, that of his "upright self" — young and naive-looking, free of the external trappings of costume and overt pose. The portrait, in many ways, recalls the young Don Juan.

The most famous artist thought to have created a portrait of Byron is the French Romantic painter Theodore Géricault (see Plate 6). Although there is some question about the authenticity of this picture,[24] its quality and the claims made for it seem to me sufficient to warrant including it in this discussion. Géricault is noted for his famous picture *The Raft of the Medusa,* showing the victims of a shipwreck *in extremis.* He is also known for the Romantic quality of his military pictures, and for a series of portraits of the criminally insane. Géricault's portrait of Byron, if it was taken from life, must have been painted in 1816 when both men were in Italy. This portrait is related to the pictures of the insane in that it, too, shows a typically Romantic interest in extreme states of mind, in this case that of artistic introspection. The head is, as usual, turned towards the right, but the oversized hand with the finger pointing towards the temple is unique in Byron portraits. The position of the hand is obviously an allusion to the role of poet, indicating the cerebral and imaginative faculties involved. The eyes seem somehow to be looking up into the head, enhancing the feeling of powerful

PLATE 1. Six Byron portraits. Photo courtesy of Jack Wasserman.

PLATE 2. Full-length portrait of Byron by George Sanders. Copyright reserved. Property of Her Majesty the Queen.

PLATE 3. Byron by Richard Westall. By permission of the National
Portrait Galley, London.

PLATE 4. Byron in Albanian dress by Thomas Phillips. By permission of the National Portrait Gallery, London.

PLATE 5. Miniature of Byron by James Holmes. Reproduced from *The Connoisseur*, 1911.

PLATE 6. Byron by Géricault. By permission of the Musée Fabre, Montpellier, France.

PLATE 7. Bust of Byron by Bertel Thorvaldsen. Copyright reserved.
Property of Her Majesty the Queen.

PLATE 8. Byron by Vincenzo Camuccini. Property of the Galleria San Luca, Rome.

PLATE 9. Engraving of a drawing of Byron by George Henry Harlow. By permission of John Murray.

PLATE 10. Bust of Byron by Lorenzo Bartolini. Reproduced by permission of the South African Library, owner of the bust.

PLATE 11. Byron by William Edward West. Reproduced by permission of the Scottish National Portrait Gallery.

PLATE 12. Sketch of Byron by Alfred d'Orsay. By permission of the Victoria and Albert Museum, London.

isolation and inwardness. The dark brooding countenance with its heavy lowering brows accentuated by the dramatic lighting creates a mood to accompany the role of Romantic poet.

The first of the two busts of Byron that were executed in his lifetime was created by the well-known Danish neo-classical sculptor Bertel Thorvaldsen (see Plate 7). It was Thorvaldsen who carved the large Byron monument in 1829 that is now in the library of Trinity College, Cambridge. Of particular interest, when Byron in 1817 sat for his first bust in Rome, is the clash of personality between the neoclassical artist, whose style has been characterized as that of "cold precision and reasoned clarity,"[25] and Byron, in whom love for classical antiquity and the neoclassicism of Pope existed side by side with flamboyant Romantic emotionalism. Thorvaldsen's account of his meeting with Byron clearly reflects the opposition of their personalities:

> Byron placed himself opposite me, but at once began to put on a quite different expression from that usual to him. "Will you not sit still?" said I — "you need not assume that look." "That is my expression," said Byron. "Indeed?" said I, and I then represented him as I wished. ... Byron when he saw the bust, said: "It is not at all like me; my expression is more unhappy." He intensely desired to be so exceedingly miserable.[26]

In effect, Thorvaldsen rejected Byron's role and then cast him in another one more congenial to the sculptor's own temperament.

Thorvaldsen regularizes the features of Byron's face much as he does the hair, which he distributes in neat corkscrew curls around the head. There is something frozen about this representation, which seems to depict the solemnity of the occasion of the creation of the bust. Byron felt this solemnity, and it made him uncomfortable. The strong streak of superstitiousness in his nature was aroused, and he was made uneasy by the thought that there was "something of a posthumous character" in a bust. Byron sought to counteract his discomfort with a characteristic resort to irony. Later, while sitting for Bartolini's bust, he told Medwin he thought the English mania for busts somewhat ridiculous, saying they were silly except for players and prizefighters, generals, orators, or cockfighters. "Portraits ... may be burnt or hung in effigy — or rot in attics," he said, "but of what use are these busts but to make lime of?"[27] "A picture," he explained in his "Detached Thoughts," "is a different matter — every body sits for their picture — but a bust looks like putting up pretensions to permanency — and smacks something of a hankering for *public* fame rather than private remembrance" (*BL&J,* 9:21).

Byron sat for another portrait while in Italy, executed by Vincenzo Camuccini, a Roman painter who was not primarily a portraitist. Camuccini was noted for the liveliness of his work, and indeed this portrait (see Plate 8) is the only one that manages to capture the playful charm and insouciance that formed a large part of Byron's personality. If Camuccini errs in giving Byron an earlobe he did not possess, his presentation reflects the spirit of the man that eluded many other artists.

George Henry Harlow, another well-known London painter and a pupil of Sir Thomas Lawrence, made at least two portraits of Byron. The later of these was sketched in Venice in 1818 and shows Byron's long hair as well as the weight he had put on at that time. The earlier portrait (see Plate 9), executed in 1815 while Byron was still in England, has an expression of aristocratic hauteur and boredom that makes it a candidate for the Childe Harold side of Byron's self-presentation. Marianne Hunt, no admirer of Byron's, gave the coup de grâce to this image of him when she remarked that it "resembled a great school-boy, who had had a plain bun given him, instead of a plum one."[28]

A second bust of the poet was carved in 1822 in Pisa by Lorenzo Bartolini (see Plate 10). A Tuscan sculptor and a onetime pupil of Jacques Louis David, Bartolini shared with his friend Ingres a desire to reform the neoclassical school of which David was a prime master. Bartolini's bust stresses reality rather than the idealizations of the neoclassical mode. Although the sculptor makes certain concessions to the conventions of his medium by giving Byron thick hair that falls over his forehead and by leaving the pupil and iris unincised, Bartolini's work is realistic in that it represents Byron as an aging and tired man. This is clear from the deep lines in his cheeks and the weary smile that plays about the corners of his lips.

Byron was not happy with the bust, but he ruefully acknowledged its accuracy in a letter to Murray:

> Of my own [as opposed to a bust of Teresa Guiccioli also executed by Bartolini] I can hardly speak, except that it is thought very like what I *now am* — which is different from what I was of course, since you saw me. [*BL&J,* 9:122]

And in a later letter:

> it may be like for aught I know — as it exactly resembles a superannuated Jesuit. — I shall therefore not send it as I intended. ... I assure you Bartolini's is dreadful — though my mind misgives me that it is hideously like. If it is — I can not be long for this world — for it overlooks seventy. [*BL&J,* 9:213]

Medwin also testified to the accuracy of the bust, which he saw in a clay model.[29]

The experience of the American portrait painter William Edward West is similar to that of Thorvaldsen. West, while in Italy in 1822-23, was requested by the New York Academy of Fine Arts to paint Byron's portrait. Once again, West's account describes Byron striking a pose that the painter promptly rejects. West reports that at first Byron was a "bad sitter" who either talked all the time or "assumed a countenance that did not belong to him, as though he were thinking of a frontispiece for 'Childe Harold.'"[30] West's words again point up the confusion between Byron the man and Byron the Byronic hero, a confusion that Byron himself engendered and helped perpetuate.

West goes on to tell how he came to know Byron better and melted the poet's reserve. He then painted the highly conventionalized, neoclassical portrait we now have (see Plate 11). This portrait is one of the few in which the sitter's eyes meet those of the viewer. Yet the eyes, and indeed the entire countenance, are relatively expressionless, demonstrating West's inability or unwillingness to make anything of the opportunity that eye contact affords. What can be done may be seen by comparing the West portrait to the one by Camuccini in which eye contact is responsible in great measure for the liveliness of the portrait.

Finally I turn to the sketches of Count Alfred D'Orsay, a French Count and an amateur artist who was traveling in the entourage of the voluble Countess of Blessington. The drawings of Count D'Orsay, done in May 1823, have the immediacy that is often the advantage of the sketch over a finished work. They show Byron's thinness and frailty and even the ill-fitting clothing about which Lady Blessington complained.[31] As with the Bartolini bust, Byron felt the drawings to be accurate and was disturbed by the image they showed him of himself. He writes to Lady Blessington in May 1823:

> I have a request to make to my friend Alfred [D'Orsay] ... viz. that he would condescend to add a *cap* to the gentleman in the jacket, — it would complete his costume, — and smooth his brow, which is somewhat too inveterate a likeness of the original, God help me. [*L&J,* 6:204]

These later portraits (that is, the Bartolini bust and the D'Orsay sketches) might well have been distressing to Byron, for they show the premature aging that prefigured his early death (see Plate 12).

Byron feared and dreaded the depredations of time. Cantos I and II of *Childe Harold,* for example, are full of the fear of time and the changes it may produce. As a poet, however, he could transcend time through the celebration of past events, through fame, and through fixing moments in his own experience. These moments could also be arrested through portraiture, as Byron himself suggests in a letter to his college friend William Harness in March 1809. At this point in his life Byron was in serious financial difficulty, yet he commissioned Sanders to paint the portrait and miniature discussed above. And he also paid to have miniatures made of his circle of friends from Cambridge. He writes to Harness:

> I am going abroad if possible in the spring, and before I depart, I am collecting the pictures of my most intimate Schoolfellows, I have already a few, and shall want yours or my cabinet will be incomplete. — I have employed one of the finest miniature painters of the day to take them, of course at my own expense. ... it will be a tax on your patience for a week, but pray excuse it, as it is possible the resemblance may be the sole trace I shall be able to preserve of our past friendship & present acquaintance. — Just now it seems foolish enough, but in a few years when some of us are dust, and others are separated by inevitable circumstances, it will be a kind of satisfaction to retrace in these images of the living the idea of our former selves, and to contemplate in the resemblances of the dead, all that remains of judgment, feeling, and a host of passions. [*BL&J*, 1:197-98]

Byron's motives for the creation of the portraits seem to be the same as some of his motives for his literary creation. That is to say, Byron uses portraiture to fix what he valued, to remove it from the alteration of time. Peter Manning in his recent *Byron and His Fictions* says that Byron is haunted by "the capriciousness of fame, the little likelihood of preservation, the universality of transcience, and the treachery of memory." Byron must therefore, according to Manning, "at every moment perform himself anew."[32] The portraits, then, are another means of performance and preservation.

As we have seen, Byron could only present himself to the artist; the role he chose was then mediated by the artist. For the most part, Byron managed an attitude of amused detachment towards these mediations. He was, of course, capable of displaying a jocular, ironic attitude about matters of great concern to him, and the amount of time and money expended on these portraits is an index of concern. In two instances, however, Byron manifests different attitudes toward his portraits. In both cases the particular portraits were engravings made from paintings, and the strong negative reaction stems from something about the engraving rather than the portrait itself. What is noteworthy here is the obsessive quality of Byron's attention.

These two instances relate to engravings made from a miniature by Sanders and from one of the Phillips portraits. In each case Murray had planned to use the engraving as a frontispiece to a volume of Byron's writing. Concerning the engraving from Sanders, Byron wrote Murray in October 1812:

> I have a *very strong objection* to the engraving of the portrait & request that it may on no account be prefixed, but let *all* the proofs be burnt, & the plate broken. ... I beg as a particular favour that you will lose no time in having this done. ... Pray comply *strictly* with my wishes as to the engraving. ... P.S. — Favour me with an answer, as I shall not be easy till I hear that the *proofs* are destroyed. [*BL&J,* 2:224-25]

Byron was similarly obsessed in 1814-15 by the second engraving from one of the Phillips portraits. In one of his many letters on this subject, he tells Murray he has no opinion on the engraving but states that Mrs. Leigh and his cousin do not like the picture (*BL&J,* 4:145-46). Once again, in a letter to Murray in April 1815, he insists upon the destruction of the prints and the plate:

> Do not forget to bring or send the *plate* of the print — which I must have given up — & nothing will ever convince me it is given

up till I have it here. — If tomorrow is inconvenient for you to call here any other morning will do. [*BL&J,* 4:287]

There is something "official" about a frontispiece portrait. It seems to bear the stamp of approval of all concerned, and this approval was refused by Byron to the two engravings in question. He was violently opposed to having the engravings, which he felt misrepresented him in some significant way, placed side by side with his writing.

In considering these portraits of Byron, I cannot but be struck with their variety, with the difference in the representation of physical characteristics of what is, after all, one man. (One does not find this sort of difference, for instance, in the portraits of Pope as collected by Wimsatt.) There is, perhaps, some explanation for this variousness in the way Byron presented himself, in the way he affected his contemporaries. People who knew him speak of his extraordinary presence. John Galt and Lady Blessington both describe his appearance as "prepossessing."[33] According to J. H. Browne, who saw Byron near the end of the poet's life,

His Lordship's mode of address was peculiarly fascinating and insinuating. . . . All who ever saw Byron have borne testimony to the irresistible sweetness of his smile, which was generally, however, succeeded by a sudden pouting of the lips, such as is practised sometimes by a pretty coquette or a spoiled child.[34]

In addition to Byron's immense charm and presence, mobility and changeability seem to have been significant characteristics, making of his countenance an ever-shifting stage on which his emotions had full play. Galt, in his biography of Byron, remarks:

The beauty of his physiognomy has been more highly spoken of than it really merited. Its chief grace consisted, when he was in a gay humour, of a liveliness which gave a joyous meaning to every articulation of the muscles and features: when he was less agreeably disposed, the expression was morose to a very repulsive degree.[35]

Coleridge, meeting Byron in 1816, testifies to the expressiveness of Byron's face in more flattering terms:

> If you had seen Lord Byron, you could scarcely disbelieve him — so beautiful a countenance I scarcely ever saw — his teeth so many stationary smiles — his eyes the open portals of the sun — things of light, and for light — and his forehead so ample, and yet so flexible, passing from marble smoothness into a hundred wreaths and lines and dimples correspondent to the feelings and sentiments he is uttering.[36]

The varied nature of Byron portraits is also accounted for, in part, by the various preconceptions of his associates. Even as a young man, before he was famous as a writer, his reputation as a profligate member of the *beau monde* preceded Byron everywhere. To Lady Hester Stanhope, "he had a great deal of vice in his looks."[37] Consistently, people expressed their views of him in terms of clear preconceptions of various kinds. Most often these preconceptions were colored, as we have seen, by what people had read, or at least heard of Byron's writings, or by their conceptions of the way he embodied the role of poet. Thus, Lady Blessington:

> The impression of the first few minutes disappointed me, as I had, both from the portraits and descriptions given, conceived a different idea of him. ... I looked in vain for the hero-looking sort of person with whom I had so long identified him in imagination.[38]

Everyone expected Byron to play the role assigned to him in his or her own imagination. Sometime before Lady Blessington met Byron she had hoped "he may not be fat, as Moore described him to be at Venice; for a *fat poet* is an anomaly, in my opinion."[39]

Time and again people spoke of Byron in terms of preconceived notions based on their own ideals. Trelawny says that in "external appearance Byron realised that ideal standard with which imagination adorns genius."[40] While some, like Lady Blessington, were disappointed, others were agreeably surprised. One of these was an American, George Ticknor, who visited Byron in 1815:

> Instead of being deformed as I had heard ... he is remarkably well built, with the exception of his feet. Instead of having a thin and rather sharp and anxious face, as he has in his pictures, it is round, open, and smiling.[41]

One wonders what pictures Ticknor saw. It is significant, though, that he had seen pictures of Byron and that by 1815 some of the portraits had circulated sufficiently to have been seen by an American visitor to London. (Perhaps he saw the Phillips portraits that were on display at the time, but the "thin ... anxious face" argues otherwise.)

Yet another preconceived view comes from Stendhal, who met Byron in Italy in 1816. It is not surprising that Stendhal's preconception has a strong literary cast:

> J'ai dîné avec un joli et charmant jeune homme, figure de dix-huit ans, quoiqu'il en ait 28, profil d'un ange, l'air de plus doux. C'est l'original de Lovelace, ou plutôt mille fois mieux que le bavard de Lovelace. ... C'est le plus grand poète vivant, Lord Byron.[42]

It is amusing that Stendhal sees Byron as Lovelace. One wonders if he was the first to do so, since now Lovelace is often seen in a sort of reversal, as a Byronic figure in advance of his creator. Surely there is a connection between Stendhal's view of Byron as Lovelace, the predatory male, and Byron's view of himself, quoted earlier, as Don Juan.

It must have been exasperating, even if sometimes entertaining, for Byron to be faced with such a number and variety of expectations. That he himself helped to create them is beyond dispute. Nevertheless, it is not surprising, given his nature, that these expectations elicited the responses they did, that sometimes he sought to fulfill them and other times to flout them dramatically.

The variety of representations testifies partly to the protean nature of Byron's self-presentation. It also testifies to the power of both his reputation as a writer and an eccentric *bon vivant*. These factors colored the view of nearly everyone who came into contact with Byron, and the portraitists were no exception. His effect on people was such that it amounted to a type of enchantment. All of these factors, then, combined to make the creation of a dispassionate, accurate representation of Byron difficult to attain.

In the verbal descriptions and in the portraits there are sets of clues as to what Byron looked like. But would we know him if we saw him on the street? I think so, and yet in the instant of recognition we would be modifying many of the portrait images we now have. Lady Blessington sums the matter up astutely:

> I am sure, that if ten individuals undertook the task of describing Byron, no two, of the ten, would agree in their verdict respecting him, or convey any portrait that resembled the other, and yet the description of each might be correct, according to his or her received opinion; but the truth is, the chameleon-like character or manner of Byron renders it difficult to portray him; and the pleasure he seems to take in misleading his associates in their estimate of him increases the difficulty of the task. This extraordinary fancy of his has so often struck me, that I expect to see all the persons who have lived with him giving portraits, each unlike the other, and yet all bearing a resemblance to the original at some one time. Like the pictures given of some celebrated actor in his different characters, each likeness is affected by the dress and the part he has to fill. ... so Byron, changing every day, and fond of misleading those whom he suspects might be inclined to paint him, will always appear different from the hand of each limner.[43]

It seems that Byron, with his insistence on his mutability, with his chameleonlike qualities, has the last word. It is appropriate that this should be the case. In spite of the corpus of his writings and his voluminous letters and journals, the definitive portrait of the man is beyond our reach. Legend feeds on mystery, and the Byron legend is no exception.

NOTES

1. *Lady Blessington's Conversations of Lord Byron*, ed. Ernest J. Lovell, Jr. (Princeton, N. J.: Princeton University Press, 1969), p. 220.

2. Ibid., p. 71.

3. F. G. Kitton, "Some Portraits of Byron," *The Magazine of Art* 17 (1894): 252-58.

4. W. A. Shaw, "The Authentic Portraits of Byron, Parts I and II," *The Connoisseur* 30 (1911): 155-62, 251-60.

5. R. R. Tatlock, "A New Byron Portrait," *The Burlington Magazine* 45 (1924): 256-61.

6. Doris Langley Moore, "Byronic Dress," *Costume,* No. 5 (1971): 1-13.

7. New Haven, Conn.: Yale University Press, 1965.

8. *Medwin's Conversations of Lord Byron*, ed. Ernest J. Lovell, Jr. (Princeton, N.J.: Princeton University Press, 1966), p. 8 and n.

9. Ibid.; Moore, as quoted by Kitton, "Some Portraits of Byron," p. 257.

10. Edward John Trelawny, *Records of Shelley, Byron and the Author* (London: Pickering and Chatto, 1887), p. 18; *Lady Blessington's Conversations,* p. 6.

11. Marianne Hunt, from the letterpress on an engraving of her silhouette of *Byron,* published by Ackerman, 6 October 1826; reprinted in *Byron*, a catalog of the exhibition at the Victoria and Albert Museum (London, 1974), p. 106.

12. *Medwin's Conversations,* p. 8.

13. Cited in Leslie A. Marchand, *Byron: A Biography* (New York: Alfred A. Knopf, 1957), 1:259.

14. Cited in Marchand, *Byron,* 3:1,257; *Lady Blessington's Conversations,* p. 5.

15. Cited in Marchand, *Byron,* 3:1,256.

16. *Lady Blessington's Conversations,* p. 5.

17. See *Medwin's Conversations,* pp. 7-9; *Lady Blessington's Conversations,* p. 6.

18. *Lady Blessington's Conversations,* p. 5.

19. Moore, "Byronic Dress," p. 2.

20. R. C. Dallas, *Recollections of the Life of Lord Byron, from the Year 1808 to the End of 1814* (London: Charles Knight, 1824), pp. 287-88.

21. Quoted by William T. Whitley, *Art in England, 1821-1837* (Cambridge: At the University Press, 1930), p. 89.

22. Quoted by William T. Whitley, *Art in England, 1800-1820* (Cambridge: At the University Press, 1928), p. 225.

23. Cited by Marchand, *Byron,* 1:438.

24. The Musée Fabre of Montpellier, which owns the picture, exhibits it as Byron by Géricault, the catalogue of the Frick Collection lists it as such, and a number of articles in art magazines concerned with Romantic art accept the title and attribution. However, the picture does not appear in major *catalogues raisonné* of Géricault's work. On June 8, 1979, I spoke with Lorenz Eitner of Stanford University, a leading expert on Géricault. Eitner claims the "Byron portrait" is a total misattributon, being neither by Géricault nor of Byron.

25. Lorenz Eitner, "Bertel Thorvaldsen," *Encyclopedia of World Art* (New York: McGraw-Hill, 1959-68), 14:56.

26. Quoted by Marchand, *Byron,* 2:693.

27. *Medwin's Conversations,* p. 7n.

28. Quoted by Marchand, *Byron,* 3:1,010.

29. *Medwin's Conversations,* p. 7n.

30. Quoted by Shaw, "The Authentic Portraits of Byron," p. 258.

31. *Lady Blessington's Conversations,* p. 6.

32. Peter J. Manning, *Byron and His Fictions* (Detroit, Mich.: Wayne State University Press, 1978), p. 243.

33. John Galt, *The Life of Lord Byron* (London: Colburn and Bentley, 1830), p. 59; *Lady Blessington's Conversations,* p. 5.

34. Quoted by Marchand, *Byron,* 3:1,093.

35. Galt, *Life of Lord Byron,* p. 324.

36. Quoted by Marchand, *Byron,* 2:597.

37. Ibid., 1:259.

38. *Lady Blessington's Conversations,* p. 5.

39. Cited in "Memoir of the Countess of Blessington," *A Journal of the Conversations of Lord Byron with the Countess of Blessington* (London: Richard Bentley & Son, 1893), pp. xliii-xliv.

40. Trelawny, *Records of Shelley, Byron and the Author,* p. 18.

41. Quoted by Marchand, *Byron,* 2:533.

42. Quoted by Peter Quennell, *Byron in Italy* (New York: The Viking Press, 1941), p. 50n.

43. *Lady Blessington's Conversations,* p. 72.

Byron's Letters and "Journals": A Note

WILFRED S. DOWDEN

When Thomas Moore finished his biography of Byron in 1830, he had in his possession a number of Byron's letters that have subsequently never come to light. Had they passed to Lord John Russell, as did Moore's own journal, a collection of his letters, and other papers, they probably would have been preserved. Though Lord John, in his zeal to protect Moore's good name and those of other contemporaries who were still on the scene, willfully and deliberately defaced the manuscript of Moore's journal in order to produce the bowdlerized *Memoirs Journal and Correspondence of Thomas Moore* (1853-56), there is no evidence that he destroyed any of the manuscript material that came to his hands. Since Moore was careful of his own papers, there is no reason to believe he would have been careless of any other manuscript material in his possession, particularly that of a friend whom he loved and admired. We may therefore assume that they were extant at the time of Moore's death in 1852.

In preparing Moore's own journal for publication, I have recently found several entries made in 1842 that indicate that he still had Byron's letters and "Journals" by him at that

time. His son Russell had just returned from India in poor
health, and Moore was once again faced with a chronic
problem; he needed money to cover a note made by his son.
On 1 and 2 March 1842, there is the following entry in his
journal, an entry that was omitted from the Russell edition of
1853-56:

> March, 1, 2 &c. [Tuesday-Wednesday] Have made up my mind,
> as some resource in my present difficulties, to dispose of the
> autographs of those letters of Byron which have been published
> — being constantly teazed by people applying for scraps of his
> writing, and having already given away far more than I ought, I
> must now see what they will fetch in the market for myself —
> Have been occupied with Bessy these two evenings past, looking
> over and sorting the letters — must also carefully expunge from
> the autographs most of those passages for which I substituted
> *stars* in their present published form — In one or two instances
> perhaps I may venture to restore the original, where the objects
> of his satire have passed away from the scene — but these
> instances are few, if any and the attacks upon Rogers are *deadly*.
> I was in hopes I should be able to avail myself also of his
> Journals — but they can hardly ever, I think, meet the light —
> certainly never while any one connected with or interested in
> Lady Byron remains alive. They are therefore a worse than
> useless deposit with me.

On 3 and 4 March Moore recorded in his diary portions of
letters from Byron that he had not included in his published
edition of 1830. Before selling them, he planned, as he says,
"to expunge the *starry* parts from the original letters" and
"shall here preserve whatever I think may be safely preserved
— at least safely in *Manuscript*." There follow several
excerpts, some of which discuss Lady Byron and acquaintances such as Rogers and Hobhouse. The excerpts will
appear in an appendix to one volume of the new edition of
Byron's letters, being prepared by Professor Marchand.

He proceeded with his plan to sell the Byron material, and
on the ninth recorded that he enlisted the aid of his wife in
arranging the letters; by this time, however, he was showing
signs of reluctance:

9th. Having with the aid of the "neat-handed Bessy" [*MS damaged*] arranged and packeted all the letters, set off for town [*MS damaged*] merchandize "and muckle may it speed!" as the old Scotch song says — though, for every reason, it is with misgivings and regret I find myself driven to such a mode of raising the supplies —

Nevertheless, he persisted and on the tenth met with his friend Moxon. Here, for the first time, he tells how many of Byron's letters were in his possession:

Saw Moxon to-day about my autographs, having called upon Evans yesterday evening on the subject. Both thought they were sure to sell well — so much as four pounds has been sometimes given for a letter, and as these amount to 160 in number, an average of two pounds, or even one for each letter would more than suffice for my immediate exigency —

On Friday the eleventh, Moxon called upon him again to discuss the sale of the letters, suggesting that Moore might dispose of them in a private sale, particularly "to 'the Americans' (who are great hunters of autographs)." Though this method was likely to bring in less money than a public sale, Moore seemed inclined toward it.

In the meantime, Moore had been negotiating with the autograph dealer Evans. He was to have met with the dealer on Monday, the fourteenth, but "some business ... intervened and our autograph matters were deferred till next day." Would the course of Byron scholarship have been altered had fate not granted Moore an additional day in which to let his misgivings grow? Suffice it to say that his judgment of the propriety of his proposed course of action shifted radically during that day, as is evident from the following entry in his journal, made on 14 and 15 March:

[Monday] — Went to Evans, according to appointment after breakfast, but some business which he had to attend to immediately, intervened, and our autograph matters were deferred till next day — In the mean time, my feelings on the subject, from maturer consideration, cannot better be told than in the following note which I wrote on this day to my sweet Bess — "My spirits, I confess, have a little sunk as to my prospects; for I greatly fear that a public sale of the Autographs would, in the eyes of the world, be thought not quite right; while a private one, while it would be almost as well known, would not bring any thing like the same amount of money — In short I feel any thing but comfortable on the subject, and (much as *you*, I fear will dislike the alternative) the very best thing I can do, under the circumstances, will be, I think, to accept the loan of Nell's money, pay her the same interest the Longmans do, and give her a right over these and others as her security. It will then be known only to our selves, *I* shall be saved from what in *this* world I dread most, any tarnish on my "fair fame," and poor Nell will, I know, feel all the happier on thus being made useful to those she loves. To all this I shall only add that *my* mind will be a hundred-fold the easier for getting over the difficulty in this manner. I mean to copy out what I have said above and send it to Nell.

15 [Tuesday] — Evans came and we looked over some of the autographs together — from what he said there seemed little doubt that it would not be difficult to get me £300 for them by private sale — but then one could not answer for their being kept private afterwards — Told him my determination to think no more at present of parting with them —

And there the matter rests. There are no further references to it in Moore's journal, and I have not found any evidence that his sister Ellen (or Nell) had possession of the letters and "Journals." Mr. John Grey Murray and I spent an afternoon at Longmans Publishing House searching through other documents in the metal box in which I found the manuscript of Moore's journal, but we discovered no letters by Byron and nothing resembling a copy of his "Journals."

Furthermore, though this box was used by Moore for storing his valuable papers and contained such documents as contracts with the Longmans for poems and notes for loans from the firm, there was no note for a loan from his sister. Ellen died in 1845 and anything of this nature would have reverted to her brother. By that date Moore was experiencing loss of memory and showing signs of the senility that marred his last years, but he was not careless of his legal papers or his manuscripts. There is no reason to believe that he destroyed or lost the Byron documents.

As for the curious reference to the "Journals," the one certain fact is that Moore had in his possession in 1842 something that he was unwilling to put up for sale for the same reasons that Byron's Memoirs were destroyed in the first place. The entry suggests that Moore did in fact have a second copy of the Memoirs, a theory that has tickled the fancy of scholars and is strengthened by Washington Irving's reference in his own diary, made at the time of his visit to Moore in 1824:

> Thursday June 17 [1824] ... ret[d] home about 1/2 past 9 — & went to my room at 10 but remaind readg Lord Byrons Ms: Memoirs till 1/2 past 12.
> Friday 18. Rose at 7. Read more of Lord Byron while dressing[1]

When referring to the destroyed Memoirs, however, Moore seldom, if ever, called them the "Journals," using instead the term "Memoirs." On the other hand, he almost always called the diaries that he published the "Journals." Yet, if these were the documents he meant, why the reference to Lady Byron and her acquaintances, with whom the earlier journals (those Moore published) do not deal? One is forced, therefore, to assume either that Moore forgot temporarily what was contained in the Journals that he published or that he did in fact have a copy of the Memoirs. As for the first proposition, I do not find in his letters or journals for this date evidence of failing memory, which afflicted him later. Moreover, it is unlikely that he would have made such an error about an event that loomed so large in his past.

The entries in Moore's journal cited here, therefore, strongly support the theory that the letters and "Journals" (whatever they were) that Moore held in 1842 are still extant. Furthermore, since Moore was living at Sloperton Cottage in

Wiltshire while he was writing the biography of Byron and afterwards, the intriguing possibility that this material is deposited somewhere in that area cannot be denied.

NOTE

1. *Journal of Washington Irving (1823-1824),* ed. Stanley T. Williams (Cambridge, Mass.: Harvard University Press, 1931), p. 211. Byron's Memoirs were destroyed on 17 May 1824. Irving may, of course, have been referring to the journals that Moore later published, rather than the destroyed Memoirs.

Notes on Contributors

MICHAEL G. COOKE, Professor of English, Yale University, has published *The Blind Man Traces the Circle: On the Patterns and Philosophy of Byron's Poetry* (1969), (ed.) *Modern Black Novelists: A Collection of Critical Essays* (1971), *The Romantic Will* (1976), and *Acts of Inclusion: Studies Bearing on an Elementary Theory of Romanticism* (1979).

NINA IA. D'IAKONOVA, Professor of English, University of Leningrad, has published, in Russian, *John Galsworthy* (1960), (ed.) *Three Centuries of English Prose* (1962, 1967), *The London Romantics and Problems of English Romanticism* (1970), *Keats and his Contemporaries* (1973), *Byron in Exile* (1974), *Byron's Lyrical Poetry* (1975), and *English Romanticism: Problems of Aesthetics* (1978). She has also edited the Russian edition of Lamb's *Essays of Elia.*

WILFRED S. DOWDEN, Professor of English, Rice University, has published (ed.) *The Letters of Thomas Moore* (1964) and *Joseph Conrad: The Imaged Style* (1970). He is currently preparing for publication by the University of Delaware Press a six-volume edition of Thomas Moore's journals.

ERNEST GIDDEY, Professor of English and Vice-Rector, Lausanne University, has published *Agents et ambassadeurs toscans auprès des Suisses sous le règne du grand-duc Ferdinand Ier de Médicis* (1953), *Histoire générale du XVIe au XVIIIe siècle* (1975), *Samuel Rogers et son poème "Italy"* (1959), and *L'Angleterre dans la vie intellectuelle de la Suisse romande au XVIIIe siecle* (1974). He has also published articles on Byron and has been a joint president of the International Byron Council.

JAMES A. HOUCK, Associate Professor of English, Youngstown

244 Lord Byron and His Contemporaries

State University, received his Ph.D. at Duquesne University in 1971. He has published *William Hazlitt: A Reference Guide* (1977).

SUZANNE K. HYMAN is a Ph.D. candidate in English at Rutgers University and is preparing a series of articles on Byron and his portraits. She is managing editor of *Raritan: A Quarterly Review*.

ALICE LEVINE, visiting Assistant Professor at Emory University (1978-79) and the University of Minnesota (1979-80), received her Ph.D. from the University of Chicago in 1979. She has published an article on Eliot and Byron and is currently continuing her research on Byron-inspired music.

ANDREW RUTHERFORD, Regius Professor of English and Dean of the Faculty of Arts and Social Sciences in the University of Aberdeen, was educated at the Universities of Edinburgh and Oxford. He has published *Byron: A Critical Study* (1961), (ed.) *Kipling's Mind and Art* (1964), (ed.) *Byron: The Critical Heritage* (1970), (ed.) *Twentieth-Century Interpretations of A Passage to India* (1970), *The Literature of War: Five Studies in Heroic Virtue* (1979), and two collections of Kipling's short stories.

ERWIN A. STÜRZL, Professor of English, University of Salzburg, received his Ph.D. at Vienna University in 1949. He has published *Kreta, die Insel im Herzen der alten Welt* (1948), *Von Satan zu Gott: Religiöse Probleme bei Graham Greene* (1954), *Der Zeitbegriff in der elisabethanischen Literatur: The Lackey of Eternity* (1965), and (ed.) *Essays in Honour of Professor Tyrus Hillway* (1977). He is director of the Salzburg Studies in English Literature and a president of the International Byron Council.

STEFAN TREUGUTT is the Associate Director of the Institute of Literary Research in Warsaw, Poland, and a Professor of Polish Philology. He has published *Pisarska Młodość Słowackiego* (1958), *Juliusz Słowacki: Romantic Poet* (1959), *"Beniowski" Kryzys Indiwidualizmu Romantycznego* (1964). He is currently writing a book on Napoleon.

JACK C. WILLS, Professor of English, Fairmont State College, received his Ph.D. in 1966 at the University of Delaware. He has published articles on Charlotte Brontë, Goldsmith, and West Virginia folklore.

Index

245